# Grandfather's Enduring
*Love*

## Kenneth David Musser

Printed in the United States of America

ISBN 979-8-89114-218-3 (sc)
ISBN 979-8-89114-219-0 (hc)
ISBN 979-8-89114-220-6 (e)

Library of Congress Preassigned Control Number: 2025916648

2025.08.04

MainSpring Books
5901 W. Century Blvd
Suite 750
Los Angeles, CA, US, 90045

www.mainspringbooks.com

In memory of my maternal grandparents, Irvin Brechbill Hoover and Anna Zelma Lady Hoover, and my step-grandmother, Carrie Deemy Hoover, my beloved uncles Harry Dwayne Hoover, and Virgil Wenger and my father and mother David, and Faithe Musser.

In the writing of my memoir and research on mental health, I have come to understand my mother's mental illness as an abusive wife and mother, and now I am at peace.

# CONTENTS

# PROLOGUE

The Gospel hymn "The Love of God" sums up the immense enduring love of God.

> The love of God is greater far
> Than tongue or pen can ever tell;
> It goes beyond the highest star
> and reaches to the lowest hell:
> The guilty pair bowed down with care,
> God gave his Son to win;
> His erring child He reconciled,
> And pardoned for his sin
> could we with ink the ocean fill
> were the whole sky of parchment made
> Were every stalk on earth a quill,
> and every man a scribe by Trade,
> To write the love of God above,
> would drain the ocean dry,
> Nor could the scroll contain the whole
> though stretched from sky to sky.

In Psalm 136, David wrote the words "His love endures forever" twenty- six times. David writes in a way that, in every declaration of God's mighty act, there is a response. It expresses deep gratitude to a God who never fails to fulfill his promise. The Israelites were in captivity, watching people and friends die, traveling through the wilderness and hard-fought battles. Their God swept Pharaoh and his army into the Red Sea. The Israelites, to get to where they were going, undoubtedly dealt with high stress and an anxiety. Ezra, the Jewish scribe and priest who was respected by all, writes in Ezra 3:11, "Praise and thanksgiving they sang to the Lord, he is God, his love toward Israel endures forever."

In my true story, the enduring love of God will shine upon and give protection and healing to several characters. At the age of fourteen, one of our characters was at the pinnacle of death when his parents' fervent prayer and their enduring love and loyalty to their son resulted in their son becoming a world hero, leader, and five-star general. Then there is the incredible story of an eight-year-old who was supposed to die from a fiery accident but this young boy's enormous courage and the steadfast loyalty of his mother's enduring love and fervent prayer allowed this boy to become one of the greatest sports stars in US history.

The main character in our true story will have suffered within a three-year period: the loss of his wife in a fiery New Year's Day death, a loss of a beloved brother due to a threshing machine accident, and, as the man Job in the Bible, this man would suffer from the loss of his entire property. Yes, this man's enduring love and steadfast faith in his God would prevail and, as Job in the Bible, God would bless this papa with a second family—two sons and three daughters—and as Papa would state, "Now a complete family.

# INTRODUCTION

The following is a true story about a Kansas family extending over four continuous generations beginning with a papa and mama, their daughter, the daughter's son, and the son's children. It's my purpose in my memoir to express the definition of an enduring unconditional love. The papa in our story would be blessed by God with an unconditional enduring love. This papa's enduring love would last through his life's external unfavorable circumstances. Unconditional enduring love begins with God giving freely of his Son, Jesus, who was blameless to give his life on the cross for all sinners. First John 4:16 states, "And so we know and rely on the love God has for us. God is love. Whoever lives in love lives in God and God in them." The papa in our story will have been afflicted with three most unfavorable circumstances, all coming within just a little over a three-year period. First Corinthians 13:13 states, "And now there remain faith hope and love but the greatest of these is love."

An early childhood trauma, particularly those traumas that happen before the age of six, lie at the root of most long-term depression, anxiety, and psychological illness such as what happened to this five-year-old daughter who witnessed a most horrific event. As a result, this five-year-old would have her entire adult life plagued with emotional and physical illness with the result of her becoming both an abusive wife and mother.

With the papa and daughter being the first two main characters in our true story, we now come to the third character, the mother's son. The son will have suffered what I shall refer to as a double whammy, that of both witnessing abuse and himself being emotionally and physically abused. This innocent son, like so many others who have suffered this double whammy, would exhibit more anxiety, depression and self-esteem problems than youngsters who haven't been abused. The author will share five escapes or places of refuge that enabled him to be free temporarily of the emotional and physical abuse he suffered.

# CHAPTER 1

## The Hoover and Lady Families

Papa Irvin, the youngest of eight siblings, was born on December 4, 1892, the son of Benjamin and Elizabeth Brechbill Hoover, in the moonlight community of North Central Dickenson County, Kansas. One sibling died at childbirth and the other at age three. Irvin Brechbill Hoover grew up in a most conservative and spiritual home. Papa, with his five siblings, were brought up in the admonition and spirit of the Lord (Ephesians 6:4). Papa's ancestors were from both Germany and Switzerland. Both Benjamin Hoover and Elizabeth Brechbill were born in Pennsylvania, Benjamin on October 10, 1849, and Elizabeth Brechbill on August 2, 1848. They were married in Pennsylvania in 1875, and the Benjamin Hoover family moved to Dickenson County, Kansas in 1882, settling in the moonlight community ten miles northeast of Abilene, Kansas, the county seat.

In the year 1610 Mennonite refugees from Switzerland had settled near the Susquehanna River in Lancaster County, Pennsylvania. These Mennonite refugees developed a conviction of a triple allusion to the Trinity—that of baptism by immersion, feet washing, and plainness in dress. These German and Swiss Mennonites would become known as the River Brethren about this time in 1778. These German immigrants and Mennonite refugees from Switzerland started a revival movement along the Susquehanna River at Marrieta in Lancaster County, Pennsylvania, in the year 1878. The name River Brethren stemmed from new converts being baptized in the Susquehanna River. These River Brethren were led by Jacob and John Engle. During the American Civil War, when required by the Union government of the United States to register as a body that held

1

nonresistance values, the name Brethren in Christ was adopted. Benjamin and Elizabeth Brechbill Hoover were members of the Brethren in Christ. Around the year 1870, a good number of these Brethren in Christ migrated to North Central, Kansas, settling in Dickenson County, Kansas, with Abilene being the county seat.

The BIC Church several times a year, held what's called a love feast, a communal meal shared among Christians. The love feast consisted of taking Communion of bread and wine, the taking of bread as a symbol of the body of Christ and the taking of wine refers to Christ's blood that he shed on the cross for all sinners. The love feast also consisted of feet washing, a time of quiet reflection of humbling oneself to wash another's feet. It was at one of those love feasts that young Irvin would meet a beautiful young teenage girl, Anna Zelma Lady, born on August 12, 1893, near Talmage, Kansas, and later taught in rural schools. Like the Hoover family, the Lady family also migrated from Pennsylvania to North Central Kansas in 1870s. Both the Hoover and Lady families were devout Christians and members of the BIC Church.

Let me share a bit about these two families. As the generations came and went, tragedy after tragedy would follow both families. Anna Zelma Lady was one of eleven siblings, born to Samuel and Mary Olive Frey Lady; the first being Sherman Stanton dying in infancy and the youngest Emma Lois, died at a year and a half with the oldest surviving child Harvey born in 1892. Harvey with his wife Naomi Kern Lady were missionaries at the Matopo mission in Rhodesia South Africa. They had gone for a rest at the Mtshebezi mission. While going on a visitation with one of the African natives, Harvey took with him a gun. The missionary Brethren always took a gun along to get meat as game was plentiful. While stepping down a ditch, Harvey stumbled with the gun and the gun discharged into his right arm, just below the shoulder, mangling the flesh and shattering the bone. Five hours after the accident, just before his last breath, Harvey's last words were, "I am going to be with Jesus."

Another tragedy in this immediate family was the death of Harvey and Naomi's only child, David Wesley. In September of 1929, Naomi was home on her first furlough. On September 20, 1929, David died of lockjaw caused by his smallpox vaccination at the age of eight. There would yet be many more tragedies to come for both the Hoover and Lady families.

The author of our true story would be able to visit Naomi Kern Lady in the summer of 1966 at the Messiah Home on Paxton Street in Harrisburg, Pennsylvania. As a teenager, the author always had a passion visiting with the elderly. The author was to find out what a precious soul Naomi Kern Lady was. The last time our author visited Naomi, she would give him the Bible that her husband Harvey would win souls for Jesus in Africa.

Irvin and Anna began a courtship which blossomed into romance. On February 1, 1917, Irvin Hoover and Anna Zelma Lady were united in holy matrimony. Our true story of the Irvin Brechbill Hoover family now begins. Irvin and Anna were a devout Christian couple. It can't be overemphasized how beautiful Anna was with her wavy blond hair. Irvin and Anna went into farming near Talmage, Kansas, located twelve miles northwest of Abilene, Kansas, the county seat of Dickenson County. On March 19, 1918, Anna gave birth to a daughter, Rozella May, followed by another daughter, Virgie Juanita, born on September 12, 1919. Anna gave birth yet to three more daughters: Faithe Alberta, born on October 24, 1921; Eunice Elizabeth, born on Christmas Day 1923; and Mary Lou, born on September 12, 1926. At this time in our story, Irvin will become known as Papa and Anna will be known as Mama.

# CHAPTER 2

## Fatal New Year's Day of 1927

The time is New Year's Eve 1927. The two oldest daughters, Rozella and Virgie, would spend New Year's Eve sleeping overnight with an aunt and uncle. At about 4:30 a.m., New Year's morning, there came the ringing of the telephone. Cattle had gotten out overnight at a neighboring farm and the farmer called to ask for Papa's help in rounding up the cattle. Papa immediately got up, dressed, and rode on his horse the half-mile to his neighbor's farm. Meanwhile Mama had awoken around 6:00 a.m. Three-month-old Mary Lou was fast asleep upstairs in her crib. At about 8:00 a.m., five-year old Faithe and three-year-old Eunice had awakened and, in their bare feet, shuffled down the stairsteps. Both girls could smell the aroma of fresh-baked bread. Faithe sat on a dining chair while Mama put Eunice in a high chair. Mama was cooking a special New Year's morning breakfast for the girls, when suddenly, without warning, a small can of kerosene that had been placed on the reservoir above the stove fell onto the hot oven, instantly scattering flames all over Mama. Mama instinctively ran out of the kitchen door, rolling onto the grass, screaming in anguish so loudly that papa, a half- mile away, could hear the anguished screams.

Papa, sensing something was drastically wrong, hurried home galloping on his horse. Five-year old Faithe would be left traumatized and helpless, in a state of shock, witnessing her mama on fire. Upon arriving home, Papa quickly put out the fire with blankets. The fatal freakish accident happened around 8:30 a.m., New Year's morning, and Mama lived for five hours. Astoundingly Mama's beautiful face and lovely wavy blond hair were not touched. Mama Anna was the most beautiful of her siblings.

Apparently the wind had blown the flames from her neck downward. Five-year-old Faithe recalled hearing her Papa say, "If I only had been there, I would have taken a blanket and smothered out the flames." On Mama's deathbed, she was to have said to her mother, Mary Olive, "Please take care of my babies."

Of utmost importance, it must be remembered that at the young tender age of five, daughter Faithe was the oldest witness on the scene of seeing her mama burning to death. At such an early age, this horrific event would be the catalyst which would wreak havoc on Faithe's emotional and physical well- being for the remaining eighty-one years of her life. Papa was by no means wealthy and the youngest daughter Mary Lou was only three months old. One rich young couple offered Papa a large sum of money to adopt three-month- old Mary Lou. There were a few seconds when Papa thought that might be for the best, but then Papa was to have said, according to daughter Faithe, "With God's help, I'm going to keep my five daughters together." I'm sure that's the way Mama would have truly wanted it. Reflecting these many years later, what an act of Papa's unconditional enduring love for his five daughters, especially for three-month-old Mary Lou.

# CHAPTER 3

## The Years 1927–1930 Brings More Tragedy

Papa was now a young widower at thirty-five, left with five young daughters, ages ranging from seven to three months. Mama's parents, Samuel and Mary Olive Frey Lady, would move into Papa's home and for the next three years, with their unconditional enduring love, would help Papa out with the bringing up and spiritual nurturing of the young daughters. The days would come and go, and many days Papa would come home so tired and somewhat depressed. Then one evening, after a hard day's work, Papa saw his daughters playing softball out in the large front yard and something snapped in his mind and he thought to himself, *That's what I have to live for.* Yes, the emotional trauma had already started in young Faithe's life as she relates the following, "Then the day of the funeral came, and when at the cemetery, I saw mama's casket and I said, "Don't put Mama in that big hole." Papa was such a loving and devoted father. The following happening is told by daughter Faithe. "On Saturday evening, Papa would always want to take us to a small town called Industry, located in North Dickenson County. Grandma Lady wouldn't always let him as she would always say that we needed to get to bed early as we had to go to Sunday school the next morning. Papa would listen to her occasionally, but one Saturday night, he told Grandma that he was going to take us with him. We girls always loved that, it was fun. Papa would give us each a penny and we would have fun spending it. Then Papa would buy a large sack of candy, and when we got home, he would make five piles and then count the candy out, making a nice handful of candy for each of his daughters. That would be a big highlight in our lives."

As did Job in the Bible, Papa suffered physically. Daughter Faithe tells of the following, "One time, Papa's body was covered with open sores called carbuncles—big sores—all over his body and they were extremely painful. They would last for some time. Even Papa's doctor was puzzled as to how they ever started. Thank the Lord Papa was healed." However, Papa was still to experience more traumatic events.

It was wheat harvest time in mid-June of 1929, wheat being Papa's main source of income. Papa and his older brother Harry, fourteen years Papa's senior, and several hired hands were harvesting wheat with a threshing machine which had a pulley belt moving at a fast rate of speed. When suddenly, with no warning, brother Harry got his arms caught in the pulley belt and his entire body was sucked into the threshing machine, killing Harry instantly. Papa idolized his older brother Harry, and some eight years later, on May 31, 1937, Papa would name his tenth and last child Harry, after his dearly beloved brother. Papa's one consolation was that brother Harry was a devout Christian who went home to heaven to be with his Lord and Savior, Jesus Christ, for all eternity.

The time was the first week of May 1930. Papa had met a lovely Christian lady from Dallas Center, Iowa, Carrie Deemy, at a church-related function at the Dallas Center BIC Church. Papa began corresponding with Carrie. One day, Papa would tell his five daughters that, "You had always called your birth mother Mama but you are to call this lady, your stepmother, Mother. The wedding date had been set for May 22, 1930. The ladies at the Bethel BIC Church had made beautiful dresses for all five daughters. The 1930s were often referred to as the dirty thirties, not only because of the numerous dust storms but many natural calamities called cyclones—now known as tornadoes—were a frequent happening. The region from Central Texas, northward to Northern Iowa, and from Central Kansas and Nebraska, east to Western Ohio, has long been known as Tornado Alley. One of the worst cyclones struck in early May of 1930 in North Central Kansas.

At this time, Papa, his five daughters, and Papa's parents-in-law Samuel and Mary Olive Lady, were renting and living on a farm owned by Lloyd Knisely near Talmage, Kansas, some fourteen miles northwest of Abilene.

In about twelve days, Papa was to marry Carrie Deemy from Dallas Center, Iowa, when the unthinkable natural calamity hit the Knisely farm. It just happened that Divine Providence had the youngest daughter, Mary Lou, not yet four years old, staying overnight at an aunt and uncle's home. How many times does our Father in heaven protect his children with his guardian angel?

Daughter Faithe tells of the following event, "Grandpa and Grandma Lady had safely gotten down to the basement in the far southwest corner safely. We four girls were upstairs in bed, and the windows were all broken and glass was all over the floor. We girls were all barefoot as Papa took two girls in his arms down to the cellar, and then Papa went up and got the last two girls, taking them down to the cellar. Just as Papa had gotten the last two girls to safety, the house moved and the stairwell was closed off. Had Papa gone back upstairs to get three-year-old Mary Lou, they both likely would have perished." Just another instance of the good Lord being our loving shepherd, sending protection for his children. Our Father in heaven does know what lies ahead for each of his children, just as he did for Papa by having Mary Lou away from home that night. I would like to emphasize, "To God be the glory, great things he hath done."

Daughter Faithe tells of how the beautiful dresses made by the church ladies' sewing circle were gone, neighbors having reported seeing the dresses over a mile away. Ironically Papa had left his wedding suit at a cleaners fourteen miles away in Abilene. Once again, God's guardian angel had looked out for Papa. The ladies' sewing circle hastily made dresses again for the girls. Papa's favorite horse was still standing with a 2x4 lumber driven through its belly, and Papa had to shoot it to put it out of its misery.

Papa then had to write a letter to his soon-to-be bride Carrie, telling her that there was nothing nice to bring her home to and Carrie wrote back and said, "A tent or a cottage, why should I care." This phrase sums it all up of the selflessness and love that Carrie was so blessed with. What a wonderful loving wife, Mother, Stepmother, and Grandmother Carrie would become. Carrie came from a loving Christian home in Iowa to live in a newly built chicken house temporarily until the new house could be rebuilt to replace the house completely leveled by the cyclone.

# CHAPTER 4

## Papa's Blessed by God with a Second Family

On May 22, 1930, Irvin Hoover and Carrie Deemy were united in marriage at Carrie's home church, the Dallas Center, Iowa, BIC Church, with the Reverend Savannah Landis officiating. Sometime after their wedding, a neighbor friend asked Papa, "How can you go on living after all that's happened to you?"

Papa's reply to him, "Look at those five little angels over there, that's what I have to live for."

Each of Papa's five daughters were musically talented. On Sunday morning, the five daughters would go up front of the congregation at their home church, the Bethel BIC located ten miles northeast of Abilene, Kansas, in the moonlight community of Dickenson County. Daughter Faithe recalled the following, "People called us the stairstep sisters as that's how we looked, each of us almost two years apart. We would also sing at other local churches. We each had a talent for music, especially singing and playing the piano. We weren't bashful in singing as we enjoyed it." Both Faithe and Mary Lou were so blessed by the good Lord with a special talent. Faithe, in her teenage years up through her adulthood, would be able to play the piano by ear, without any notes, while Mary Lou had the special talent of yodeling.

Papa Irvin and Mother Carrie would be blessed with five children over the first seven years of their marriage. Papa would finally get his sons, three to be exact. Herbert Curtis was born in 1931, and a little tidbit on the name

Herbert Curtis. Herbert was named after then-Quaker-born President of the US, Herbert Hoover. Herbert's middle name was named after then-Vice-President Charles Curtis whose ancestry was Native American. Curtis's mother Ellen, was Kaw, Osage, and French; while his father Orren was of English, Scot, and Welsh ancestry. A second son, Glenn, was born in 1932; a daughter, Carol, born in 1934; another daughter, Delores, in 1935; and a son, Harry Dwayne, born on May 31, 1937. Papa would now state "a complete family."

Still there were to be more traumatic events to befall on Papa. According to daughter Faithe, "One Sunday, we were in church which was always the case. A neighbor came into our church and told Papa that our chicken house was on fire, burned to the ground with all the chickens gone." This was indeed a great loss as Papa depended on the egg money to help buy our groceries."

Daughter Carol relates the following, "When Harry was age nine or ten, he had climbed up inside the silo and I remember Harry falling through an opening in the scaffold when he was about halfway to the top. Harry was unconscious, and when one of his brothers carried Harry to the house, we thought he was going to die." Harry did fully recover with fervent prayer going up on Harry's behalf.

# CHAPTER 5

## *Papa and Job*

When I reflect on Papa's tragic losses, whether they be natural calamity or tragic accidents, the family man Job in the Old Testament comes to mind. Most people when hearing the name Job, think of a righteous man who suffered unjustly. Job exemplifies the person who questions why good people suffer. In the course of one day, Job receives four messengers, each one bearing separate news that his livestock, servants, and ten children have all died due to marauding invaders as natural catastrophes. Job tears his clothes and shaves his head in mourning but he still blesses God in his prayers. Satan appears in heaven again and God grants Satan another chance to test Job. This time Job is afflicted with horrible skin sores. His wife encourages him to curse God and to give up and die but Job refuses, struggling to accept his circumstances. Job didn't deserve his tragic losses. Even Job's friends tried to convince him that these things happened to him because he sinned but Job knew better. In Job 1:8, we read the Lord called him, "A blameless and upright man who fears God and shuns evil." Yes, the perseverance of Job held steadfast. Job lost seven sons and three daughters and, in the end, due to Job's enduring faith in God, through all his losses and health, God gave him seven new sons and three new daughters. Job 42:12 tells us that the Lord blessed the latter days of Job more than in the beginning.

Just as in Job's situation, Papa Irvin didn't blame God for his tragic losses. Papa, like Job, persevered through great suffering and loss. Like Job, Papa embraced God and Papa's faith in God sustained him. After Job's tragedy had passed, Job said to God, "I have heard of you by the hearing of the ear, but now my eye sees you" (Job 42:5). Yes, Papa suffered mightily, but due to his steadfast faith in God, the Lord would reward Papa with a lovely second wife, Carrie, who was so blessed by God in her unconditional love to the five stepdaughters; and Papa, like Job, was blessed with five more children, and Papa was able to say, "Now a complete family."

# CHAPTER 6

## Faithe's Trauma and Growing into Adolescence

Let's get back to that innocent five-year-old who at the tender age of five, witnessed her mama burning to death. Researchers have studied and found that children with post traumatic disorder, also known as PTSD, are likely to experience a decrease in the size of the hippocampus, a brain structure important in memory processing and emotion. Various studies have been made of children who were suffering from PTSD as a result of their undergoing physical, emotional, or sexual abuse, witnessing violence, or experiencing lasting separation and loss. In their studies, they found that the younger a child was at the time of the loss, the more likely they were to develop mental health problems, including anxiety, depression, and abusiveness. Can you think of a more violent death than of a child witnessing her mother burning to death? This is a lasting earthly separation for this five- year-old and her mother.

Let's now take a closer look at the early childhood life into adolescence of daughter Faithe who now becomes the second character in our true story. The following incident shows us of the unconditional love of Papa for his daughter Faithe. Faithe tells about a family of children at her elementary school who always had peanut butter sandwiches. Faithe relates, "It smelt so good and so tempting. Every day, they had peanut butter sandwiches and we had cold egg sandwiches. I was soon to take my eighth-grade examination. All students had to bring their noon lunch. I will never forget what Papa did, never will I forget. He went to the grocery store and bought fresh-baked bread, lunchmeat and cheese, banana and orange, and a candy bar for lunch. That was for the day of my exams, and yes, I passed the examination."

Faithe tells of the morning when she and Eunice missed the school bus due to their getting around late doing their chores. Faithe recalled, "Due to our being late, Papa let me drive his good white Pontiac to school. We got along fine and made it just in time when classes started. On the way home while driving, I was behind our school bus. The students looked out the back window and noticed it was us. I was going to show off going around the bus—with the result of hitting the fender of the bus. I pulled over and stopped to see the damage of the car. The fender was dented just a little bit, not as bad as I thought it would be. I was afraid to go home and tell Papa that I had wrecked the car, so on the way home, just a bit out of the way, we went to a machine shop. We asked one of the men working there if he would fix the fender. He looked shocked and said, 'No, not now. That will take some time.' He had recognized us as Irvin Hoover's daughters. There was nothing to do but go home and tell Papa which we dreaded terribly. We got home and saw Papa at the barn. I drove the car into the garage and went and told Papa that I had wrecked his car awful! I thought that was the way to handle it—making it sound worse that it was. He said, 'Let's go see it.' He said, 'Is that all?' As Eunice and I rode the bus the next day, the students had a lot of fun with me about hitting the bus. I was terribly embarrassed. I don't remember about the bus, if it was wrecked, but I'm sure that Papa saw that it was taken care of as Papa was a good friend of the bus driver. That was another time it didn't pay to show off. It was just foolish." Just think about trying to do that today, of going around a bus. There was a mischievous side of young Faithe, right?

It's mid-August 1938, and Faithe was about to enter her senior year at Chapman High. Faithe had lost all desire for studying and Papa needed a hired hand as the oldest son Herbert was only eight years old. Faithe didn't go back for her senior year; instead she became Papa's hired hand. Faithe would drive the tractor while Papa drove the combine. Faithe did one great job, and as a reward, Papa gave her fifty dollars, the exact amount a hired hand's wages were. It was at the age of eighteen that Faithe would begin working as a waitress for the Callahan sisters' family restaurant located on North Second Street in Abilene. The Callahan's were extremely generous to Faithe.

# CHAPTER 7

## Faithe Goes West: Marriage: Black Widow Scare

At the age of nineteen, in the early fall of 1940, Papa put Faithe on the train headed for the Golden State of California. Faithe planned to work as a maid in rich homes. Papa had contacts through the local BIC Church in Upland, California. Faithe really didn't like that line of work and she found work as a nurse's aide at the Upland General Hospital. Upland was a suburb of Los Angeles located forty miles due east of LA. While working in Upland, Faithe met a young college student who like Faithe was a native of Abilene, Kansas. This college student's name who was attending Upland College was David. Ironically some seven or eight years earlier, both had first met while attending a church function, a love feast, held at the Abilene, Kansas BIC Church. As to their initial meeting, David was in a fight with another boy his age, Wilmer, who was much bigger than David. The other boy was getting the better of David and it was Faithe who came to David's defense. When David was fifteen, his parents Noah and Vesta Musser, moved to Upland, California.

While Faithe was busy working at the Upland General Hospital, David was furthering his education, studying for the ministry, attending Beulah College in Upland. David was extremely athletic and played basketball on the Beulah College varsity basketball team. Quite often, for recreation, David and friends would often hike up Mount Baldy in the San Gabriel Mountains with an altitude of 4,193 feet. Faithe would often accompany

David on these hikes. David's older sister, Frances, had just graduated from Beulah College.

After dating for several months, Faithe and David's relationship had become serious and soon blossomed into romance. David and Faithe became engaged, and on August 12, 1943, David Wesley Musser and Faithe Alberta Hoover were united in marriage at the Abilene, Kansas BIC Church, officiated by Faithe's uncle, Chris Frey. Chris was a younger brother to Mary Olive Lady, Faithe's maternal grandmother. David would graduate from Beulah College in May of 1944. Before their marriage, David had to be honest with Faithe and told her that it would be hard financially on them for a while as back in the mid-to-late 1940s, a minister's pay, some months, came to a measly ten dollars a month.

Shortly after David and Faithe's marriage, Faithe had quite the scare. Both David and Faithe were in bed sleeping, when unknowingly a black widow spider began crawling up the neck of Faithe. You know the saying, "God's angels will look over his children," well this evening it came true. This night God protected his child. Only God knows, but David opened his eyes looking at Faithe and seeing the "orange-colored hour glass female black widow on Faithe's neck, defly swept the black widow off of Faithe's neck, possibly saving Faithe's life from the poison venom of the female black widow. The male black widow isn't poisoness, but the female is. A full grown the female black widow usually has a red or orange hour glass on the ventral surface underside of the abdomen. The female black usually has large venom glands, and its bite can be deadly to humans.

# CHAPTER 8

## David's Ministry Begins in Kentucky and Kansas

After David's graduation in late May of 1944, David and Faithe took a church home mission assignment with the BIC Church; their destination would be at Knifley, Kentucky, a small rural area in the Kentucky hill country. David and Faithe would serve at Knifley for one year. On August 2, 1944, a son was born to David and Faithe, Kenneth David Musser, the third character and the author of our true story. I was born in Garlin, Kentucky, in a house on top of the Kentucky hill country. About the only exciting happening in my first year of life was that I had colic and almost died from pneumonia.

In the summer of 1945, the Lord called Daddy to take the pastorate of the Bethel, Kansas, BIC congregation located ten miles northeast of Abilene. This was daughter Faithe's home church while growing up. Daddy would pastor at Bethel from 1945–1952. My parents were extremely grateful that Grandpa Hoover lived only two miles from both the church and our home. Grandpa would provide us with much needed food including milk, chicken, beef, and lots of veggies from Grandma's garden. Just a note about the Bethel church: it was there in 1895 at the BIC Church general conference that the first five dollars was given toward BIC foreign missions for Africa.

Daddy began his pastoring at the Bethel Brethren in Christ Church, and while pastoring there from the years 1945–1952, a native of the Bethel church would become the first female ever to be appointed as a mission superintendent. As a boy of three and a half, I faintly remember of Sarah Bert. Sarah Bert had been a somewhat frail and sickly young lady of thirty-four years. Sarah had a desire to trade the blustery plains of Kansas for the Windy City of Chicago. It wasn't the bright lights of Chicago that Sarah had an interest in but a desire to serve at the Chicago fledgling mission. After much prayer and meditation, Sarah couldn't get peace of mind as to if she should make the change. Being raised up in the church, Sarah was aware that when first-century believers had important matters to settle, they would cast lots. So in her naive mind, she thought what was good for first-century believers was good for nineteenth-century believers. However, Sarah had a problem—she didn't know how lots were cast in the first century. But Sarah did know how lots were cast in the nineteenth century and that was by the flip of a coin. If one side came up, it would be Chicago; if the other side came up, she would forget the city. The die was cast. The flip was made with the Chicago side coming up and the next fifty years were history.

Sarah passed away on Wednesday, January 28, 1948, at the age of eighty- eight years. The following was told to me by my daddy, the pastor at Bethel at the time. "As Bishop M. M. Book was conducting the service, the sky began to darken and a typical afternoon Kansas storm developed which continued even after the service had been completed. In the meanwhile, undertaker Ray Danner, Bishop M. M. Book, and the mourners waited patiently for the storm to pass over. As the storm began to cease, Deacon Alvin Hoover stepped outside to ascertain if the burial could take place. At that moment, a lightning bolt hit the church with so much velocity that Deacon Hoover wondered if anyone in the building had been struck. The Lord, in his mercy, protected all in the building. However, the bolt had torn a hole one and a half and two feet in diameter in the church ceiling. Later it was suggested that Satan was giving payback to Sarah for her faithfulness regarding his nefarious works. In due time, the church ceiling was plastered over. But as the plaster dried, it shrank and left a large round mark in the ceiling. Whenever worshippers entered the church and gazed to the ceiling, they could be reminded of the faithfulness of one of their former members and to follow the Lord's leading in their life."

At this time, in the mid-to-late 1940s, in Dickenson County, Kansas, there was a shortage of schoolteachers so Daddy would improvise and, with his BA degree, was able to teach at elementary schools. In the fall of 1946, Daddy accepted a teaching position as principal of a one-room elementary school, Rainbow, in Northern Dickenson County. There was one occasion that I'll never forget which took place at Rainbow. There was a family get together night, and at the age of four, I recall of dribbling a basketball around older students. My love of basketball started young.

On June 18, 1948, our family would welcome a new addition to our family with the birth of a ten-pound baby boy, Charles Wesley, named after the eighteenth-century English songwriter of some 6,500 hymns, Charles Wesley. My paternal grandmother, Vesta Musser, had traveled to Central Kansas to help with Mother and newly born grandson. I recall, as though it was yesterday, of driving home with baby Charles on old Highway 40 with Grandma Musser holding the baby. In 1948 Daddy would accept a new position as principal at the Detroit Elementary School located on old Highway 40, four miles east of Abilene. It would be an increase in pay for Daddy and the school had four classrooms. Daddy taught sixth, seventh, and eighth.

# CHAPTER 9

## Traveling on a Greyhound

That summer of 1950, Mother and I took a Greyhound bus, from Abilene bound for the state of Pennsylvania, to visit Mother's two sisters, Rozella and Virgie. Mother and I would join up with Aunt Mary Lou and her daughter, Janet, in Kansas City, Missouri, where Aunt Mary Lou's husband, Dale Eshelman, was an MD. Yes, the same Mary Lou, the three-month-old infant asleep in her crib that fateful New Year's of 1927. As a five-year-old on that trip, I have so many special memories such as the street cars running on the tracks in the city of Pittsburgh. To a five-year-old, the city seemed immense.

On July 12, 1950, Janet would celebrate her third birthday while we were visiting at the farm of Aunt Rozella and her husband, John Thrush, and family. I remember well of Janet holding her small birthday cake with three candles and blowing the candles out. Over the years, Janet and I would become very special friends. I recall, for the first time, of seeing lightning bugs flying around on Uncle John's large front lawn. Those lightning bugs really struck up my curiosity as I kept trying to catch them. Aunt Rozella had five children: Johnny, eight years; Irvin, four; Rozanna, three; Mahlon, two; and Mary Lou, a year old. My highlight at their farm was riding on one of their horses.

I had already met Aunt Virgie and her husband Glen and family as they had previously lived on a small farm just three miles east of Abilene, Kansas, right along old Highway 40 East. Their children: Glenda, age nine; Irwin, age seven; Gerald, six; Faithe, five; Joyce, four; and Vivian, not quite a year old. Daughter Faye would be born in 1953. I had a blast with my Hess cousins as they had a goat farm. However, my biggest thrill on that 1950 trip was getting to see, for the first time, my dearest great-grandmother Mary Olive Frey Lady who, in only fifteen months, would go on to be with her dear Lord and Savior, Jesus, for all eternity. Great-Grandpa Lady had passed away in 1934 at his daughter Eunice's home in Grantham, Pennsylvania, where Messiah College was located.

I must share a bit about my time of going to the Bethel church. As a first and second grader, I had a wonderful Sunday school teacher. Her name was Naomi Hoover whose husband Alvin, was a deacon at the Bethel Church for years. Every Sunday I remember Naomi giving us a size of a postcard picture of a Bible character or a biblical event. Oh, how I loved collecting these cards. As a three and four-year-old, we lived only a mile from the Bethel church in a home that my parents rented from the other deacon at Bethel, Roy Landis and his wife, Bessie. During the seven years that I would attend Bethel, from 1945–1952, there were no boys my age and there were two girls, Marjorie Allen and Ruth Bert. However, I had a couple of good boy friends in Myron Hoover, a son of Alvin and Naomi, a year younger than me and Donnie and Ken Crawford, one year older and Ken a year younger.

Soon after returning home that summer of 1950, I would be entering first grade. I still have the photo that Mother took of me on my first day of school with my little green lunch pail. Oh how I enjoyed reading the three small color reading books about Sally, Dick, and Jane. From these three small books would be the root of my becoming an avid lifetime reader. My favorite teacher, through all my elementary and secondary schools, was Ms. Betts who so inspired me to read. There also were the early afternoon naps. As a first grader, I have vivid memories of Daddy coaching his track team on the side street in front of the school for the one-hundred-yard dash. The four eight graders running the one-hundred-yard dash were John McDonald, Larry Kiem, Robert Bistline, and Dale Mills. Dale would go on to be a great football running back at Southwest Missouri State where he was a little college All-American. Tragically Dale was killed in an automobile crash in his early '20s.

# CHAPTER 10

## *Christmas 1950*

It's nearing Christmas 1950 as I'm in first grade. Our family was planning to spend Christmas with my great-uncle Samuel and great-aunt Lois Lady. Great-Uncle Samuel was a younger brother of my Grandma Anna who burned to death. My parents were going to hold a week of special Christmas musicals and stories and plays for children at the Dallas Center, Iowa, BIC church where Great-Uncle Samuel Lady was the pastor. I do remember Daddy playing Christmas songs with his accordion. It would be the last time that I can recall Daddy playing his accordion. I do remember being up front singing Christmas carols with other children from Uncle Samuel's church. Christmas Day in 1950 came on a Monday and I remember the Christmas present that I got from Uncle Samuel and Aunt Lois, a black train engine. Great-Uncle Samuel and Aunt Lois's youngest child, Ruth, was only two years older than me.

Ruth and I would become good friends, and during my cruel and lonely world in the late 1960s, Ruth had me over for dinner numerous times in the Colonial Park area in East Harrisburg. I remember on our drive home from Uncle Samuel's, we were in heavy snow and that Daddy had to put chains on the tires. How many times do I remember Daddy putting chains on tires during my childhood as back then, there were no snow tires?

# CHAPTER 11

## The Years 1951–1952

During the summer of 1951, I would spend a couple of nights at the Abilene General Hospital as I had my tonsils and adenoids taken out. I remember as soon as I got home from the hospital, Mother gave me vanilla ice cream and I've been and ice cream lover ever since.

I must share a bit about Daddy and his basketball coaching. Daddy had played a lot of basketball in his high school and college years and he really knew the Xs and Os of coaching. When I was ages five and six, Detroit Elementary played Talmage Elementary in basketball, located fourteen miles northwest of Abilene. Detroit didn't have a gymnasium, so both years, Detroit had to play at Talmage. Talmage was a much larger school than Detroit. In all four games, Detroit defeated Talmage. However, after Daddy left Detroit as principal, it was a 360 turnaround as Talmage always defeated Detroit, just a statement of Daddy's knowledge of coaching. In the summers while living in Detroit, Daddy did some farming for a local man. I would get to ride on the tractor with Daddy. I recall there being walnuts all over the farmer's front yard, falling from a walnut tree.

The summer of 1951 in North Central, Kansas, was a wet one, an understatement. It was on Friday, July 13, called Black Friday by some meteorologists, that the costliest and most devastating flood in Kansas State history swept down the Kansas River Valley. Manhattan Kansas known as the Little Apple, a city of forty thousand had its business district covered with eight feet of water. Roads being washed away and railroad tracks moved. Can you believe that this was the very week the annual BIC General church conference was being held in Manhattan, located forty miles east of Abilene, Kansas. I recall Daddy driving us the four miles south to Abilene to Northeast Seventh Street where my Great-Uncle Luther and Great-Aunt Mildred Lady lived. A third cousin of mine Janice Hoover, and I were wading in water up to our knees. Janice's grandfather and grandmother, Jesse and Ruth Hoover, only lived a block from Great-Uncle Luther Lady's, Luther was the two-year-younger sibling of Anna who burned to death. Jesse Hoover and my Grandpa Hoover were first cousins. The flood claimed twenty-eight lives and more than one million acres of land were flooded. I remember Daddy driving through this flooded area. Again I must make mention of my dear precious great maternal grandmother, Mary Olive Lady. Great-Grandma made two aprons, one for Daddy and the other for Mother's first cousin, Mahlon Engle, for their working in the kitchen at the general conference. I'm so honored that Daddy, shortly before his death at ninety-seven, on August 26, 2018, gave me that same apron. While living in Detroit and years after, Daddy had a frozen walk-in locker at a mom-and-pop store, Dewey Steelsmiths. As a young boy, that was so awesome, being able to walk into the frozen locker.

In the fall of 1951, Daddy would accept a new assignment as principal of a one-room eighth grade elementary school, East Buckeye, located six miles north of Abilene. Can you believe that of the twenty-one students at East Buckeye, fifteen were first cousins with the surname of Kuntz? Our new home would be a former elementary 1890s schoolhouse. The irony is that the East Buckeye school district extended to only one-half mile from our new house located on Highway 15. This would be a real bummer for me as I would have to attend Talmage Elementary, located seven miles from our home, the Talmage that could never beat Detroit in basketball. I would enter second grade at Talmage with Mrs. Underhill being the teacher.

One day Mrs. Underhill asked me to go to the front of the class to recite a short reading. Shortly after beginning the reading, I began stuttering, forcing to get the words out but they wouldn't come. I remember my classmates laughing at me as I returned to my desk. This would be the first of hundreds of times during my life that I would be living out traumatic acute anxiety. I've always had a very hard time throughout my life with beginning sentences with the vowels, A, E, I, O, U. Most remarkably is that many times during my life, I've gotten up in front of a large gathering, such as a church service, family reunions, without stuttering at all. I feel like I'm a natural at public speaking.

# CHAPTER 12

## *The Abuse Begins*

In March of 1952, several startling occurrences began happening in our home. Going on sixty-eight years ago, I remember the following happening as though it was just yesterday. I witnessed my mother slapping Daddy in the face with profanity-laced language. I'll go to my grave remembering that first slap that Mother gave Daddy. Reflecting many years later, I've come to the realization, at that very moment was the beginning of my being emotionally abused and traumatized. This continual slapping and cursing of Daddy had the beginning of knots being torn up inside of me. I had referred to the phrase "the double whammy" as I began my story. The first phase had started that of witnessing Mother's abuse of Daddy, and within days, I would personally be hit by the second whammy.

For no reason at all, Mother began to punish me. My punishment was being sent to the cold outside cellar, being locked up with mice crawling around me. I would be locked up for two to three hours at a time. Our house was in the country with open fields all around us, the reason for there being mice. To this very day, I have a fear of seeing a mouse. My three children have known for years of that fear; now they will know where it had its roots. This outdoor cellar would become my personal dungeon, my albatross for the next three years. My brother Chuck was never abused like this. This double whammy of Daddy and myself would continue up through the age of seventeen, almost ten full years. The harsh reality is that for nearly sixty-five years, I had absolutely no idea of the traumatic abuse that I received at the hands of my mother and the impact that this abuse would impact my life. Please believe me, it's only in the last nineteen months, while researching and writing my memoir, that I've come to know of these two double whammies. Reflecting back these many years later, I've come to the sad realization that I was robbed of my childhood by my mother.

I feel that this is the appropriate time in my memoir to share with the reader my five escapes or places of refuge that I sought out during the years of my being emotionally and physically abused.

1. My most important refuge would be my priceless unforgettable memories of my time spent on my Grandpa and Grandma Hoover's farm. Here was where I, an emotionally traumatized boy, would receive true unconditional love that I would never receive at home. My most cherished boyhood memories are those summers spending with Grandpa and Grandma, Aunt Delores, Aunt Carol, and Uncle Harry and the unforgettable memories of my priceless time spent in the big red barn.

2. I can't overemphasize the importance of the world of sports as a safety net from my years of traumatic abuse. Proof of this will be the large amount of sports that I will share in my story. From the ages of eight through sixteen, I would literally spend hundreds and hundreds of hours shooting basketball in solitary. The radio would become a haven of rest and safety in my listening of many sporting events. If there was a live sporting event on the radio, I would find it. To be completely honest, I'm not sure if I would be here today on God's earth if it wasn't for sports. Sports was so therapeutic for a lonely abandoned boy.

3. The Abilene, Kansas, Public Library would become my home away from home where I would find peace and contentment. When first moving to Abilene, halfway through my fifth grade, I immediately sought out the public library through my senior year of high school in 1962. Beginning as a sixth grader, I would daily devour the sports pages of three newspapers. It was there at the library where I would come to memorize the birthdate and years of death of all thirty-four presidents as well as many of the first ladies. What priceless unforgettable memories I have of the Abilene Public Library. Next to my Grandpa and Grandma

Hoover's farm, the best moments of my child into adolescent years were spent at the public library.

4. Believe it or not, our family vacations would become such a fun and joyous time. I can never remember there being a family argument on our three major vacations: the trip to Ohio and general church conference in the summer of 1952, to the Grand Canyon and California in 1953, and the Black Hills in South Dakota in 1956. Reflecting these many years later, I've come to realize that these trips were a refuge of happy family times for both Mother and myself, so therapeutic for both of us.

5. The fifth and final refuge for me would be my love of Kansas State history as well as my love for my hometown of Abilene and Dickenson County. Included in my memoir will be that of two native Kansas sons who would both prevail over near-death experiences with the help of their parents' enduring unconditional love and prayer. One boy would grow up to be a great general and US president, the other a track-and-field superstar who became the greatest mile runner in his era and an 1870 lawman who became President Eisenhower's hero.

# CHAPTER 13

## The Ohio Trip and Childhood Trauma Defined

It's late June 1952, and our family is driving to the BIC annual church conference in West Milton, Ohio, a suburb of Dayton, Ohio. Chuck had just turned four and I was just a month away from turning eight. What memories I have of driving on the large bridge over the mighty Mississippi River. Our first destination would be the state of Kentucky, my birthplace. I would view the house where I was born high on the Kentucky hills. We visited Reverend Elam Dohner and his wife who had taken over for Daddy at the Knifley Church home mission. To this day, Mrs. Dohner made the most delicious strawberry shortcake that I've ever had.

After lodging at the Dohners, we left for West Milton, Ohio, for the annual BIC conference. Daddy at that time, was on many BIC conference committees. The highlight of that conference for me was seeing my first ever helicopter. Someone had helicoptered to the conference, and for a seven-year- old, that was so awesome.

The following is taken from research about childhood trauma, by Dr. Kathleen Kendall in the National Institute of Mental Health. Dr. Kendall defines childhood trauma as the experience of an event by a child that's emotionally painful and distressful which often results in lasting mental and physical effects. My suffering of this double whammy has led to a life of chronic depression and acute anxiety which has left me so short of my full potential. My biggest lifetime regret is not having been a history teacher and a basketball star which I'll share later.

In an article in *Psychology Today*, it makes mention that extreme trauma or anxiety may stunt children's growth. Psychologists have known that children who suffer severe emotional abuse often grow slowly or not at all, a condition called failure to thrive. The following is a statement from psychologist John Cacioppo of the University of Chicago, "Isolation is so damaging because infants and young children depend on social stimulation to shape their minds." Yes, the sad fact is that I was isolated, abandoned for hundreds of hours, from ages eight through ten, in that cold outdoor cellar.

I never realized until doing research on my memoir, of the many years of vitamin D that I was missing out on without sunshine. Let me emphasize that it wasn't in God's plan for a child to be kept inside, in darkness, during daylight hours. Sunshine is part of a child's growing cycle. Yes, that was physical trauma of being in the dark with no sunshine. I was kept locked up in what I refer to as my albatross. The definition of albatross is a psychological burden that feels like a curse. I recall, as a teenager, of a great- uncle of mine, a brother of my maternal grandmother who burned to death, saying to me, "You are so short, is it because of your homelife?" I have no idea of how he came up with that statement but I've been haunted by it for years. Was he aware of my abuse?

New research from the UK has found that exposure to family problems or child abuse will leave a child with a smaller cerebellum. For me, the emotional and physical abuse started at about eight and lasted until age of seventeen. The normal age that damage has been done is ages eight to eleven. Shockingly the ages that I was locked up in that albatross outdoor locked-up prison was ages eight to ten. Just several statistics regarding height in my immediate family: my brother Chuck is 5'11", my late daddy was 5'8", and my son, David, is 5'10" and a half and I'm barely 5'4".

# C H A P T E R   1 4

## *Fervent Prayer and Enduring Love*

Dwight David Eisenhower was born on October 14, 1890, in a modest two- story-frame house in Denison, Texas. Dwight was the third of seven sons, born to David and Ida "Stover" Eisenhower. In 1892 the Eisenhower family moved to Abilene, Kansas. David Eisenhower would be employed at the historic Belle Springs Creamery where the manufacture of butter, ice cream, and ice would be made. The Eisenhower family roots run deep in Dickenson County, Kansas, history. Ike's great-grandfather Jacob Eisenhower, a deeply religious man, followed other Pennsylvania River Brethren families in 1878 to the Belle Springs area, just southeast of Abilene. The President's parents, David and Ida Stover, met while students at Lane University in Lecompton, Kansas. David was studying mechanical engineering while Ida was studying music. David Eisenhower and Ida Stover were married in 1885 in the university's chapel. Through family connections, David Eisenhower was hired as a mechanic in the Belle Springs Creamery engine room.

One afternoon while running home from school, young Dwight almost lost a leg after falling while racing down a wooden platform. The knee became swollen, turning a dark shade—a result of blood poisoning. Ike was in and out of consciousness for over two weeks. Dr. Conklin examined little Ike's leg and was attempting to reach for a saw, drawing a line just above the knee. Doc Conklin said to Ike, "If I do this now, I can save the rest of the leg. The longer I wait, the more I'll have to take off." Little Ike would shake his head, no death seemed better.

"You can't take any of my leg off," Ike told the doc.

Doc Conklin went downstairs and told both parents, "Ike's not wanting his leg cut off. Doc was urging Ike's parents, David and Ida, to give him permission to cut off the leg.

When Edgar, known as big Ike, little Ike's oldest brother, came home, Ike cried out to Edgar, "Promise me you won't let Doc cut off my leg. I'd rather be dead than crippled." Edgar gave Ike his word. For two days and nights, Edgar, as a loyal brother, remained right outside the bedroom door; while inside the bedroom, Ike would be continually biting on a fork to keep from screaming. Ike's pain was agonizing. The leg was swelling up like a balloon about to burst. Luckily for Ike, his parents refused to give the doc permission to cut. Both parents' thinking was, *If it's God's will for Ike to die, not even the sharp singing bone saw could save him.* Doc Conklin applied an alcohol carbolic acid to help keep infection from spreading to the rest of Ike's body. Dwight became unconscious and he was struggling to breathe. Death seemed so imminent, and then miraculously, Dwight's breathing began to improve and the swelling was decreasing and Dwight's fever diminished. Dwight would live after all, not by brother Ed's help nor by Doc Conklin but both Ida and David were certain it was through fervent prayer and God's will. Somehow Ike was possessed with an inner will and strength given by God to have survived. Ike missed so many school days that he was forced to repeat his freshman year. James 5:16 tells us, "The effectual fervent prayer of a righteous man availeth much." Prayer was of extreme importance in the life of this family. One night a week, the Eisenhower family gathered in the parlor to read the Bible, with the boys taking turns reading a passage of the Bible. Before Ike was eighteen-years-old, he had read the Bible through twice, from Genesis through Revelation.

To sum this true story up, you have an illustration of enduring love. As it was with Edgar who stood right outside Ike's bedroom for two days and two nights. David and Ida Eisenhower were steadfast in their loyalty to both sons, little Ike and big Ike, Edgar who valiantly stood by his dying brother for two full days. The Eisenhower family was loyal to a fault. The family stood firm with their son's wishes that he remain whole and nothing else was acceptable.

Irvin Brechbill Hoover and Ann Zelma Lady Hoover
The wedding of my Grandfather Irvin Hoover and my
Grandmother Anna Zelma Lady on February 1, 1917

Irvin Brechbill Hoover and Carrie Deemy Hoover The wedding of my Grandfather
Irvin Brechbill Hoover and Carrie Deemy my Step-Grandmother on May 22, 1930

The five daughters pictorial in 1928 left to right Rozella, Virgie, Faithe, Eunice, Mary Lou

The Pennsylvania bus trip July 1950 when 5 years old. The
great-grandchildren with Mary Olive Frey Lady
Front row left to right Joyce Hess, Faithe Hess, Janet Eshelman, Great Grandma
Lady Irvin Thrush, Rozanna Thrush Standing in back far left Irwin Hess, myself
the towhead, Jerry Hess back of me Far back Johnny Thrush, Glenda Hess

The result of Explosion of Grandpa Hoover's house, on May 31, 1953

My first day of 1<sup>st</sup> grade

My mother and Grandpa thrashing wheat in the summer of 1938

# CHAPTER 15

## *The 1952 Presidential Election*

The time it's the fall of 1952, Tuesday, November 4, 1952, and the US is voting for the thirty-fourth president of the US. My lifelong love of history and politics would be rooted in this 1952 presidential election. As an eight- year-old, I had my ears right up to the kitchen radio listening to the roll call of the states. Why was that 1952 election so special for me? the Republican candidate for President had spent his entire boyhood into adolescence growing up in my native beloved hometown of Abilene, Kansas, the five-star general, the supreme commander of the Allied forces in WWII, President of the prestigious Ivy League school Columbia University, Abilene's own native son was running for President of the United States—his name Dwight David Eisenhower, better known as Ike.

The presidential slogan for the 1952 Republican Party was "I like Ike." How did the Eisenhower boys get the nickname Ike? Ike was an abbreviation for their last name Eisenhower. By adulthood only Dwight was called Ike.

Ike's main challenger for the 1952 Republican Party for president was Robert A. Taft the oldest son of former President Howard Taft. Taft was the front-runner for the Republican nomination until Thomas Dewey and other moderates convinced Eisenhower to run. It's ironic that Taft who lost to Ike, became senate majority leader of the Republican Party. Six months later on July 31, 1953, Taft died from pancreatic cancer. As an eight-year-old already interested in politics, I remember his passing well.

On June 4–5, 1952, Ike came home to Abilene and I was able to see Ike, memories to last a lifetime. Ike's advisers decided that General

Eisenhower should make the announcement of his running for president on the Republican ticket in his hometown of Abilene. They felt that the small-town flavor would add to his popularity and that local color was needed, sort of like a windowsill type of thing. They wanted old friends talking to reporters about old-time memoires with Ike. The Abilene train depot on Northwest Second Street is just several blocks north of the Eisenhower center and home. I shall forever remember the train approaching the depot. I recall seeing the renowned CBS broadcaster Edward R. Murrow being there. I recall my family later that morning, being in attendance of the laying of a cornerstone for the building of the Eisenhower Museum. At around 3:00 p.m., on June 4, 1952, Abilene held the largest parade the town had ever seen. There were bands, horses, floats. The climactic moment of the parade came when several floats were pulled by convertibles depicting a stage in Ike's life. June 4, 1952, would be the first of three times that I would get a live view of Abilene's favorite son.

On that Tuesday evening November 4, 1952, Daddy drove us the four miles south on Highway 15 to Abilene and the site of the hometown newspaper, *The Reflector Chronicle*, located then at Third and Spruce Street. The *Reflector* had put up the continuous election updates on the front window. The election result was a landslide victory for Ike. The final voting result was Eisenhower, 442 electoral votes, and Adlai Stevenson, 89 electoral votes. The popular vote—Eisenhower 33,936,204 to Stevenson's 27,314,992 votes. I vividly recall there being large posters of "I like Ike" which became the presidential slogan for the Republican party in 1952.

During Ike's eight-year administration, there were four occasions when Ike visited Abilene. The population of Dickenson County, Kansas, has roughly stayed at around twenty-one thousand throughout the decades, and my guess is that well over 75 percent of the residents showed up to cheer on Abilene's favorite son. There was a parade with marching bands from local high schools and state colleges. Ike and Mamie would be riding in the open limousine, constantly waving to the crowd.

The Eisenhower Museum was completed in 1954. Both Daddy and Uncle Herbert worked on the building of it. In addition, there's the much larger Eisenhower Library where ground was broken on October 13, 1959, and on May 1, 1962 then-vice-president Lyndon Johnson would join the retired president in the dedication of the Eisenhower Library. What's so convenient for visitors is that both the museum and library are located just several blocks from the Eisenhower home.

I must share a tidbit about my beloved Grandpa Irvin Hoover. My dearest Aunt Carol Hoover Wenger shared the following with me. She relates, "Your Grandpa Hoover, on Ike's first visit to Abilene, walked past Secret Service, enabling him to shake the hand of Ike, shocking the security guards." Yes, my Grandpa Irvin Brechbill Hoover was one unforgettable character.

Another little-known fact, the Brethren in Christ Church in the late 1800s to mid-1960s had two bishops, one serving South Dickenson County and the other in charge of North Dickenson County churches. The bishop in charge of South Dickenson was Ray Witter who just happened to be a first cousin of Ike's. As a young boy, I got to know Ray very well as he was an evangelist and a bishop and pastor. Bishop Witter would travel the entire US as an evangelist. Even though Ray Witter was a first cousin to Ike, never once in his life did Bishop Ray Witter vote for the president of the US.

# CHAPTER 16

## A Massive Heart Attack

The date was August 14, 1955, and President Eisenhower flew into Denver, Colorado, for what he was calling a work-and-play vacation until October. Ike planned to go fishing at Byers Peak Ranch in the Rocky Mountains and playing golf in the city of Denver's many golf courses. Ike would experience a massive heart attack on September 24, 1955, which I remember well. It turned out to be on a golf course where historians and medical experts now surmise Ike's heart attack began. Feeling ill after a round of golf at the Cherry Hills Golf Club in Southern Denver, Ike returned to his in-laws at the Doud home. Ike had turned in early the evening of September 23, awaking to chest pains in the early morning of September 24. A cardiac specialist was summoned from Fitzsimons Army Hospital to conduct an electrocardiogram which confirmed that President Eisenhower had suffered a massive heart attack. Wife Mamie moved into an adjoining suite at the Fitzsimons Army Hospital. This suite was decorated in all pink for her, including a pink toilet seat.

While in the hospital, recovering on his birthday, October 14, the White House Press Corps gave Ike a set of maroon pajamas—his uniform of choice—along with a western necktie. The pajamas also featured five stars on each collar, denoting his army rank. A month after his heart attack, Ike made his first public appearance on October 25, 1955; and on that day, a sixth gold star appeared in the center of his collar, a gift from Dr. Paul White given to Ike for good conduct. On November 11, Armistice Day, President Eisenhower was released from Fitzsimons Army Hospital. Ike, in his farewell brief speech from the hospital, closed with the following statement, "So I leave with my heart unusually filled with gratefulness, to Denver, to the people here—in fact to everyone who has been so kind."

I recall, as a twelve-year-old, watching on TV the second inauguration of President-elect Eisenhower on Monday January 21, 1957. The Dickenson County Public School System was closed in honor of their native son. Chief Justice Earl Warren administered the presidential oath. The inaugural parade was highlighted with a mammoth float—408 feet long and mounted on 164 wheels—which introduced the theme "liberty and strength" through consent of the governed. It was such a treat to watch our hometown Abilene cowgirl majorettes with their marching and baton twirling. Just a sidenote about Ike's second inauguration, it's the first time that a president was inaugurated for a term limited by the constitution (Twenty-Second Amendment) which stated that no person shall be elected to the office of the presidency more than twice.

# CHAPTER 17

## Presidential Train Rides to Their Eternal Rest

President Eisenhower and wife Mamie, retired to his farm at Gettysburg, Pennsylvania, located close to the Civil War setting at Gettysburg. President Eisenhower passed away in Washington, DC, on March 28, 1969, at the age of seventy-nine. I would like to mention two presidential train rides to each final resting place. The first is President Eisenhower and the second, my hero in US history, Abraham Lincoln. President Eisenhower's casket traveled by train on March 31, 1969, from the Washington National Cathedral to his hometown of Abilene, Kansas, arriving at his beloved Abilene on April 2, 1969. A crowd, estimated at one hundred thousand people, had come to Abilene to pay their respects to their native son. Located right across from Ike's boyhood home is the Place of Meditation where Ike was interred with firstborn son, David Dwight, called Icky, who died on January 2, 1921, from scarlet fever. Wife Mamie passed away on November 1, 1979, at age eighty- two. Both Ike's and Mamie's graves are covered with a marble slab.

I've read many books on, whom I consider the greatest US President, Abraham Lincoln, born near Hodgenville, Kentucky, on February 12, 1809, in a log cabin which I've been so fortunate to visit. Lincoln passed away on April 15, 1865, from an assassin's bullet. On April 21, 1865, Lincoln's body was loaded onto a nine-car funeral train carrying 300 through 180 cities and seven states and readied for the 1,700-mile trek home to Springfield, Illinois, his hometown where he would be buried on

May 4, 1865. The train would make several stops. At each stop, Lincoln's coffin was taken off the train, placed on an elaborately decorated horse-drawn hearse, and led by solemn processions to a public place for viewing. In cities as large as Columbus, Ohio, and as small as Herkimer, New York, thousands of mourners flocked to pay tribute to the slain president. In Philadelphia, Lincoln's body lay in state in the east wing of Independence Hall, the same site where the Declaration of Independence was signed. Newspapers reported that people had to wait more than five hours to pass by the president's coffin in some cities. This goes to show you what a beloved president he was.

Lincoln's funeral train was dubbed "The Lincoln Special." His portrait was fastened to the front of the engine above the cattle guard. Lincoln's eldest son Robert, accompanied the body as well as Lincoln's son Willie who had died in 1862 at the age of eleven from typhoid fever. Willie's body had been disinterred from a plot in Washington, DC, so he could be buried alongside his father at the family plot in Springfield. Mary Todd Lincoln, the widow of Abraham Lincoln, passed away in 1882 and lies at eternal rest with both Abraham and son Willie.

As a young boy who suffered from much emotional abuse, I would devour many books about sports and history and my all-time favorite hero in American history is Honest Abe. Let me share a little-known story about the sensitiveness of Lincoln. One day, Congressman Thaddeus Stevens from Lancaster, Pennsylvania, and one of the leaders of the radical Republican Party in the house of representatives in the 1860s accompanied an old lady from Lancaster to the White House, seeking a presidential pardon for her son. The son was condemned to die because he went to sleep while on post at duty. Lincoln granted the request and was to have said, "I couldn't think of going into eternity with the blood of that poor boy on my hands. It is not to be wondered at that a boy raised on the farm and in the habit of going to bed early should go to sleep during the night watch. I cannot consent to sentence him for such an act." Lincoln penciled a note in silence and handed it to the mother and said, "Here, madam, is your son's pardon."

The old lady's gratitude knew no bounds. Tears accompanied her words of thanks to the president. When she and Mr. Stevens reached the outer door of the White House, she burst out excitedly, "I knew it was a lie. I knew it was a lie."

"What do you mean," asked Mr. Stevens.

The woman replied, "When I left home, a neighbor said I would find Mr. Lincoln an ugly man. The truth is that he is really the handsomest man I ever saw in my life."

Let me share a talent of Honest Abe which I found in the Lancaster, Pennsylvania, *Intelligencer* journal, written by Joseph Roda, a retired attorney who resides in Lancaster County. Quoting Roda, "While Lincoln was a master of the long speech, he was equally a master of the short. Consider the Gettysburg Address, only 272 words, and his second inaugural only 701." Again Roda, states, "Consider also the statements like 'the world will little note nor long remember what we said here, but it can never forget what they did here,' or with charity towards all, with malice towards none." If only our politicians in 2020 had the integrity and the humbleness of our sixteenth and greatest President of the US.

Let me share another little known fact about Lincoln. For fifty-one years, Lincoln never wore a beard, but during the 1860 presidential campaign, Lincoln received a letter from a little girl named Grace Bedell who lived in Westfield, New York. Grace wrote that she had seen his portrait and thought he would look better with a beard. She promised that if he let his whiskers grow, she would try to persuade her older brothers who were Democrats to vote for him. Lincoln wrote back to her on October 19, 1860:

> Your very agreeable letter of the fifteenth is received. I regret the necessity of saying that I have no daughter. I have three sons, one seventeen, one nine, and one seven years of age. As to the whiskers, having never worn any, do you not think people would call it a piece of silly affection if I should begin it now?
>
> Your very sincere well-wisher,
> A Lincoln

Lincoln, however, soon changed his mind on the subject. When he was on his way to Washington to be inaugurated, the train stopped at

Westfield, New York. Remembering young Grace Bedell, Lincoln inquired after her. It was soon discovered that she was present. The president asked her to come forward so Grace might see that Abe had allowed his whiskers to grow at her request. She timidly obliged, and Abe lifted her up and kissed her while the crowd roared its approval. Abe wore a beard ever after. Can you believe that Abraham Lincoln has had sixteen hundred books written about him? The Library of Congress some years ago numbered that many books that have been written about the martyred "Great Emancipator." Furthermore, Lincoln's Gettysburg Address is the most memorized speech in the world.

# CHAPTER 18

## Ike the All-Around Athlete

Let me share several other little-known facts about the five-star general and supreme commander of the Allied Forces in WWII. After graduating from Abilene High School in 1909, Ike worked at the Belle Springs Creamery, 6:00 p.m. to 6:00 a.m., seven days a week. With his creamery earnings, Ike supported Edgar through two years of college at the University of Michigan. The plan was for Edgar to work the next two years for Ike's schooling. Instead Ike won an appointment to the US Military Academy at West Point, New York, and, as the saying goes, the rest is history.

Ike was an all-around athlete. At Abilene High, Ike starred in both baseball and football. Of all the US Presidents, Ike was arguably the most natural athlete. In the summer after graduating from Abilene High, Ike played centerfield in the Kansas league under a synonymous name "Charlie Wilson" as Ike didn't want to have his amateur standing jeopardizing in his going to West Point.

The great athlete Jim Thorpe, who I consider the greatest athlete in the first half of the twentieth century, had all of his gold medals taken away at the Helsinki, Finland, 1912 Olympics due to his playing amateur baseball. In that 1912 Olympics, Thorpe won the cherished decathlon. Thorpe was the first Native American to have his medals taken away. When being admitted to West Point, Ike's number one priority was to play football. During Ike's sophomore season, Ike came in at running back due to an injury to a running back. All Ike did was to score sixteen touchdowns in four straight games. In 1912, in what was to be an epic game, Army played the legendary Thorpe and the famed Carlisle Indian school. In that game, Ike took a ferocious hit to the knee by Thorpe.

Late in that 1912 season against Tufts University, Ike twisted his knee so badly, and for the rest of his life Ike would have a sensitive knee.

One other unknown fact concerns the well-known presidential retreat of Camp David in Maryland's Catoctin Mountain Park. This presidential retreat opened in 1938 by FDR and was called Shangri-la, after the fictional Himalayan paradise. Ike, however, wanted a less formal name so he renamed it in 1953 in honor of his five-year-old grandson, David Eisenhower. Shangri- la was just a little too fancy for a Kansas farm boy that he wrote in a letter to his boyhood Abilene friend Edward Swede Hazlett. There you have the historical legend of Camp David.

Ike smoked three packs of cigarettes a day, picking up the habit while he was a student at West Point and quitting only a few years before he became President. His initial attempt involved excising tobacco and the related accoutrements from his daily life but it didn't work out so Ike went in the other direction. Ike related, "I decided to make a game of the whole business and try to achieve a feeling of some superiority when I saw others smoking while I no longer did." Ike crammed cigarettes and lighters into every nook of his office. Ike related, "I made it a practice to offer a cigarette to anyone who came in and I lighted each while mentally reminding myself as I sat down, *I don't have to do what that poor fellow is doing.*"

Cabinet meetings opened with a silent prayer, and on more than one occasion, in a moment of adversity, Ike said he felt the need for divine assistance. The need for prayer was deeply ingrained in Ike as a boy, and Ike often quoted, "Freedom itself means nothing unless there is faith."

A grand house over the last century in Abilene, has been the Seelye Mansion located on North Buckeye Street, the main North South Street in my native hometown. The mansion was built in 1905 by Dr. A. B. Seelye. His two daughters went to school with the Eisenhower boys. However, the Eisenhowers were from the other side of the tracks, being the poor south side of Abilene. For this reason, the boy who was to become president of the US had to use the side door to enter the mansion as he was not good enough to enter through the front doors. Legend has it that Mamie Eisenhower agreed to move back to Abilene upon Ike's retirement with one stipulation—that they live in the Seelye Mansion. But the Seelye sisters wouldn't sell so Ike didn't move back to Abilene until after his death.

Ike was just an ordinary student but he was an outstanding high school and college athlete and had he not suffered repeated knee injuries (playing football and thrown from a jumping horse during cavalry training), he very well could have become a professional baseball player or football coach instead of a General and President. Historians, writers, and diplomats have analyzed Eisenhower inside and out, trying to find out what gave him such a worldwide good-guy hero image. There have been other great generals and presidents—but probably never again one like Ike. Ike never lost his common country boy touch with the people. Ike enjoyed shaking up some of his white- tie audiences in this country and abroad with stories about the rip-roaring days of the West where he was raised. No high position Ike ever held went to his head. Most importantly, Ike never forgot his humble beginnings in Abilene and spoke often of his beloved hometown, and his hero was none other than Marshall Thomas Smith who lies buried only one hundred yards from Ike's parents in the Abilene cemetery.

As a lifetime scholar of US and world history, I consider Sir Winston Churchill the greatest political leader of the twentieth century. Churchill was a British statesman, army officer, and writer. He was Prime Minister of the United Kingdom from 1940 to 1945 when he led the country to victory in the Second World War and again from 1951 to 1955. Amid the developing "Cold War" with the Soviet Union, he publicly warned of an "iron curtain" of Soviet influence in Europe, and Churchill was the leader against the spread of fascism. Due to Churchill and Eisenhower working closely during World War II, both became vast friends. Ironically, after retiring from public service, both men took up the hobby of oil painting. On retiring to Gettysburg in 1961, Ike took up "oil painting," and Ike painted a portrait of Winston Churchill against the Prime Minister's advice. Churchill was an accomplished artist, whose paintings have been hung in the Louvre in Paris. Churchill told Ike, "I do not paint portraits of people—only trees and mountains—because they don't talk back." Ike painted Churchill's portrait in 1954. It now hangs in the Walter Reed Hospital, where Eisenhower died in 1969.

# CHAPTER 19

## The Thanksgiving Blizzard of 1952

Just weeks after the 1952 presidential election, the National Weather Service had put out a warning for a snow blizzard heading for North Central Kansas on Thanksgiving November 27. On Thanksgiving eve, November 26, Daddy had walked the two miles to East Buckeye Elementary as he thought that by evening, he might not be able to drive home. The snow had started out lightly that morning, and by noon, it was snowing heavily and the winds had picked up to over forty miles per hour sustained.

While at school, Daddy would relate the following, "All I could see while looking out the school windows was a blanket of heavy snowflakes dropping down from the heavens. There wasn't a soul in sight. I could just barely make out the outline of the road but no car tracks. Most of my students had been picked up by about noon with an early dismissal. I had gotten ready to head home and prepare for tomorrow's holiday. Now it looked like Thanksgiving 1952 might not happen at all for any of us. No one was going to get out in this blizzard. I glanced back at the five children of Homer and Sarah Kuntz. Their parents were stuck and unable to make it out to the school. 'I'm afraid we're going to be here for a while,' I told the children after getting a call from their daddy Homer. 'Maybe we'll be here all night.'

"'But where will we sleep?' little Twila said, her face filled with worry. 'I'm cold,' Edward added, and 'I'm hungry,' Dwight said. Warren and Dorland nodded. I took out the sandwich and apple from the lunch I hadn't eaten and divided it among them as I was too nervous to eat anyway. Somehow it was up to me to keep the children safe and calm. At least we were inside but we'd lost power earlier that morning, and with no heat, already our breath hung in the frigid air. How long could the kids hold out in this chill? And what about my own kids? I'd called my wife, Faithe, hours ago to tell her I'd be home soon but that was before I knew about the Homer Kuntz family. Faithe was home alone with our boys. Who was caring for my family while I was stuck here? Had they lost power? When I left the house in the morning, Faithe was full of plans for Thanksgiving. I wasn't feeling very thankful now. I picked up the phone to update my wife. However, when the operator tried to place the call, nothing happened."

"I'm sorry but that line is dead," Daddy was told.

While back at our home, Mother heard someone yelling. Mother went to the door and looked out. Our neighbor Bert Zook was standing out in his lane, hollering over the howling wind to Mother, "David's stuck at the school. Your phone line is down but David got through to my house." Mother waved in acknowledgement and came back inside. As an eight-year-old, I recall thinking to myself, *Could God's angel's protect Daddy at the school?* as little did we know of the five Kuntz children being there with Daddy.

At about 5:30 p.m., there came a knock at our front door. Mother opened the door and was startled to find two young men and a young woman huddled together on the porch. They were covered with snow, their cheeks red from the wind. "We're students at Kansas State," one of the men said. "We were on our way home for Thanksgiving when my car slid into the ditch. Would you have any room for us?"

"Why, of course," Mother replied. "Come inside and get warm by the fire." Mother then made a fresh pot of coffee.

Mother later remarked how she had prayed for angels to protect Daddy but God had also heard Mother's silent plea for company. Several minutes later, there came the sound of feet stomping on the front porch. Mother opened the door, only to find two men—linemen for Kansas Power and Light. "Our truck slid into the ditch," one of the men said.

"Please come in," Mother replied. The two KP and L men warmed up with what was still fresh coffee, when about ten minutes later, there came still another knock at the front door, a bread man's truck had slid off the road and gotten stuck.

He said, "I just made out a faint light in the window leading to your front door. Would you have a place I could stay?" Mother immediately let him in and warmed him up with another fresh pot of coffee. Certainly God had answered Mother's silent plea for company.

Back at the school, Daddy would rack up in his mind for ideas to keep the kids moving. "We'd play tag and duck, duck, goose, and Simon says." *What now*, Daddy would think. Heavy curtains hung from the windows and Daddy pulled them down and draped them around the children, but still, they couldn't stop shivering. Daddy later remarked of trying to stay calm but he could feel the fear, a sense of dread building up inside of him. Daddy would later tell us, "It was getting pitch-dark save for the flickering light of the candles. We huddled together. I could hear little Twila sniffling, trying not to cry. I thought about Faithe and how she was coping, all alone with my two sons, and Homer and Sarah Kuntz, how frightened they must be. I'd never felt more alone, cut off from everyone."

And then Daddy remarked, "I heard a rustling, the door flew open, a shadow filled the doorway—'Uncle Harry,' the children shouted together. Mrs. Kugler called me and swore she wouldn't be able to sleep one wink, knowing I was in this icebox. I hitched up the horses and, well, we better get going." Mrs. Kugler was a member of the East Buckeye school board and she was such a vocal resident that no one could refuse her request.

Daddy recalled, "We held each other in the back of the wagon while Harry urged the horses, a team of Percherons, through the drifts." A Percheron is a breed of draft horse that originated in the Western France, usually gray or black in color, strong and muscled, and known for their intelligence and willingness to work. "I would spend the night at Brian Curren's home while Harry Kuntz took his niece and nephews home with him. Lying on a warm guest bed that night, I thought about everything that had happened. Boy, would I have a story to tell Faithe. *She'll never believe it*, I thought as I drifted to sleep."

While back at our home, Mother had a dilemma with five men and a young lady to host on this Thanksgiving Eve, what was Mother to do? Fortunately our neighbor Bert Zook heard Mother's call for help. Bert hustled over to our place and he offered to take the bakery driver and the two young college men for the night. Mother was still left with the two KP and L men and the young lady. Mother put the two men in the spare room and the young lady slept with Mother. Our phone line was down but Bert just happened to have two telephone lines. Daddy would call Bert on the line that was working and then Bert came over to let us know that Daddy and the five Kuntz children were safe and sound.

On Thanksgiving morning, Mother made the two men and the young lady a hearty breakfast before setting out to find their transportation. On Thanksgiving morning, Daddy arrived home on Brian Curran's horse with whom he had stayed the night. What a joyful reunion it was. And boy, did Mother and Daddy have one unbelievable story to tell the other. And with a little icing added to the cake, KP and L had a magazine that was put out monthly with our photos in it. Since Mother had kept their two employees sheltered through the blizzard, they came to our home to interview Mother, Chuck, and me. On Thanksgiving, it was just the four of us for dinner but our house and our hearts had never been more thankful knowing that we lived in a community of angels.

Christmas 1952 was to be so special for this boy of eight. This boy had sent Santa a letter, telling him how good a boy he had been in 1952 and asking Santa to bring him a basketball for Christmas. And did Santa Claus come through for this lad in giving him the best Christmas gift he would ever receive in a Wilson basketball? Uncle Harry in his high school shop class had made me a basketball backboard, and Daddy bought me a rim and a net and put a pole in the backyard ground, and I, for the next two full years, would be in basketball heaven, a haven of safety, away from my "albatross" prison abuse. I would shoot hoops for hours even with a two-inch blanket of snow on the ground.

# CHAPTER 20

## Fort Riley, Kansas

During the summer of 1951 and '52, Daddy would take several summer courses at Kansas State University in nearby Manhattan, Kansas, known as the Little Apple. Manhattan was located on Highway 40 East, forty-five miles from our home. Daddy needed to complete several college courses to enable him to keep his permanent teaching certificate for the State of Kansas Board of Education. For six Saturdays, Daddy would drive to Manhattan and it was a special treat that I always got to go with him. Those Saturday drives with Daddy will forever live in my heart, priceless moments with Daddy to live a lifetime. Daddy drove old Highway 40 East which took us through Junction City. Located between Junction City and Manhattan is Fort Riley, Kansas, home of the big red one, the First Infantry Division. In the fall of 1866, shortly after the Civil War, Major General George A. Custer would take command of the Seventh Calvary Regiment at Fort Riley, and at that time, the Union Pacific Railroad reached the fort. The military police were always looking for speeders. Daddy was always so very careful driving the speed limit which was twenty miles an hour. Daddy's classes normally ran from 8:30 a.m. to 3:30 p.m. with a half-hour for lunch. I had access to a reading room where I always had a couple of books.

A man who in the future was to become a legendary sports figure and a living milestone for racial equality, had been assigned in April 1942, to a cavalry unit at Fort Riley, his name was the immortal Jackie Robinson. On April 15, 1947, Jackie would break the Major League Baseball color barrier, becoming the first black player. Robinson, while a student at UCLA, was the first person to letter in four major sports: baseball, basketball, football, and track. Believe it or not, Jackie's worse sport at UCLA was baseball, hitting only .097. In his first baseball game, playing for the Bruins, Jackie had two stolen bases and went 4-for-4. Robinson only played one season of baseball at UCLA. His two top sports were football and track. Robinson led the nation in punt-return average in both 1939 and 1940, and Jackie's career average of 18.8 yards per return ranks fourth in NCAA history.

Robinson, with several other blacks, were rejected for OCS at Fort Riley because they lacked leadership abilities. Robinson took his plight not to army officials but to a more commanding figure—Joe Louis, known as the "Brown Bomber," whose reign as the world heavyweight champion was from 1937– 1949. Louis would become one of the greatest heavyweights of all time. Joe Louis along with Jackie Robinson was serving in the US Army at Fort Riley, Kansas. Joe Louis, a black like Robinson, took several other blacks, along with Robinson's grievance, to the secretary of defense; and within a matter of days, Robinson and other blacks were enrolled in OCS. What cherished memories I have of Saturdays with Daddy at K-State.

# CHAPTER 21

## Baseball Cards and Memorization

The time is the spring of 1953 at Talmage Elementary. At lunch break, a friend and I took the short two blocks' walk to Talmage's ma and pa store. I had heard from friends that this 1953 Bowman baseball card set was special with a colored set of 160 cards and a black-and-white set of 54 cards. I was in baseball heaven and my baseball card collecting had started. This 1953 Bowman card was by far the most popular card ever. A Mickey Mantle card—very good or excellent—sells for $1,950, just unbelievable. As for my Bowman cards, either I lost the cards or Mother threw them away. Recently I purchased a reprint set of both the color and b and w for a special price of $69. Did this take me back to my childhood days. Today a minted set of the 1953 Bowman goes for about $ 10,000. It was at this time, in the spring of 1953, that I was at recess at Talmage when I first heard the name Mickey Mantle, the future legend. This was the beginning of my love for Major League Baseball.

My younger brother Chuck and I would improvise in making a little extra cash. We lived right along Highway 15, a main north south artery which ran the entire state of Kansas. Back in the 1950s, the landscape would be littered with pop bottles and Chuck and I hit a gold mine. We would walk two miles on both sides of the highway and did we strike gold. At that time a pop bottle came to three cents which bought me a lot of baseball cards. The future first lady of the US, Lady Bird Johnson's, action to beautify America was still some fifteen years in the future.

From the late 1940s through the '50s, two Major League teams dominated, The New York Yankees of the American League and the

Brooklyn Dodgers of the National League. These two teams would meet in the 1947, 1949, 1952, 1953, 1955, and 1956 World Series. You were either a Yankee or a Dodger and I was a die-hard Dodger. Them Bums, another name for the Dodgers, were never able to win that seventh and final game. On a spring Saturday in 1953, my friend Dwight and I were playing catch in his long lane. His father came walking by and said to us, "You boys always have to be for the two best teams, the Yankees and Dodgers." Dwight was a Yankee fan and I, a Dodger. Those were Bert's exact words. This is just another instance of my left temporal lobe, located right below the temple, the memory part of the brain, enabling me to retain the exact words.

Yes, the good Lord has blessed me with an exceptional memory. There were many times when I was in my prison dungeon that I had my baseball cards and sports magazines being a refuge for me. Already as an eight-year-old, I had memorized the entire starting lineup of all 16 Major League teams, all 16 managers, and many of the coaches and pitchers. Let's see, that's eight positions times 16 teams which comes to 128 players, 16 managers—a total of 144. That doesn't even include pitchers, so I had at least two hundred players memorized. I would recite them all to my aunts, uncles, and grandparents who were completely astonished.

# CHAPTER 22

## The Explosion

The date was May 31, 1953, my late beloved uncle Harry's sixteenth birthday, and I'm spending a month at my beloved grandparents. The setting, a cow pasture. Uncle Harry and I were leading the dairy cattle in from the pasture for morning milking. When suddenly, there was a loud cracking boom. My initial reaction was that it was thunder but an older and wiser sixteen-year-old Uncle Harry knew better. What had happened was that there was a leak near the furnace in the cellar, and when the hot water heater came on, that ignited the explosion. For some unknown reason that only God knows, all of us had gotten up about a half-hour later than usual that morning. Normally, at the precise moment of the explosion, Grandpa, Uncle Harry, and I would be sitting around the dining table chatting, while Grandma, Aunt Carol, and Aunt Delores would be preparing breakfast. Where we all would normally have been sitting at the dining table eating breakfast, right above in the ceiling were fork prints, kitchen utensil prints punctured into the ceiling. The dining room floor and been blown up where we would have been sitting. Miraculously not one of us were injured, although several days later, I fell halfway to the basement and as a result, had a nasty scar for years on my left side. We would all end up living out of the washhouse for the next three weeks.

# CHAPTER 23

## *The California Trip*

The summer of 1953 would be extremely busy for Grandpa Hoover's as well as my family. On July 7, 1953, Aunt Carol was united in marriage to Virgil Wenger with my daddy officiating at my home church, the BIC in Abilene. Uncle Virgil had recently been deployed in the Korean War and was a graduate of Abilene High. Two weeks later on July 21,1953, Uncle Herbert would tie the knot with Gladys Gish at her home church, the Upland, California, BIC Church with Daddy again officiating. To this day, I have no idea how Grandpa and Grandma Hoover got the house fixed up and then drive the 1,500 miles to California.

Just days after Aunt Carol's wedding, our family embarked on a seventeen-day trip. These family trips were my happiest times with Mother and Daddy. There was no arguing, no slapping, and best of all no cellar prison. Our first stop took us South to Greensburg, Kansas, to tour the world's deepest hand-dug well at 109 ft. deep and 32 ft. in diameter. A spiral- like staircase took you deep down into the well. Our trip resumed on Route 66 West to the magnificent Grand Canyon, carved out by the Colorado River. As an eight-year-old, I was just in awe of the canyon's layered bands of red rock and the majestic beauty of its mile-deep geologic wonder.

After leaving the Grand Canyon, a once in a hundred happened. We were driving through a small town shortly after leaving the Grand Canyon, and lo and behold, we saw a car with a Kansas license; and would you believe who it was—my uncle Glenn Hoover, the second oldest child of Grandpa and Grandma Carrie. Uncle Glenn had a passenger, a cousin of

Mother's, Pauline Frey. I was completely dumbfounded. What are those odds? Pauline was the daughter of my great-grandmother Mary Olive Frey Lady's youngest sibling Lawrence Frey. We chatted for a bit and traveled on. Our next stop would be Needles, California, the last stop for gasoline before entering the Mojave Desert, the driest desert in North America. No, not once had there been an argument, just wonderful therapy for our family.

Our destination brought us to my paternal grandparents, Noah and Vesta Musser, Daddy's parents who lived in Upland, California, a suburb of Los Angeles forty miles to the east of LA. Living with my Grandpa Musser's was my aunt Francis, an elementary school teacher, and my aunt Faith, only 16 years old. There was a sixteen-year age difference between Aunt Francis and Aunt Faith, the oldest and youngest siblings. A brother, John, also lived in Upland. As I'm writing in January of 2020, my aunt Francis just recently passed away at the age of ninety-nine. Daddy officiated at the July 21, 1953, wedding of Uncle Herbert and Gladys Gish. What a treat it was to see an ocean for the first time in my life. What's so truly amazing about the Pacific is the fact it covers one-third of the planet earth's surface.

Mother and Daddy had so many friends to visit from their previously living in Upland. I shall forever remember our visiting the amusement park in Buena Vista, California, Knott's Berry Farm. It was the only time in my life that I would be dining with both my paternal and maternal grandparents at the same time. It was at Knott's Berry that Chuck and I had our photo taken on a mounted horse waving with our cowboy hats. I have that photo tucked safely away sixty-seven years later. A rather humorous event took place one evening at the Upland municipal swimming pool— well, maybe not so humorous to a few ladies. After our swim, Aunt Fran didn't hesitate in taking me with her to the women's shower and dressing area. As an innocent eight- year-old, I didn't think anything of it. However, I'll always remember the shock on the ladies' faces when seeing me, but apparently Aunt Fran didn't see anything wrong with it. I do remember sharing a bed with my aunt Faith. I'll forever remember the picnic at the Upland City Park with Aunt Eunice and family. We had a softball game with Uncle Gordon and son Vaughn and a childhood friend of Daddy's in Abilene, Maynard Book, and his seven- year-old son, Morris Book. I also got to meet my Great-Aunt Sarah Hoover, the widow of my great-uncle Harry whose limbs were torn off in the threshing machine in the summer of 1928. On our last day in Upland, Grandpa Musser drove us up to Mount Baldy in the San Gabriel Mountains with an elevation of 4,193 feet. Grandma Musser had made a delicious fried chicken dinner for our picnic in the mountains.

Upon leaving Upland, we were now about thirteen days into our trip and still no arguments, no fighting, no cursing, no slapping. It was such a therapeutic vacation for an eight-year-old, away from my albatross. We drove northeast to Sequoia National Park which was just so breathtakingly beautiful with the 300-ft. high General Sherman Tree. By volume, the General Sherman is the largest known living single-stem tree on God's earth. The General Sherman Tree was named after the American Civil War general William Tecumseh Sherman, in 1879, by naturist James Woolverton who had served as a lieutenant in the Ninth Indiana Cavalry under Sherman during the Civil War. So breathtakingly beautiful was the majestic Mount Whitney, the highest summit in the contiguous US at 14,505 ft. We were so fortunate in that we got to see a black bear and her cub while driving up Mount Whitney. Sequoia National Park is known for its many black and grizzly bears. As our seventeen-day trip was coming to an end, we were still to see a most beautiful part of the US in the state of Utah; Zion National Park and Bryce Canyon. At Zion, we found a nice campground and camped out in God's beautiful creation. Bryce Canyon was my highlight with its orange and pink colors just left you standing in awe, so majestic, so breathtakingly beautiful. Not once on that seventeen-day trip did Mother or I fight as the wonderful beauty of God's great handiwork had our attention. I must share a car game that Chuck and I had on our long road vacations. We would each pick four or five car models and we would keep track of our cars coming toward us. We also played the State license plate game where we would have our own states.

# CHAPTER 24

## Losing a Best Friend and More Trauma

Has anyone ever experienced the euphoria of a high and then, in a 360 turnaround, the depths of a low? That's what I experienced on our arrival home the last day or two of July 1953. My precious pet dog Trixie, wasn't there to greet us nor was she at Bert Zook's as the two oldest sons, Dwight and Duane, were to check daily on Trixie. Bert told Daddy that Trixie was at a nearby farm. The farmer an acquaintance of our family, told Daddy that he was missing some chickens. His thinking was that Trixie had killed and ate them. I remember telling Daddy that it could have been a fox as foxes were known to frequent the area. What a way to celebrate my ninth birthday on August 2. I thought that Daddy had taken Trixie out to Grandpa Hoover's to have either Grandpa or one of my uncles shoot Trixie. One day soon after I lost a best friend, Daddy came home with a new Wilson baseball glove. I was grateful to have received it, however, it was little consolation to a boy whose heart had been broken in losing his precious Trixie.

Let's forward some fifty-six years to about 2009 with Daddy calling me on his smartphone. Daddy said, "Ken, I've something to tell you that I've been living with for years. Ken, I'm the person who shot Trixie." I was a bit dumbfounded and somewhat shocked. I forgave him, just thinking of how much of a burden this must have been weighing on him all those years. Ironically it was the second time that Daddy had a part in my losing a pet dog. As a four-year-old, I had a dog named Tony. When backing out of the garage one day, Daddy accidently ran over Tony, killing her. My heart was broken when losing Trixie.

Let me share what would become a most traumatic happening for me. A friend of mine at Talmage Elementary was having a Saturday birthday party. Lynn was a year younger than I. Back in the early 1950s, Saturday birthday parties were a big deal. My parents gave me a silver dollar, along with a card, as Lynn's birthday present. That was a large sum of money to give as a birthday gift in the 1950s. I put the silver dollar into the card. The time came for the opening of Lynn's gifts. Upon Lynn's opening of the card, there was no silver dollar. I told Lynn and his mother that I had put it in the card and somehow mysteriously slipped out of the card. On arriving home, I told Mother what had happened as Daddy was at JC Penny working. Mother didn't believe me, and when Daddy arrived home, Mother told Daddy what had happened. She had talked Daddy into believing that I had taken it. Here I was, an innocent nine-year-old and my parents not believing me. A child needs to feel loved, to feel secure, and most importantly, he must have his parents' trust. Sadly I never felt loved, I never heard those three magic words—I love you—from either parent. I was being completely honest and had told the truth. Wasn't I living in a God-fearing home? That Sunday afternoon, my parents drove me back to Lynn's home and I was forced to lie. Thankfully Lynn and I remained good friends. The sad conclusion to this story is that neither family knew the truth. However, most importantly, God did.

# CHAPTER 25

## Finding Solace and Comfort in Grandpa Hoover's Big Red Barn

I was so extremely fortunate as out of Grandpa Irvin's two marriages and ten children, there are thirty-six first cousins. Of the first five children born to Papa Irvin and to Mama Anna, only one of those first five daughters would remain in Kansas. Both Rozella and Virgie married and moved to Pennsylvania, Eunice would marry and live in California, Mary Lou would marry and would live in Puerto Rico and Missouri. That left only my brother, Chuck, and me as the only two grandchildren to grow up in Kansas, and I never lived more than ten miles from Grandpa and Grandma Hoover. That leaves only fifteen grandchildren born to the second five children. Of those fifteen grandchildren, just three were born before Grandpa's passing in 1961. In the summers of 1951–1952, Daddy and Mother would travel to Dallas Center, Iowa, to hold Bible school for four weeks. Chuck would always go with them but I always chose to go to Grandpa Hoover's, so of the thirty-six grandchildren, I was the only grandchild who got to spend premium time with the best friend I've ever had on God's earth, my beloved Grandpa Irvin Hoover.

Grandpa Hoover knew of my love of basketball, so at the age twelve in 1956, Grandpa put up a basketball goal for me with the help of Uncle Harry. Grandpa was aware that I would shoot basketball for hours in solitary at home often shooting basketball hoops in the Kansas snow. This is just another instance of Grandpa's unconditional love for me and knowing what a lonely grandson needed. I recall numerous times when Uncle Dale Eshelmans would make the 170-mile trip to Dickenson County, Kansas, that Uncle Dale, Daddy, and my uncles and myself would have some great three-on-three basketball games. These were memories, the best moments of my life, at my heaven on earth—Grandpa and Grandma Hoover's farm. Often my cousin Janet Eshelman from Kansas City would come up to Grandpa Hoover's for two to three weeks and what fun Jan, my brother, Chuck, and I would have playing in the hay in the red barn on the second loft. What fun we had playing hide and seek in the hay. Jan was also athletic and we would play softball in Grandpa's large front yard.

Those four weeks at Grandpa's became my Utopia, freedom and escape from my dungeon prison. It was in Grandpa's big red barn, in the milking area, that a traumatized abused grandson could enjoy his sports. Yes, in a red barn. In the milking area Grandpa had an outlet with a radio. Day after day I would turn on the radio to the Mutual Broadcasting Network. From 1950 through 1954, Mutual would have a Major League game of the day with the late Al Helfer doing the play-by-play. Amazingly Helfer's play-by-play of the of the Major League game of the day went around the entire world along with it being on the Armed Forces Radio network. I would have with me my baseball and glove, playing make-believe games with my beloved Brooklyn Dodger team. It was in this big red barn that a boy's gaping black hole in his heart, starving for love, found that in my grandparents' unconditional love. What great memories I have of Grandpa's dog Rusty. As a four- to eight- year-old, Rusty and I were inseparable until Rusty died in 1952. It wasn't long until Grandpa Hoover got another dog, a German shepherd named "Shep," who, for the next seven years, would become a wonderful companion.

Those summers at Grandpa's I was not at a loss for reading. Grandpa's subscribed to a weekly newspaper the *Grit*, so popular in rural America during much of the twentieth century. Grit was founded in 1882 in Williamsport, Pennsylvania, and later based in Topeka, Kansas, in Heartland Mid-America. The *Grit* was rural America's favorite weekly newspaper for over a century. Approximately thirty thousand children collected dimes from more than seven hundred thousand small-town homes during the 1950s. I would simply devour the *Grit*. I read every single page. The *Grit* included local news items, editorials, and tidbits. The *Grit* was founded by Dietrick Lamade of Williamsport, Pennsylvania, and his son, Howard, became the top executive with Little League Baseball, helping to build it into an international event, and there you have it—the Little League World Series which is played annually in South Williamsport, Pennsylvania the last two weeks in August with teams from all over the globe.

It's a crispy cool late October morning in 1953 and I was in for a special treat. My school Talmage had an off day and I had spent the night at Grandpa Hoover's. I was walking down Grandpa's long lane with Uncle Harry and shep Grandpa's German shepherd dog. I was riding in a yellow school bus for what would be the first and only time. Uncle Harry, a junior at Chapman High, would be my host. Believe it or not, this would be the only day in my twelve years of school that I would ever ride on a bus. While at Talmage, from grades 2 through 5, I would ride in a car driven by "Bunny" Schuman.

My Grandpa Hoover had gotten a television about five years before my parents. It was season 1 of the hit TV series *I Love Lucy*. The date was April 28, 1952, a Monday, and my family's at Grandpa Hoover's to watch a most memorable episode of *I Love Lucy*. This episode of Lucy would become one of the most popular and my favorite *I Love Lucy* episode. It's about Lucy being locked up in a freezer. Lucy and Ethel decide to make money by buying a used walk-in freezer when they unwittingly buy seven hundred pounds of beef and then try to sell it to customers at the butcher shop. Lucy, when getting some beef for a customer, accidently gets herself locked inside the freezer with the result of Lucy having icicles in her hair and face desperately looking out seeking help from Ricky, Ethel, and Fred who are in shock looking in. Yes, just another occasion of the very best times of my life having been spent at the best grandparents in the world.

# CHAPTER 26

## *The Brilliant Coach*

It's early December of 1953, Daddy's last year of teaching, and the Dickenson County schools held a basketball league for all elementary schools. The games being held at DCCHS, Dickenson County Community High School better known as Chapman High, located twelve miles east of Abilene on Route 40 East. Most students living in the country attended Chapman with a minority attending Abilene.

The games were played late afternoon once or twice a week on alternate weeks. How I loved watching Daddy coach the X's and O's. There was East Buckeye's star player, point guard Eddie Rider along with a fine player in Warren Kuntz. I imagined myself out there with Eddie playing as the shooting guard. I must give Mother credit where it's due. She really got into the game and we were East Buckeye's biggest cheerleaders. Each school was placed in a bracket according to enrollment. East Buckeye was in class C out of four classes. As this was Daddy's last year of teaching, Daddy would go out a winner coaching East Buckeye to the class C championship in Dickenson County. Every now and then after a game, Daddy would drive the twelve miles west on US 40 into Abilene. Our destination was the Wagon Wheel restaurant located at Third and North Cedar Street. The restaurant owner Francis Steele, was a good friend of Daddy's and what a treat it was eating that delicious hamburger and french fries. Just an added note, all of Grandpa Hoover's ten children attended Chapman High, also known as DCCHS, Dickenson County Community High School.

My favorite time of the year was the annual Dickenson County basketball tournament held at Abilene City Hall for two Saturdays in early to mid- March. It would be held two consecutive Saturdays with schools with the same enrollment placed in brackets. The tournament was a double elimination and there was plenty of delicious hot chili along with hamburger and french fries.

One game will forever be etched in my memory bank. It's a Saturday afternoon in early March of 1954 and Daddy would coach his last game ever. East Buckeye was in the championship game in C-bracket. The game pitted two fierce archrivals—Chronister and East Buckeye. The game was like a backyard brawl as the schools were located only six miles from each other with all students knowing one another. It just so happened that the principal of Chronister was Myron Lady, a first cousin of Mother's, and like Mother, a grandson of Mary Olive Frey Lady. Myron was a novice at basketball so he had another lady cousin Larry Lady coach the team. Mary Olive Lady would be a great-grandmother to both Larry and me and a grandmother to Myron. In several years, Larry would become a star basketball player in the state of Kansas and would attend Kansas University on a basketball scholarship. It was like one big family tree coaching against one another. Reflecting some sixty-five years later, I've come to realize that going and cheering wildly for East Buckeye was so therapeutic for both Mother and me. We could let our emotions go. The game came down to the final ten seconds when our star, Eddie Rider, hit a game-winning field goal and Daddy retired as a true champion coach.

# CHAPTER 27

## *Family Fun Time*

I so looked forward to Saturdays. Some Saturdays Daddy would drive us the four miles to Abilene in the morning; and other times, we drove into Abilene in the evening. On our Saturday morning trips, our destination was the local five-and-ten-cent store, Duckwalls. Duckwalls five and ten and JC Penny were the two busiest stores in Abilene. If we drove to Abilene early morning, we would stop at Duckwalls which had a restaurant and Aunt Carol and Aunt Delores were waitresses. What a treat that was to have my aunts serving breakfast. On some Saturdays we would drive to Abilene at night. Our family had a Saturday evening ritual. Daddy would park either on North Cedar Street or on North Broadway. These were the two busiest streets in Abilene and we would sit in our car for at least an hour or two, watching the shoppers walk by. As Daddy was a minister, teacher, and assistant manager at JC Penny, so many walkers recognized Daddy and we weren't at a loss for chat. I must make mention about a fun time at Duckwalls five and ten. From the 1940s through the '50s was the boom time for comic books. At the end of the shopping aisles at Duckwalls were stands of comics as *Superman, Blondie, Dick Tracy*, the *Lone Ranger* just to name a few.

I must make mention of a special happening at Christmastime. JC Penney in the late 1940s through the mid-'50s had, at Christmas, a toy land in the back of JC Penny on the second floor. How exciting it was to a boy of eight and nine to visit the toy land. Priceless forever memories of JC Penny.

After long family trips in the summers of 1952 and 1953, we stayed closer to home in both 1954 and '55. This meant one of two things for me: either I would spend hours and days in that albatross prison, the cellar, or I would shoot basketball for hours at a time in solitary. There were two summers that we visited the state capital in Topeka, Kansas. We would enter the capitol rotunda. Back in that era, you could climb the winding stairs all the way to the top. As a nine-year-old, it felt like I was climbing the summit at Mount Everest.

# CHAPTER 28

## Kansas City, Here I Come

In 1959 Wilbert Harrison had a Billboard no. 1 record song, "Kansas City." The following are several lines of lyrics of this song,

> I'm going to Kansas City
> Kansas City, here I come
> I'm going to Kansas City
> Kansas City, here I come
>
> They got a crazy
> Way of loving there
> I'm gonna get me some
>
> Well, I might take a train
> I might take a plane
> But if I have to walk
> I'm going there just the same

About every other summer we would make the 170-mile trip to Kansas City, Missouri, to visit Aunt Mary Lou and family. I recall twice when making the Kansas City trip, that we visited the largest drugstore chain in the US. Located at Thirty-Ninth and Main in Kansas City, Missouri was the giant Katz drugstore. At Katz you could get your prescriptions filled, have a shake at the giant soda fountain, visit the legendary pet department to look at the alligator, parrots, and monkeys which were for sale. Two brothers, Ike and Mike Katz, founded the chain in 1914, sons of Ukrainian immigrants. The Katz brothers opened the landmark store in 1934 and designed the store with a three-hundred-car parking lot. There weren't even three hundred cars in that neighborhood at the time. The Katz brothers had the foresight to open the store and it became the world's largest cut-rate drugstore. The Katz drugstores were more than a place to pick up prescriptions or smokes. They were where memories were made and friendship and romance blossomed.

Katz grew to include sixty-five stores in five states. Due to the coming of self service in the late 1960s and early 1970s, stores like Katz began disappearing from the retail scene. Katz later merged with CVS pharmacy. One landmark of Katz drugstore was the large signature cat on top of the drugstore.

Aunt Mary Lou's husband Dale Eshelman was an MD and like our family, a huge sports nut. I shall never forget the summer trip of 1954 as I would have the dream of a lifetime fulfilled. Uncle Dale took Daddy, Janet, and myself to see my first ever Major League baseball game. Our destination was the old municipal stadium on Brooklyn Avenue to watch the Kansas City A's playing the powerful Cleveland Indians who in that summer of '54, would win a record 111 games. The Indians would lose only 43 games that year in what was still a 154-game-schedule. What a team of future baseball Hall of Famers that Cleveland team had in pitchers Bob Feller, Bob Lemon, and Early Wynn and then first African American to play in the American League in Hall of Famer Larry Doby. The Indians manager was Al Lopez, a star catcher in his playing days, and he would become a Hall of Fame manager. The greatest player on that '54 Indian team would be "Rapid" Bob Feller who pitched three no-hitters in his storied career and an unbelievable twelve one- hitters. What's so remarkable about Feller's 1946 season is that just after returning from WWII, Feller threw a record 348 strikeouts which stood for nineteen years until a brilliant lefty, Sandy Koufax, in 1965 had 382 strikeouts. Feller in that 1946 season, started 42 games, including 36 complete games, including 10 shutouts with a 26–15 record and an era of 2.18, just a remarkable feat coming right after serving in WWII. Let me mention, these Bob Feller records in the 1946 season have been frozen in my left temporal lobe of the brain for over six decades. I've memorized Bob Feller's hometown of Van Meter, Iowa, since a boy of nine.

The following are two quotes from two Major Leaguers who I consider the two greatest players in the 1940s and 1950s. A quote from the "Splendid Splinter" Ted Williams, generally regarded as the greatest hitter ever, says of Feller, "The fastest and best pitcher I ever saw during my career."

Hall of Famer Stan the Man Musial says, "Feller was probably the greatest pitcher of our era." The Kansas City A's poor in talent during the 1950s had one of the greatest first basemen in Major League history in Vic Power, a native Puerto Rican who was a great hitter as well as one of the greatest fielding first baseman ever. I recall Feller entering this game at municipal stadium in relief as he was on the downside of his career.

Uncle Dale had as two of his patients and friends, legendary manager Whitey Herzog and Roger Maris from Fargo, North Dakota. Maris, along with the greatest switch hitter in Major League history from Commerce, Oklahoma, Mickey Mantle, would form the M&M boys in the season of 1961. In that 1961 season, Mantle would hit fifty-four home runs while Maris hit sixty-one, breaking the hallowed Bambino's record of sixty. It so happened that in the 1961 season, Major League Baseball went to a 162-game schedule, up from what had been the standard 154-game schedule for decades. The baseball commissioner at the time, Ford Frick, was a contemporary and a friend of Babe Ruth. Frick made sure that an asterisk was put next to Maris's record. During the final days of that 1961 season, as Maris was trying to break the revered sixty homer season of the Babe, Maris became so stressed out that small clumps of hair began falling out of his hair. The hostile New York media considered Maris unworthy as a record breaker successor to the Babe and Maris was constantly booed by New York fans. It was on the last day of the season that Maris hit his sixty-first record-breaking homerun off Boston Red Sox hurler Tracy Stallard. Tragically Roger Maris passed away from Non-Hodgkin's lymphoma in 1985 at the young age of fifty-one.

# CHAPTER 29

## Kidnapped

It's early June of 1954. Chuck and I were out front playing when a big international truck pulled up along our front lawn. It was Uncle Harry who waved to us and Chuck and I instinctively got into the truck with Uncle Harry who was driving wheat from the harvest. It was wheat harvest time for the state of Kansas which produces one-fifth of the US wheat supply. It was a four-mile trip to the feed mill in Abilene. On our arrival, there were at least eight trucks ahead of us and we had at least a forty-five-minute wait. Back in the '50s, there wasn't an Amber Alert and Mother was going crazy yelling our names. Mother had run across the township road to Bert Zook's without any success. Uncle Harry would have us for well over an hour and fifteen minutes. I will forever remember as Uncle Harry drove the big international up along our front lawn. Mother ran out to Uncle Harry and boy did Mother give Uncle Harry a scolding and tongue-lashing. I will never forget how remorseful Uncle Harry was. He promised Mother this would never happen again. I do remember Mother giving Uncle Harry a loving hug before he drove off. I'll forever remember what Mother gave to both Chuck and me—a Snickers bar and I've been a Snickers lover ever since.

The summer of 1954 I would earn some extra spending money working with Daddy for a local farmer, Marion Book, who later became a minister. I recall as a fourth grader of stealing a kiss from Mary Ellen my age, who was Marion Book's daughter. I would plow for Marion on his Massy

Ferguson tractor. Plowing for Marion would bring me some extra bucks for baseball cards. Daddy had a bad accident that summer while driving a tractor for Marion. Somehow Daddy got his hand caught in a disc while plowing and really had his hand cut up badly which took a good number of stitches at Abilene General Hospital.

# CHAPTER 30

## A Family Fun Day in Enterprise

It was on Saturday 11, 1954 that we were invited for dinner to Mother's first cousin Charles Hoover, a son of my great-uncle Ben Hoover to whom I referred to earlier as giving his life to Christ shortly before his death. Enterprise was a town of nine hundred, four miles due east of Abilene. Charles wife's name was Dixie Lee and they had several children, including a daughter, Cleo Von, my age. And what a surprise a recently turned ten-year- old was in store for! After dinner, Charles turned the television on and I would see my first ever Major League Baseball game played between the Baltimore Orioles and the Washington Senators. I forgot who won that game, however the Orioles' thirty-year-old second baseman, Bobby Young, left a lasting impression on me with several great defensive plays at second base. On January 23, 1901, the small town of Enterprise had a not-so-special visitor in the lady with a hatchet in one hand and a Bible in the other hand— yes, Carrie Nation, the Temperance leader who destroyed a saloon in Enterprise.

# CHAPTER 31

## *The Catch*

It's Wednesday September 29, 1954, game 1 of the 1954 World Series with the powerful American League champions, the Cleveland Indians, against the National League champs, the New York Giants. This was a rare year that neither the Dodgers nor Yankees made the World Series. The underdog Giants were led by their twenty-three-year old superstar, Willie Mays the "Say Hey Kid" who I consider the second greatest player of all time, behind only the Babe. Mays, in my book, is the greatest five-tool player ever. A five-tool player is a player with above-average skills in hitting, hitting with power, fielding, throwing, and running. My six greatest Major Leaguers off all time: (1) Babe Ruth; (2) Willie Mays, it is almost inconceivable that a power hitter, standing barely five feet ten, weighing 175 pounds, could hit 660 home runs and at the same time could have 338 lifetime stolen bases. Willie Mays standing as the no. 2 all-time Major League player is unquestioned. Willie Mays recently was the number one ranked centerfielder in baseball history by Bill James in "The New Bill James Historical Baseball Abstract; (3) Ted Williams, the Splendid Splinter, who could actually see the baseball on contact with the bat; (4) Walter Johnson the "Big Train," who won 417 games with a Major League record of 110 shutouts and one of the few state of Kansas natives who played Major League Baseball; (5) Hank Aaron; and (6) Tyrus "Ty" Cobb, the "Georgia Peach." Barry Bonds could very well be in that select company except for the fact that he's a cheater who was caught using performance-enhancing drugs, not exactly a poster child.

That 1954 Indians team was special, winning a record of 111 games. I can recite their entire starting lineup, 1b Vic Wertz, 2b Bobby Avila, SS

George Strickland, 3b Al Rosen, the 1954 American League MVP, C Jim Hegan, lf Al Smith, center field Larry Doby, Rf Dave Philly. I can also rattle off the entire starting lineup for the underdog Giants: 1b Whitey Lockman, 2b Davy Williams, SS Alvin Dark, an LSU football star and later Major League manager, 3b Hank Thompson, C Wes Westrum, left f Monte Irvin, a black player in the Hall of Fame, center field Willie Mays, and right f Don Mueller who led the National League in hits in 1954 with 212. Yes, for sixty-five years, both teams starting lineups have been frozen in my left temporal lobe

And brother was I in baseball heaven as the administration had the game sent to each class via the public address system. The World Series was a shocker as the Giants defeated the heavily favored Indians in a sweep of 4–0. The 1954 World Series will forever be remembered for "The Catch." In the tenth inning of game 1, "the catch for baseball lore" happened. Cleveland hitter Vic Wertz hit a long drive to dead center field. Willie Mays running at full speed with his back to the infield, would make a miraculous over-the- shoulder catch to rob Wertz of extra bases. An unsung hero in that 1954 World Series was a lightly regarded pinch-hitter Dusty Rhodes. In that '54 World Series, Rhodes batted six times and had four hits, including home runs off two future Hall of Famers Early Wynn and Bob Lemon. Yes, here you have a young boy whose empty heart was aching and starving for love who would have to find his solace in memorizing hundreds of sport facts dates in his left temporal lobe.

The following are several stats for making Babe Ruth, "the Sulton of Swat," the greatest baseball player ever. The Babe had 714 home runs, 2,873 hits, lifetime batting average of .342—just astronomical for a power hitter— and 2,213 RBI's. The Babe began his major league career as a pitcher, winning ninety-four games, while losing only forty-six, with a lifetime "ERA" of 2.28. Ruth could have been a Hall of Famer as a pitcher as well. Ruth hit long home runs, a feat unusual for any player in the pre-1920 dead ball era. For forty-three years, Ruth had the world series record for most scoreless innings pitched until Whitey Ford broke it in the 1961 world series. The Babe's remarkable offensive achievements led American league in home runs twelve times, bases on balls, "or walks," eleven times, and RBI's an incomparable sixteen times.

# CHAPTER 32

## Acute-Anxiety and a Young Boy Defies All Odds

It's Mid-October 1954, and my time as a student at Talmage Elementary is winding down. The Dickenson County schools would hold a declaration contest. Being an extremely expressive boy, I was nominated by my class and teacher to memorize a reading. The speech had to do about a father. Memorizing was not a problem for me as I was a "natural" of being blessed with an exceptional memory. My practicing for the speech went great. However, when I got up in front of the judges and the crowd of people, I simply froze. I fought to get the words out, stuttering awfully. Acute anxiety has always been my "Achilles's heel." It was a time of personal humiliation. That "double-whammy" PTSD had yet again left me to live out a traumatic experience.

A very special guest was visiting our school, his name was Glenn Cunningham, a native of Elkhart, Kansas. Cunningham's life story is truly incredible. It's about a boy who was to die. His true story beautifully illustrates the incredible power of determination and of a mother's enduring love. Glenn with his thirteen-year-old brother Floyd, had the job of coming to school early every day so they could use kerosene to start the heating of the potbellied stove. It was to make the school warm for the arrival of the teacher and students. Someone had accidently put gasoline into the kerosene container. When Floyd went to put what was thought to be kerosene into the potbellied stove, fire ignited killing Floyd instantly. The classmates and teacher arrived to find the schoolhouse engulfed in flames.

To their horror, they found Floyd dead and eight-year-old Glenn had lost all the flesh on his knees and shins and all the toes on his left foot, also his transverse was practically destroyed.

From what was to be Glenn's deathbed, the dreadfully burned semiconscious boy faintly heard the doctor telling his mother that her son would surely die which was for the best as the horrific fire had devastated the lower-half of Glenn's body. But the brave boy didn't want to die. Glenn semiconscious, made up his mind that he would survive; and somehow, to the amazement of the physician, Glenn did survive. Yet when the mortal danger was past, Glenn again heard the doctor and his mother speaking quietly. The mother was told that since the fire had destroyed so much flesh in the lower parts of his body, it would almost be better if he had died since he was doomed to be a lifetime cripple with no use of his lower limbs. His mother steadfastly refused to let the doctor amputate.

From the waist down Glenn had no motor ability. His thin scarred legs, just dangling, all but lifeless. Glenn had no feeling or control in his legs yet his determination to walk was stronger than ever, and coupled with hours upon hours of a new type of therapy, Glenn was going to beat the odds. Glenn was still confined to a wheelchair. One sunny day Glenn's mother wheeled him out into the yard to get some fresh air. That day instead of sitting, Glenn threw himself from the chair. Glenn pulled himself across the grass, dragging his legs behind him. Glenn worked his way to the white picket fence bordering their lot; with great herculean effort, Glenn raised himself up on the fence. Then stake by stake, he began dragging himself along the fence, resolving that he would walk. He started to do this daily until he had worn a smooth path round the yard beside the fence. Glenn could finally stand up straight, then walked haltingly with help, then walked by himself, and then miraculously, run. Glenn had such a positive attitude as well as a strong religious faith. His favorite Bible verse was Isaiah 40:31, "But those who wait on the Lord shall renew their strength, they shall mount up with wings, like eagles, they shall run and not be weary, they shall walk and not faint."

At Kansas University, Cunningham became known as the "Kansas Flyer." After all he had overcome, Glenn must have felt as though he was soaring like an eagle. In February 1934, in New York City's famed Madison Square Garden, this young man who wasn't expected to survive, who would surely never walk, who could never hope to run, this determined young man, Glenn Cunningham, was considered as the greatest American miler of all time. Glenn received the James E. Sullivan award as the top amateur athlete in the US in 1933. In 1934 Glenn set the world record for the mile-run at 4:06.8 which stood for three years. Glenn competed in the 1,500-meter event at the 1932 and 1936 Summer Olympics, finishing fourth and second respectively. While on the ship traveling from the US to Germany in 1936, Glenn was voted most popular athlete by his fellow Olympians. Yes, this was the Olympics that Reich Chancellor Adolf Hitler had built a new 100,000-track- and-field stadium in Berlin, outdoing the Los Angeles games in 1932; and yes, Hitler was out to show the world that the Aryan people were the dominant race. Well, a young black American, Jesse Owens, proved Hitler wrong. Owens won four gold medals in the 1936 games at Berlin including the one-hundred-yard dash, the long jump, 4×100 relay, and the 200 meters.

Glenn Cunningham went on to earn a master's degree from the University of Iowa and a PhD from NYU. Later in life Cunningham, with his wife, helped ten thousand needy and abused children. It was such a privilege, as a ten-year-old, to have met this true champion who had defied all odds to overcome a most horrific traumatic experience. Just like David and Ida Eisenhower were steadfast in their loyalty to Ike, likewise Mrs. Cunningham's faith and enduring love for her son was like a rock, another example of the fervent power of prayer.

I'll forever cherish the Sunday afternoon hikes that Daddy took with Chuck and me. About a quarter-mile from our house was a large wooden area with a creek. These hikes would last a good hour. No matter whether Daddy had two services to preach on a Sunday, which was always the case, Daddy still found that priceless time to spend with Chuck and me. I will forever remember the touch football games that Daddy had with Chuck and myself in our yard next to the township road. As busy as Daddy was, he always found premium time with Chuck and me.

I have one more memory to share at the time that we lived along Route 15. My Great-Grandma Mary Olive Frey Lady's younger brother Lawrence lived only about one hundred yards south of us, along Highway 15. What's so remarkable is that there was a twenty-one-year age difference between the oldest sibling, Mary Olive born in 1870, and the youngest,

Lawrence born in 1891. I would often walk down and visit Great-Uncle Lawrence and his wife, Grace. In 1930, their large farmhouse was burned to the ground, just another instance of a Lady family tragedy. Great-Uncle Lawrence and Great-Aunt Grace lived in a very small house but their home was filled with their genuine hospitality. Great-Uncle Lawrence was deacon for many years at the Zion BIC Church. As a young boy growing into adolescence, I always enjoyed visiting with the elderly and I spent much valuable time at Great-Uncle Lawrence's and Great Aunt Grace's.

# CHAPTER 33

## The Move to Abilene

During the Christmas holiday of 1954, we moved the four miles south on Highway 15 to Abilene. Our new home would be the church parsonage located at 204 NE Seventh Street. Daddy took over the pastorate of the Abilene BIC church in January of 1955. I was extremely excited about our move to Abilene as I was so familiar with the town due to our weekly trip and of Daddy being assistant manager of JC Penny. I was to be comfortable with the fact that I would no longer have an outside locked up prison cellar; however, the parsonage had a basement that, sadly, I was to become very familiar with.

I began the second half of my fifth grade at Garfield Elementary which had grades 1 through 5. For decades in Abilene there were three elementary schools named after assassinated US presidents. There was Lincoln, located south of the railroad tracks, only one block from the Eisenhower homestead, the elementary school that Ike attended. McKinley, named after assassinated President William McKinley in 1901, located on Abilene's west side, and Garfield, located in North Central Abilene, named after James A. Garfield, assassinated on September 19, 1881, after serving only six and a half months as president. In recent years a middle school, Kennedy has been built. Throughout the decades, Abilene's population has remained at seven thousand.

What was so convenient was that our church was located at Seventh and Buckeye, only two blocks from the parsonage, and Garfield was only three blocks from the parsonage. When walking to school with my brother, Chuck who was in first grade, we would walk right past the red brick building that Abilene's favorite son, Dwight David Eisenhower, graduated from high school in 1909. In my only half-year spent at Garfield, I have so many great memories and one not-so-great memory. A wonderful memory was the morning open playing of the army song, "Caissons Go Rolling Along." We would march around the room to the playing of the song. It was dedicated as the army song on November 11, 1956, Armistice Day, and the army band performed it at President Eisenhower's inaugural parade on January 20, 1953. Memories of this song have lasted a lifetime.

It just seemed like I always had to have a ball in my hands. Several weeks into beginning classes at Garfield Elementary, the unthinkable happened. I was throwing a basketball with another student before the start of class. It's just my luck that I threw the ball, breaking a school trophy. My fifth-grade teacher Ms. Burgett, sent me to the principal's office of Mr. Lee Horst. I was fortunate that I only got off with a reprimand. It might have been in my favor that Mr. Horst was a friend of Daddy's from his teaching days in Dickenson County. For the longest time, even into high school, I had to live with the words *trophy breaker*. Two boys in that fifth-grade class, Charles and Arthur, continued the saying into high school. I'm an extremely sensitive person and I a hard time living with that.

Another favorite memory from Garfield was the comic book festival. Students, parents—anyone—could bring comic books and there were hundreds of comics. The Golden Age of Comic Books was from the late 1930s to the mid-1950s. Technically the Golden Age of Comics took place between 1938 and 1956. During this era, the superhero archetype came along, many well-known characters were introduced, including Superman, Batman, Captain Marvel, and Wonder Woman. At this comic festival you were able to buy a set of ten comics for a dollar. I would only be at Garfield for half a year as my sixth grade and junior high years would be spent in the former Abilene High, located right across from our BIC Church at Seventh and Buckeye.

It was in the spring of 1955 that a new style of baseball card was made of the Bowman set. It's distinguishing horizontal design, showing players as if they were appearing on a large brown-bordered color television set. Next to the 1953 Bowman set of color and BW cards, this would become one of the most popular sets ever. This 1955 Bowman card is one of the few sets to never have been reprinted. If it is reprinted, you can be sure that I'll purchase it. Throughout my memoir, I will refer to pop music recordings which have helped me at periods during my down and depressive times throughout my life. One pop hit I'll forever associate during my five months at Garfield Elementary in that spring of '55 is the million-seller hit, recorded by the late Doris Day, "Que sera sera whatever will be will be the futures not ours to see que sera sera."

> When I was just a little girl,
> I ask my mother what will I be.
> Will I be pretty? Will I be rich?
> Here's what she said to me,
> "Que sera sera,
> Whatever will be, will be.
> The futures not ours to see,
> Que sera sera."

# CHAPTER 34

## Abilene Begins as a Stagecoach Stop

In 1854 the Kansas territory was organized, and on January 29, 1861, Kansas was admitted to the Union as a free state, the thirty-fourth state to join the Union. In 1857 Dickenson County was organized under territorial law. The county measures thirty-six miles north to south and twenty-four miles east to west. Abilene began as a stagecoach stop, and in the same year, this stagecoach setting was established by Timothy Hersey and named Mud Creek. Elizabeth Hersey, wife of Timothy Hersey is credited with naming Abilene from Luke 3:1 in the Bible, meaning "city of the plains."

Abilene was a sleepy little town until 1867 when a livestock dealer from Illinois, Joseph G. McCoy, saw Abilene as the perfect place for a railroad from which to ship cattle from. McCoy chose Abilene for this railroad due to the abundance of grass and water in the area of North Central, Kansas. In 1867 the Kansas Railway Union Pacific pushed westward through Abilene, and in the same year, Joseph G. McCoy purchased 250 acres of land north and east of Abilene on which he built a hotel, the Drovers Cottage, and McCoy built stockyards equipped for twenty thousand heads of cattle and stables for their horses. In the year 1871, more than five thousand cowboys herded six hundred thousand to seven hundred thousand cattle to Abilene and shipped by rail to Kansas City, Kansas. Abilene became the furthest point north of the Chisholm Trail which started in the post-Civil War.

The Chisholm Trail originated in Southern Texas and ran about one thousand miles. The Chisholm Trail is named for Jesse Chisholm, a half- Cherokee trader from Tennessee who originally created the trail to transport goods from one trading post to another. Texas ranchers using the Chisholm trail started on the route from either the Rio Grande or San Antonio and joined the Chisholm Trail at the Red River of the south, at the border of Texas and Oklahoma, and continued north to the railroad of the Kansas Pacific Railway in Abilene, Kansas, where the cattle would be sold and shipped eastward by rail to Kansas City, Kansas. And there you have it, the Red River of the south at the border between Texas and Oklahoma which takes us to the modern-day annual football game played each fall at the Texas State Fair in Dallas, between the Texas Longhorns and the Oklahoma Sooners.

And just to think in 1867 Joseph McCoy referred to Abilene, Kansas, as a very dead place with dozens of log huts and not a single roof house could be found in Abilene. Just a little tidbit, at some point in 1871, the exact date is unknown, Jesse James, Frank James, and Cole Younger stayed covertly overnight at the Drover's Cottage Hotel. The James brothers used Abilene as a staging ground where they rested their horses and purchased daily fresh clothes and ammunition as they raided surrounding areas. The James brothers never caused a single problem in Abilene due to an informal agreement with Town Marshall Wild Bill Hickok that he would leave them alone if they left Abilene alone. During the peak of the cattle drive in 1871, Drovers Cottage had an average of 160 guests a day, just remarkable. As of 1868, Drovers Cottage had forty bedrooms and was lavishly furnished which surprised many visitors who did not expect to find such a luxurious hotel in a small town in the West.

Abilene, Kansas, from the 1860s–1880s was known as the queen of the Kansas cow towns; and Abilene, not Dodge City, was known as the wickedest town in the West. The River Brethren, later to become Brethren in Christ, settled in North Central, Kansas, from the years 1877–1879. It's around the years 1887–1888 that the BIC founded churches at Belle Springs and Rosebank in South Dickenson, while in North Dickenson, three churches were founded: the Abilene BIC, my home church; the Zion BIC, located seven miles north of Abilene on Highway 15; and the Bethel BIC where Daddy pastored from 1945–1952.The Abilene BIC Church was the home church of the Eisenhower family. They would always sit in the same front pew. Dwight had carved his initials into the front bench, "DDE," standing for Dwight David Eisenhower.

# CHAPTER 35

## The Legend of Thomas Smith

Another most influential character in early Abilene was Thomas Smith, also known as Tom "Bear River" Smith. Thomas Smith grew up in New York City where he served as a police officer and professional middleweight boxer. In 1868 Smith was involved in the accidental killing of a fourteen-year-old boy after which he resigned and began working for Union Pacific Railroad in Nebraska.

Thomas Smith received the nickname "Bear River" due to a stand he made during a skirmish with vigilantes while serving as a lawman in Wyoming. A vigilante group had lynched a railroad employee who was suspected of murder. Soon afterward, railroad employees retaliated against the vigilantes, resulting in most of the small town of Bear River City, Wyoming, being burned to the ground and a shootout between citizens and mob members erupted. Smith stood both sides off until troops from Fort Bridger, Wyoming, arrived and imposed martial law. Bear River City soon became deserted, just another railroad ghost town.

Thomas Smith has been described as having been a handsome man with a thick mustache and almost fearless nature. Prior to Smith's appointment as Abilene marshal, two St. Louis, Missouri, policemen had been hired. At this time in 1867, Abilene had become a wild cattle town and it came to the point where murders and shootings were common. The two St. Louis lawmen resigned before their first day of service was complete. Policing was all but nonexistent. In 1869 Thomas Smith was commissioned as a deputy US marshal in Abilene and Smith was insistent that he could police Abilene using hands rather than guns. Smith was a fearless man. On one occasion, shortly after taking office, Smith singlehandedly overpowered two men known for their bad temperament, "Big Hank" Hawkins and his partner, known only as Wyoming Frank. Smith banished them both from Abilene after beating them both at the same time using only his bare hands. When Smith implemented a law of no guns in the town limit, it became very unpopular with the cowboys. Smith would survive two assassination attempts. Smith became widely respected and admired by the citizens of Abilene.

On November 2, 1870, Smith and a temporary deputy, believed to be named James McDonald, attempted to serve a warrant to two local farmers, Andrew McConnel and Moses Miles. The two men were wanted in connection with the murder of another Abilene man John Shea. Smith and McDonald located the suspects in a small settlement ten miles outside of Abilene. A gunfight erupted in which Smith was badly wounded in the chest. Smith returned fire and wounded McConnell. Smith's deputy fled the scene and as Smith was mortally wounded, Moses Miles hit him with the butt of a rifle, then took an ax and decapitated Smith. McConnell and Miles were captured and arrested in 1871, Andrew McConnell got twelve years in prison and Moses Miles got sixteen years in prison. To me it's hard to believe that they both weren't hanged. Smith was replaced as Abilene marshal by legendary gunfighter James "Wild Bill" Hickok.

To let one know of how popular and how much Thomas Smith meant to the Abilene residents, the deepest gloom blanketed Wild Texas Street where bad women and good women stood side by side on the boarded sidewalks, weeping, as the funeral procession passed toward the newly laid out cemetery. The American flag draped Smith's casket and men, women, and children stepped forward to lay flowers on the wagon around it. Walking directly behind the hearse as chief mourner was Tom's big iron-gray horse named Silver Heels, all saddled and bridled as his master had left it. Yes, Thomas J. Smith was a true living legend of historic Abilene, Kansas.

It's important to point out that Dwight Eisenhower reportedly considered Smith a personal hero, and on Ike's four visits to Abilene while president from 1953–1961, Ike visited Thomas Smith's grave each time.

President Eisenhower said in the following years about Smith, "According to the legend of my hometown he was anything but dull. While he almost never carried a pistol, he subdued the lawless by the force of his personality and his tremendous capabilities as an athlete. One blow of his fist was apparently enough to knock out the ordinary 'tough cowboy.' He was murdered by treachery." On one of Ike's four visits to Thomas Smith's grave during his administration, he had his young grandson David with him. The David and Ida Eisenhower burial plot lies only one hundred yards from the grave of Thomas Smith at the Abilene Cemetery. Here at Smith's grave, Ike read the inscription on the stone and told attentive little David the story of the famed cowboy marshal. David was wearing two toy pistols in leather holsters a gift from Grandpa.

# CHAPTER 36

## The River Brethren Arrive in Abilene

In 1879 a colony of nearly three hundred people migrated from Pennsylvania. The colony consisted of successful farm families who had brought cash gleaned from the sale of their Eastern farms. It was the largest cash inflow the county had ever seen. Called the '79er's, they were all members of the Brethren in Christ Church and were commonly called River Brethren. The group leaders later built an immigrant house near the railroad station at North Second Street in Abilene. It provided a place to stay until land could be located and living arrangements made. These colonists settled into different areas of Dickenson County. Their simple ways and distinctive garb set them apart from the other residents. Their superior farming abilities and high morals quickly gained for them a place of great respect in the area. A good number of these colonist were the Hoovers, Freys, and Ladys; however, most of my kin settled in North Dickenson County.

One of the group leaders of the religious sect 79'ser's was Jacob Eisenhower, a grandfather of Ike. Jacob Eisenhower was both a BIC minister as well as a very prosperous farmer. His prosperity is shown in that his standard wedding gift to each of his sons was a 160 acre farm as well as $2,000.00 in cash. However this wedding gift was not appreciated by son David after working for 18 months on the cotton belt railroad for forty dollars a month. In the summer of 1891, with Dwight going on two years old, the David Eisenhower family returned to Abilene, Kansas, where David's brother-in-law Chris Musser, who was foreman at the famed Belle Springs Creamery, offered David the position of "plant engineer."

David Eisenhower was plant engineer for 20 years at the creamery. David loathed farming and one wonders how successful David might have been as a farmer.

In this colony was a twelve-year-old Millard Engle born in 1867. In 1891 a twenty-four-year-old Engle was born again in the great revival of 1991. MG as he was come to be known in the Brethren in Christ church, became a two- time moderator at General Conference. I got to know Bishop Engle as he and his wife Anna, lived only two miles from our home, located on Highway 15. Engle was always recognized with his bushy beard and big bushy eyebrows and Bishop Engle had a part in the funeral of my Grandma Anna Zelma who burned to death. The following is a true happening when my late daddy was a pastor of the Bethel Kansas BIC from 1945 to 1952. On this particular Sunday, Bishop Engle was the guest minister at Bethel. Daddy was sitting on a chair and had fallen asleep. Bishop Engle looking back at Daddy seeing his eyes closed, said the words, "Isn't that right, Brother Musser?" with the result being an embarrassed pastor and a chuckle out of the congregation. Bishop MG Engle passed away into glory at the age of ninety-three in 1960.

# CHAPTER 37

## The Spring and Summer of '55

Living in town had its advantages, especially for a sports nut like myself. That first summer of 1955 I was in the Pee Wee League. I played second base for our team, the Kiwanis Club. I had always been a contact hitter and I struck out only three times that summer. Our star pitcher was Don Duffy a year ahead of me in school. Our team that summer won the Pee Wee League championship. I recall sixty-five years later, seeing my fifth-grade teacher at Talmage, Ms. Olson, being in the stands cheering wildly for me. Yes, the world of sports was where our family could always come together. I firmly believe that my competing in sports and watching Daddy be such a successful basketball coach was truly an escape, a refuge for both Mother and I from our dysfunctional homelife. The Kiwanis Club of Abilene would treat our team with a celebratory dinner at a famous Abilene landmark, Lena's restaurant. Lena was known throughout North Central Kansas for her delicious fried chicken. Lena was a close friend of Grandpa Hoover but then who wasn't Grandpa a friend of. Several times during my childhood into adolescence, my entire family of Aunts, Uncles, and Grandpa and Grandma Hoover would dine together at Lena's. President Eisenhower had dinner three times at Lena's and his choice was steak. It became a custom that when people dined at Lena's on their birthday, she would come from the kitchen and give them a swat with a special paddle which they then signed.

On a Tuesday, December 4, 1956, is a memory of a lifetime for me. On that night, Grandpa Hoover celebrated his sixty-fourth birthday at

Lena's with family. Yes, I'll forever remember the paddle that Grandpa got from Lena.

My first spring living in Abilene I would pick up my first regular job. It would be mowing our large church lawn at Seventh and Buckeye. And yes, the excellent marks that I received would bring me more mowing jobs. Living on the same block as my family was my Great-Uncle Luther Lady and Aunt Mildred residing at 210 NE Seventh. It was while living with her son Luther Lady, that my Great-Grandma Lady would pass away into eternal glory in October of 1951. I also picked up mowing for Uncle Luther's. Aunt Mildred had the most beautiful garden of red roses. Uncle Luther's had the *Salina Journal*, the hometown newspaper of Salina, Kansas, a city of forty-five thousand, located twenty miles due west of Abilene, delivered daily to their home. I would walk the fifty yards to Great-Uncle Luther's every evening, to read the sports section of the *Journal*. It was at Uncle Luther's one evening in late spring of 1955 while reading the *Salina Journal*, that I came upon an article about a high school basketball phenom named Wilt Chamberlain. Chamberlain attended Overbrook High in Philadelphia. In Wilt's senior year at Overbrook High, he scored 74, 78, and 90 points in three consecutive games. Chamberlain would become the most recruited high school star ever. To top it all off, Wilt chose to play basketball at Kansas University. In my estimation, Chamberlain is arguably the greatest athlete in the modern era. I'll get back to "Wilt the Stilt" a bit later.

I would get a kick out of Aunt Mildred and Mother's marathon telephone conversations. We only lived three houses from Uncle Luther and Aunt Mildred yet the two would be on the phone for two to three hours at a time. Uncle Luther's were devout Christians and members of the Abilene Wesleyan Methodist Church. Great-Uncle Luther was always on fire for his Lord and Savior, Jesus Christ. Often Uncle Luther would drive by our house in his big green 1955 Buick, and if Daddy was out in the front yard, Great- Uncle Luther would be waving out the window, yelling to Daddy, "Keep the victory, Brother Musser."

The race is called The Run for the Roses, on account of the blanket of red roses draped over the winner, and it can also be known in the US as the most exciting two minutes in sports. The setting is Churchill Downs with the Twin Spires in Louisville, Kentucky, on the eighty-first running of the Kentucky Derby. I vividly recall my being up in my bedroom at the parsonage. The date was May 7, 1955. I was a true sports nut. If there was a sporting event on the radio, my ears would be right up to it. I had heard so much talk about a three-year-old horse, Nashua, and that's the horse I was rooting for. Nashua's trainer was eighty-one-year-old Hall of Famer Sunny Jim Fitzsimmons. Nashua would be ridden by future Hall of Fame jockey Eddie Arcaro who is generally regarded as the greatest jockey in US history. Arcaro is the only rider to the present day to have won the US Triple Crown twice. Nashua's chief challenger would be Swaps with a young twenty-three-year-old superstar Wille Shoemaker as the rider.

The distance of the Kentucky Derby is one and one-quarter-mile distance on a dirt track. The race came down to the last quarter of a mile with Swaps defeating Nashua by a length and a half. I'll forever remember as a ten-year- old, of doing my best to urge Nashua to victory. Nashua would redeem himself by winning both the Preakness and the Belmont Stakes, the latter two legs of the Triple Crown of horse racing. Swaps winning time was 2:01. A bit about the two jockeys: Arcaro stood 5'2" and died in 1997 of liver cancer. A bit about Shoemaker; on April 8, 1991, in San Dimas, California, he rolled over the Ford Bronco while driving, and the accident left him paralyzed from the neck down due to his being drunk. Shoemaker passed away in 2003. I remember this race as though it was only yesterday. Yes, only a two-minute horse race would bring comfort to the aching heart of a ten-year-old suffering from traumatic emotional abuse.

# CHAPTER 38

## I'm in Baseball Heaven

The summer and fall of 1955 would be most memorable for me. My parents hadn't yet gotten a television. Our neighbor Wayne Londeen was a huge baseball fan and a coworker of my Uncle Virgil Wenger at the Abilene US Post Office. Wayne would let me come over every Saturday afternoon to watch the CBS Major League game of the week with play-by-play broadcaster, the legendary Jerome Hanna "Dizzy Dean." A brash and colorful personality, Dean is the last National League pitcher to win thirty games in a season (1934). That record still stands eighty-five years later. Dean's broadcast partner was Buddy Blattner who was a Major League player in the 1940s for the Cardinals, Phillies, and Giants. What a spectacular setting for me! I would get to see my beloved Brooklyn Dodgers play. I was in baseball heaven, getting to see my all-time favorite player jersey 14, Gil Hodges, the Dodger first baseman. My Dodgers were loaded with future Hall of Famers: catcher Roy Campanella, jersey 42; the captain, Harold "Pee Wee Reese, jersey 1; center fielder Duke Snider, jersey 4; the second baseman, the immortal 42, Jackie Robinson. In addition, James "Junior" Gilliam took over at second base for the aging Jackie Robinson. Gilliam won the 1953 National League Rookie of the year and was a key member of ten National League championship teams from 1952–1978. Tragically Gilliam joined Dodger teammates whose post major league career was marked with tragedy. Gilliam suffered a massive brain hemorrhage at home on September 15, 1978, lapsed into a coma from which he never recovered, passing away nine days before his fiftieth birthday. These jersey numbers have been stored in my left temporal lobe for sixty-five years. It felt like I was right there at Ebbets Field, cheering my beloved Dodgers on.

In 1960, the recently retired Pee Wee Reese would join Dizzy Dean as the colorman. What a broadcast team was ole Dizzy and Pee Wee. The heart and soul of the late 1940s through the '50s Brooklyn Dodgers was number 14, Gil Hodges. During the 1952 World Series against the hated Yankees, Gil went 0 for 21. His slump continued into the 1953 season. By May 23, Gil was batting an anemic .181. One Sunday during the slump, a priest arose in St. Francis Roman Catholic Church in Brooklyn and said, "It's too hot for a sermon. Just go home and say a prayer for Gil Hodges." Hodges was such a beloved Dodger that the fans did just that. Dodger relief pitcher Clem Labine quotes, "Gil Hodges was the only Dodger that never got booed in Ebbets Field. Those fans knew their baseball."

Indispensable to those Dodger teams was the catcher Roy Campanella who in his prime, was the best catcher in baseball whose true greatness seemed only partly reflected by his statistics. This view was summed up by Ty Cobb, the Georgia Peach Baseball Hall of Famer and a man not known for hyperbole. "Campanella," Cobb said, "will be remembered longer than any catcher in baseball history." At 5'9" and a half inches, weighing 190 pounds, Campy had the ideal build for a catcher. Campanella won three MVPs— 1951, 1953, and 1955.

# CHAPTER 39

## Travails of Dodgers' Post Major League Careers

The post baseball life was so extremely cruel to a number of these Dodgers. Roy Campanella a black man, was born in 1921 to an Italian father and a black mother, and in the America of the 1920s, that meant Campy was black. In the mid-1950s, realizing that he couldn't play baseball forever, Roy opened a liquor store in Harlem which prospered. It was while driving from the store to his home in Glen Cove, Long Island, in the early morning hours of January 28, 1958, Campanella suffered the injury that ended his career. His car skidded on a wet spot near the crest of a hill, crashing into a telephone pole, turning over, fracturing two of Campanella's vertebrae. A four-and-a half-hour operation by five surgeons saved his life but Campy would never again have movement below the shoulders.

In the aftermath of the accident, Campanella suffered a series of further setbacks. His first marriage deteriorated with his home having to be sold to pay off debts. Roy Campanella's gritty determination to make a life for himself in a wheelchair won him even more fame and admiration than he had enjoyed as a baseball star. Roy Campanella died of a heart attack near his home in Woodland Hills, California, on June 26, 1993, at the age of seventy- one.

Carl Furillo, nicknamed the "Reading Rifle" due to his lethal throwing arm and a native of Reading, Pennsylvania, passed away from leukemia and died of a heart attack on January 21, 1989, forty-six days before his sixty- seventh birthday. Pirate's pitcher Mel Queen learned about Furillo's rifle arm the hard way—thrown out at first base after hitting an apparent single to right field. It was one of Furillo's twenty-four assists in 1951, just a remarkable stat. The following is a quote from teammate Carl Erskine, "I remember how tough he was, how consistent of a player. When he hit a single it was like a bullet, when he hit a homer it was like a rocket." And his arm portrayed his strength. Furillo won the National League batting title in 1953 with a .344 average. After retirement from baseball, to make ends meet until his baseball pension kicked in at age fifty, Furillo took a job installing doors on the elevators at the World Trade Center. I personally remember seeing a photo of Furillo working on a high-rise building at the World Trade Center. The photo was in an article describing the travails of Dodgers players post-baseball careers.

Jackie Robinson's post baseball continued the woes and health issues of these beloved Dodgers. Jackie Robinson was born January 31, 1919, in Cairo, Georgia, and passed away on October 24, 1972, at age fifty-three. On April 15, 1947, Jackie broke baseball's color barrier as the first Afro American to play in the Major Leagues. Robinson won the Rookie of the Year in 1947, and in 1949, Robinson won the MVP of the National League with a .342 batting average. The 1997 MLB season was dedicated in honor of Jackie Robinson's silver anniversary of breaking the color barrier.

During Jackie's first year in 1947, players of the St. Louis Cardinals threatened to strike if Robinson took the field. Commissioner Ford Frick quashed the strike, countering that any player who did so would be suspended from baseball. Jackie Robinson was the perfect black to break the color barrier since he was a man of nonviolence and a man of true Christian faith. As terrible as the racial insults were made to Jackie, he never retaliated. One day Dodger captain Pee Wee Reese left his position at shortstop and went to put an arm around Robinson playing second base in a show of solidarity when fans, heckling him, became ruthless and as a result both became lifelong friends. On July 23,1962, Jackie Robinson was inducted into the National Baseball Hall of Fame in Cooperstown, New York. In 1999, Jackie was posthumously voted into the Major League Baseball All-Century team.

I've had frozen in my left temporal lobe, for over sixty years, Jackie's lifetime batting average of .311. After Robinson's death in 1972 from diabetes, in recognition of his achievements on and off the field, Robinson was posthumously awarded the Congressional Gold Medal and Presidential Medal of Freedom. On April 19, 2019, Major League Baseball celebrated Jackie Robinson's one-hundredth birthday, and Major League Baseball celebrated Jackie's life all of the 2019 baseball season. What peace and contentment this three-hour game every Saturday afternoon would bring to a boy starving for love and affection.

# CHAPTER 40

## In Air—Gunsmoke—Shooting Basketball Hours on End

It was in late summer of 1955 that I got to take my very first airplane flight. A deacon in our Abilene BIC Church and a cousin of Mother's, Lowell Hoover, had a friend who had his own airplane, his name was Mark Winger from Pennsylvania. Mark's brother Bert Winger, was the pastor of the Bethel BIC Church before Daddy replaced him in 1945. Mark took Lowell, Daddy, Chuck, and I up in his airplane and something magical was about to happen—Mark flew us right over Grandpa Hoover's farm. That truly was awesome for an eleven-year-old who could see his heaven on earth from the sky. Being up in that airplane would dwarf the forty-foot-high silo that I had climbed to the top both inside and outside.

I must make mention of a television series debuting on September 10, 1955, and ran for twenty years to March 31, 1975. The series *Gunsmoke* would have 635 episodes. *Gunsmoke,* for years, held the record of the longest consecutive run series which will soon be broken by the *Simpsons.* Aunt Delores and her husband, Uncle Darrel Kelly, lived in an apartment at the very end of our block on Northeast Seventh. *Gunsmoke* was the second western TV series premiering four days after the *Life and Legend of Wyatt Earp*, starring Hugh O'Brien. Every Saturday evening, Chuck and I would have a front-row seat watching what would become my favorite TV series in the 1950s. What a cast of characters: Amanda Blake as Kitty, Dennis Weaver as Chester Goode, Milburn Stone as Doc Adams, and, James Arness as Marshall Matt Dillon. Both Arness and Stone spent the entire twenty years acting out their parts. The towering giant bartender Glenn Strange, passed away in 1973, two years before the show's conclusion. This one hour with Aunt Delores and Uncle Darrel was so therapeutic for me, away from my albatross cellar. In September of 1955 I got my first bicycle. I was eleven and had never ridden a bike. My second cousin Sharon Lady, who lived just north of Abilene, gave me her green bicycle. It was a girl's bike but I was okay with that. I now had a bike to ride around town. Sharon's grandpa was Luther Lady, a younger brother to Mama Anna who burned to death that January 1, 1927. Sharon was my age and a younger sister of Larry Lady who coached against Daddy and East Buckeye at Abilene City Hall in March of 1954.

There was no longer an outside darkened locked up cellar but there was still a parsonage basement which now became my dungeon from 1955–1960. Unexpectedly about four years ago in 2016, totally out of the blue I got to chat via our smartphones, with Mary Jean Londeen who, along with Linda Minter, were Chuck's two best childhood friends. We were chatting and Mary Jean told me that she had a master's in education, specializing with the autistic and behavioral troubled child. I then told Mary Jean that I had just recently started working part-time with special education. Our conversation then led Mary Jean to share with me of how sorry Chuck, Linda, and she were with my being kept down in the cellar. That was truly a stunner for me. I had absolutely no idea that Mary Jean and Linda were aware of the abuse that I suffered at the hands of my mother. Now the sixty-four-dollar question—were their parents aware of this! I'm almost sure they were.

Linda had a brother Larry two years younger than I. Larry and Linda lived right across the alley from us, they were children of a minister. Their father Galen was a minister of the Evangelical United Methodist Church, the church that my late beloved Uncle Harry and his wife, Aunt Carolyn, were members of. When moving to Abilene, I brought my basketball goal with me; however, our backyard was so small and so bumpy. Larry's parents had one huge backyard and had a basketball goal set up. The Minners let me shoot whenever I wanted to and that was all the time. In their backyard, I would refine my shooting skills, literally spending hundreds of hours shooting in solitary. I can't even count the times that I would shoot baskets for four to five hours at a time. Oh, how I loved the sport of basketball—my refuge, my Utopia, an escape from Mother's continual abuse of me. I would make up in my head two basketball teams, the all-time K-State greatest players versus the all-time greats of KU, referring to the Kansas State Wildcats and the Kansas Jayhawks.

During that fall of 1955 I learned the art of juggling and guess who taught me—my daddy. One fall evening, Daddy and I were playing catch, I was always the pitcher and Daddy was the catcher. The pitching mound and the catcher's base were right in our driveway. After throwing for a while, Daddy got three tennis balls and what was to happen simply stunned me. Daddy started to juggle the three balls. Yes, Daddy was athletic but I had no idea of his juggling skills. I always had to have a ball in my hands and I quickly learned how to juggle; yes, that very evening, I mastered the three-ball juggling act. I would go around to family gatherings and would put on a juggling show, often juggling for thirty minutes without dropping one. In return, I taught my son David to juggle. However, the three of us could never quite master the art of juggling four balls. Daddy could also play a musical instrument, the accordion. As a boy of three, I remember Daddy with his accordion over his shoulder playing.

# CHAPTER 41

## Public Library—My Home away from Home

I've always been an avid reader and I have my first grade teacher Ms. Betts to thank for that. How she encouraged me to read. From that first summer of 1955 through the spring of 1962 while living in Abilene, the public library would become my place of refuge away from my tormented life in the cellar. Some sixty-four years later, I can't express enough of my love of reading and the safe haven of rest the public library became to me. During those seven and a half years living in Abilene, not one of my 150 classmates came close to spending time at the library as I did. I remember of only one time that I saw a classmate at the library and that was a friend of mine, Roger. May I also make mention that I doubt that too many of my classmates came from a dysfunctional family.

My barber Red Davis's wife was the head of the children's library who I got to know very well. Red Davis was a close friend of Grandpa Hoover's. Often Grandpa and I would get haircuts together every couple of weeks at Davis's barbershop. The first book that I ever checked out of the Abilene public library was a biography of the "Iron Horse," Lou Gehrig. Gehrig was born on June 19, 1903, in the Yorkville section of Manhattan in New York City. Gehrig would play in a record of 2,130 consecutive games which stood for fifty-six years until Cal Ripken broke that streak in 1995. I personally was not happy about that as my two all-time favorite Major League players just happened to be first basemen—great first basemen— Lou Gehrig and Gil Hodges, their jersey numbers 4 and 14 respectively.

On June 2, 1925, Yankee first baseman Wally Pipp asked the team's trainer for an aspirin for a severe headache. New York manager Miller Huggins said, "Wally, take the day off, we'll try that kid Gehrig at first base."

Pipp was later to have said, "I took the two most expensive aspirin in history." Beginning on that June 2, 1925, Lou Gehrig wouldn't miss a game until May 2, 1939, when at the young age of thirty-six, Gehrig had to take himself out of the lineup due to weakness throughout his entire body. Gehrig at the famed Mayo Clinic in Rochester, Minnesota, was diagnosed as having amyotrophic lateral sclerosis (ALS), an incurable neuromuscular disorder, now commonly known as Lou Gehrig disease. Gehrig is regarded by all baseball historians as the greatest first baseman of all time. No one is even a close second, although George Sisler who had a lifetime batting average of .340, has to get a few votes. From 1920 to 2004, Sisler held the (MLB) record for hits in a season with 257 until Ichiro Susuki had a record of 262 hits in 2004.

Lou Gehrig became known for his prowess as a hitter and for his durability which earned him the nickname "The Iron Horse." Gehrig was a Triple Crown winner once, that's of leading your league in home runs, batting average, and hits. He was American League MVP twice and a member of six world championships. He was a member of the 1927 Yankee team known as Murderer's Row, considered the greatest Major League team of all time. Of the six starting hitters in that lineup, four players would be future Hall of Famers: Earl Combs, Babe Ruth, Gehrig, and Tony Lazzeri. Lou Gehrig had a career .340 batting average, 632 slugging average, and hit 493 home runs with 1,995 RBIs. If Lou Gehrig would not have suffered his fatal illness, in my book, either he or the "Splendid Splinter" Ted Williams, who missed over five years due to service in both WWII and the Korean War, would be the all-time leader in RBIs. Now for a most shocking fact: in the thirteen full seasons he played, Gehrig averaged 147 RBIs a season. Hank Aaron, Willie Mays, and Mickey Mantle never drove in that many runs in a season once.

The pathos of his farewell from baseball was capped off by his iconic July 4, 1939, speech where Gehrig remarked, "For the past two weeks you have been reading about a bad break, yet today I consider myself the luckiest man on the face of the earth." In 1939, Gehrig was elected to the Baseball Hall of Fame, the six-year post playing career was waived due to

Gehrig's impending death. Gehrig was the first MLB player to have his uniform number—4—retired by a team. Lou Gehrig passed away at the young age of thirty-seven on June 2, 1941.

In the children's library, I would read the entire thirty some books of the Franklin Dixon Hardy Boy mystery books with Frank and Joe Hardy and their close friend, Chet, as the main characters.

> Entering the foyer leading up to the first floor of the library was always a small coffee table where free magazines were kept such as *Look Magazine*, *Life Magazine*, *National Geographic*, just to name a few. My mind was always starved for reading. One *Life Magazine* I particularly remember had a cover photo of the recently crowned Queen Elizabeth whose reign began on February 6, 1952, at the young age of twenty-six. Today in 2020, at the age of ninety-three, the queen is the longest lived and longest reigning British monarch. Queen Elizabeth's reign has now been sixty-eight years compared to Queen Victoria's sixty-four-year reign from June 1837, until her death on January 22, 1901. Another *Life Magazine* I picked up had on its cover the young New York Yankee superstar from Commerce, Oklahoma, Mickey Mantle with his wife, Merlyn, and sons. I also recall picking up a magazine, thinking it was *Look Magazine* which had on its cover US citizens Julius and Ethel Rosenberg who were convicted of committing espionage for the Soviet Union. Both were executed by the electric chair on June 19, 1953. Not yet nine, I remember that execution well.

Another *Life Magazine* had on its cover the Bobby Greenlease kidnapping. Bobby Greenlease was the six-year-old son of a multimillionaire automobile dealer Robert Cosgrove Greenlease. The Greenlease kidnapping led to the largest ransom in US history of $600,000. On September 28, 1953, Bobby Greenlease was sitting in his class at his elite Catholic school in Kansas City, Missouri, when around 11:00 a.m., one of the nuns came to retrieve him. He was told that an aunt was there to pick him up. Bobby readily took the hand of the woman, never to be seen alive again. The two kidnappers were Carl Hall and Bonnie Brown Heady. According to Heady, after she left the school with Bobby, she got into a cab to go meet with Hall nearby. They then drove into Missouri where Hall shot Bobby Greenlease, murdering him. He was dead within thirty minutes after his abduction. On December 18, 1953, a mere eighty-one days after Bobby had been kidnapped, Hall and Heady were ushered into the gas chamber. They were pronounced dead within twenty seconds of each other. How well I remember this kidnapping and execution as a nine-year-old.

Yes, the Abilene public library became my haven of rest, a place of contentment away from my daily emotional trauma. As you entered the adult library, just to your left was the reading room and newspaper sections. If I hadn't read the *Salina Journal* at Great-Uncle Luther's, I would devour both the *Salina Journal* and the *Topeka Daily Capitol*'s sports sections. Daily I would read the box scores for every Major League game. My parents had the *Abilene Reflector Chronicle* delivered daily to our home. It was at the library that I first read about Christine Jorgenson, an American transwoman, who was the first person to become widely known in the US for having sex reassignment surgery in Denmark on September 24, 1951. Her transition was the subject of a *New York Daily News* front-page story. I would also spend hour after hour in the historical section of Dickenson County, Kansas. I got to be very good friends with the head librarian, Ms. Clara Hanson, and the assistant librarian, Ms. Betty Jean Holmes.

Across from the newspaper room was a special coffee table with glass that had Dwight David and Mamie Doud Eisenhower pictured on their wedding day, July 1, 1916. The couple exchanged vows in the Denver home of Mamie's parents, John and Elivera Doud. Next they took the train to Abilene to meet Ike's parents and his brothers. In April 1952, *Life Magazine* printed the lovely wedding photo of Ike and Mamie on its cover. With a circulation of more than 5,200,000 and with ten pages of copy on and photos of Ike's life, this issue must have certainly helped Ike's campaign for president. That photo of Ike and Mamie will forever linger in my mind.

# CHAPTER 42

## *The 1955 World Series*

It's Wednesday September 28, 1955, and after a one-year sabbatical for both the Yankees and Dodgers, again they would face off in the World Series. Would this be the year that my Dodgers would finally win a World Series? In 1947, 1952, and 1953, the Yankees defeated the Dodgers in the best-of-seven series, four games to three. It was only in 1949 that the Yankees defeated the Dodgers four games to one. The 1955 World Series would be the first to be televised in color. I had to settle for radio as my parents hadn't yet gotten a television. I recall the radio announcers, the late Al Helfer and the late Bob Neal of the Mutual Broadcasting System of doing the play-by-play. The 1955 World Series was loaded with future Hall of Famers including the following Dodgers: Manager Walter Alston, the immortal number forty-two, second baseman, Jackie Robinson, catcher Roy Campanella, SS Harold Pee Wee Reese the captain, and center fielder the "Duke of Flatbush" Duke Snider. Future Hall of Famers the legendary Sandy Koufax and Tom Lasorda did not play. The following Yankee players would become future Hall of Famers: Manager "the Ole Professor" Casey Stengel, catcher Yogi Berra, SS the scooter Phil Rizzuto, center fielder Mickey Mantle, and pitcher Whitey Ford.

Game 7 of the 1955 World Series will forever be baseball lore. The Dodgers scored the only runs on a fourth inning, RBI single (after a double), and a sixth inning bases loaded sacrifice fly both RBIs by Gil Hodges. Of baseball lore happened in the sixth inning at Yankee Stadium on October 4, 1955. With runners on first and second base and one out, Sandy Amoros made a dramatic game-saving catch of a fly ball down the left field line off the bat of Yogi Berra to start a double play. Amoros after the miracle catch, threw to Pee Wee Reese and Reese relayed a strike to Gil Hodges who tagged Gil McDougald out before McDougald could get back to first base to complete the double play and as a result, the Brooklyn Dodgers would win their first ever World Series, and I recall jumping up and down on the bedroom floor, celebrating my Dodger World Series victory.

For the first time in World Series history, an MVP was selected—a twenty-two-year-old lefty "Southpaw" Johnny Podres who won games 3 and 7. Podres, in the series, was 2–0 with two complete games, an incredible era of 1.00. Podres pitched a shutout in game 7. It was the first World Series that *Sport Magazine* would give a Corvette to the World Series MVP. On September 29, 2017, the MVP of the World Series was named in honor of Willie Mays in remembrance of the sixty-third anniversary of "the catch" in the 1954 World Series. Mays never won the award himself.

The following is Ken Musser's argument for jersey 14 Gil Hodges to be in the Baseball Hall of Fame. During the decade of the 1950s, Hodges ranked second in the Major Leagues to teammate Duke Snider in both home runs and RBIs. Hodges was the league's first Gold Glove winner in 1957 and Gil also won the award in 1958–1959. On top of that, Hodges ranked tenth in total hits in the decade of the 1950s. Gil is also ranked as the greatest fielding first baseman in all the Major Leagues in the 1950s. Gil ended his sterling career with 370 home runs and 1,274 RBIs. On top of that, Hodges was the manager of the 1969 Miracle Mets, winning one hundred games and upsetting the heavily favored Baltimore Orioles, four games to one, and yes, that '69 Oriole team included future Hall of Famers Frank and Brooks Robinson and pitcher Jim Palmer.

Here's a stat that is hard to believe but it's true. Jim Palmer in his Hall of Fame career, never allowed a grand slam home run. Hodges was a man of high integrity and sportsmanship and Gil never turned down an interview. Gil always blew a kiss to his wife Joan, after hitting a home run while rounding third base in Ebbett's Field. If Gil had one vice, it's that he was a chain- smoker. Hodges was only forty-seven when he had a heart attack while playing golf on the second of April 1972, just two days short of his forty- eighth birthday. Please believe me, I've had stored in my left temporal lobe of the brain, for years, Gil Hodges' birthdate on

April 4, 1924, and his hometown of Princeton, Indiana. Let me conclude by stating that it's just a travesty that Hodges isn't in the Baseball Hall of Fame.On December 6, 2021 my favorite all-time Major League baseball player Gil Hodges was at last elected to the Baseball-Hall-of Fame. Nearly half a century after his death Gil Hodges has added to his prolific profile which includes a US Marine, All-Star first baseman, and World Series winning manager. Jerry Koosman a starting pitcher on that 1969 "Miracle New York Met Team" has the following quote; "We would have been a powerhouse for many years if Gil had stayed on with us and not passed away". It took the Veteran's committee to vote Hodges into the Hall-of-Fame but at last justice has been served.

It's a good thing that my Dodgers won that 1955 World Series as after the 1957 season, both the Dodgers and the New York Giants and their superstar the "Say Hey Kid" Willie Mays would be moving to Los Angeles and San Francisco respectively. The Dodgers moving out West got rather personal with me. It took a long time for me to forgive the late Dodger president Walter O' Malley for moving my beloved Dodgers out West.

The mid-1950s would bring with it a new fashion in hat, the Davy Crockett coonskin cap, highly popular among boys. The coonskin cap was fashioned from the skin and fur of a raccoon. Both Chuck and I had our coonskin caps along with our plastic knives, toy guns, and holsters. In 1958 was the invention of the Hula-Hoop craze which swept the world by storm, and in the years 1958–1960, world sales reached more than 100 million. The Hula-Hoop eventually died out in the 1980s but not in China and Russia where Hula-Hooping and hoop manipulation were adopted by rhythmic gymnasts. Yes, I had my Hula-Hoop and I was good at it. Our family had a Sunday evening ritual before going to evening church. We had a light supper—often ice cream and potato chips—and we had the kitchen radio turned on to a classic Western *Gunsmoke*, starring William Conrad as Marshal Matt Dillon. The radio version of *Gunsmoke* started in April of 1952 whereas the television version started in September of 1955.

# CHAPTER 43

## A Wasted Sixth Grade

Upon entering sixth grade in the fall of 1955, I attended the old Abilene High School located at Seventh and Buckeye, right across from my church. This isn't the high school that President Eisenhower attended as that's located on the block of west Seventh, next to Garfield elementary where I spent the second half of my fifth grade when moving to Abilene. My sixth-grade teacher was a former basketball player at Kansas State University at Manhattan, Kansas, the "little apple." He was a towering figure standing six feet nine inches. Why was my sixth grade a waste? Almost every day he would read stories from books and magazines of adventure, both fiction and nonfiction. It was during sixth grade that I made A's and B's. When entering seventh grade, I was at a loss in math and science classes. My sixth-grade teacher had put little emphasis on these two classes. As a result, from grades seven through my senior year in high school, I could pull no better than C's, coupled in with a few D's in math and science. Yes, it was a fun sixth grade, but a wasted one.

# CHAPTER 44

## Football on Armistice Day

During the decade of the 1950s, Abilene High School annually hosted a Central Kansas league football game on November 11 Armistice day now better known as veteran's day. Daddy, Chuck, and I would walk the nine blocks to the high school football field. I remember it as such a fun day with Daddy. On those cool November days, there was a hot dog and pretzel stand with coffee and soft drinks. This was a yearly ritual that I so looked forward to. On these Thursdays the Abilene Cowboy football team usually lost. The reason being that for years Abilene was in the "CKL" Central Kansas League, and Abilene was one of the three smallest towns. Teams like Salina had a population of forty-five thousand; Manhattan, forty thousand; Junction City, twenty-five thousand; McPherson, fifteen thousand; whereas Abilene was a town of seven thousand. Only two other schools were close to Abilene in population Clay Center and Chapman. Memories of those Armistice days with Daddy remain unforgettable.

Our first Christmas arrived in 1955 at the parsonage and Santa brought me just what I had asked for—a shiny red J. C. Higgins bicycle from Sears and Roebuck. I would ride my new bike all over Abilene, out to the municipal swimming pool, and out to my Little League Baseball practices. Christmas Day at Grandpa Hoover's was the best day of the year for me. I remember asking my parents if I could take my shiny new bike out to Grandpa's without success. Most Christmases Aunt Mary Lou and family drove the 170 miles from Kansas City, Missouri, to Grandpa's. Their oldest child Janet and I became very close over the years. Jan was extremely athletic and we had so much fun playing softball. To this day, I remember how much Janet loved Grandma Carrie's mashed potatoes and gravy. Every Christmas, Grandma would bake the most delicious apple and cherry pies. Grandma's pies could have won a blue ribbon at the Central Kansas free fair in Abilene.

# CHAPTER 45

## Television and Radio Bring Comfort to a Love-Starved Boy

As a lifetime basketball fanatic, I must share the very first time that I watched a basketball game on television. It was a bitter-cold late January day in 1956 as I was walking from downtown toward home on North Buckeye. I was walking past Sears and Roebuck when looking through the store's front window, I saw a basketball game being played on TV. A lady who worked in the business office waved and I stepped inside. It just happened that she was the wife of one of my barbers. She knew me and I was able to watch the basketball game between Ohio State and Illinois. One player immediately stood out to me, his name was Robin Freeman. Freeman stood only 5'11", short even for a college player in that era. Freeman was unconsciously swishing the net, jumper after jumper. Freeman I would later learn, would become the first player in big ten history to average 30-plus points in back to back seasons in 1955–1956. Freeman tallied 723 points as a senior in 1956. His career scoring average of 28.0 points per game ranks number 1 in Ohio State Buckeye history. That's a statement as probably the greatest player in Buckeye history is the great incomparable Jerry Lucas. Freeman in that June 1956 draft, was selected by the Pro St. Louis Hawks. However Freeman never got to play a single game in the NBA as he severed the tips of two fingers while chopping wood shortly after graduating from Ohio State in 1956. Instead Freeman went to law school and became a lawyer in Springfield, Ohio. Freeman, a two-time consensus All-American, passed away in 2014 at the age of eighty. A question for the reader—how many eleven-year-olds would stop to watch an entire college basketball game at a Sears and Roebuck? My answer—not many, zilch, nada. This is an example of an eleven-year-old starving for love and affection, being given a short time of peace and contentment watching the game he loved away from his albatross prison cellar.

One unforgettable evening took place in early 1956 with the setting being my Aunt Carol and Uncle Virgil Wenger's home. Aunt Carol had invited my family for the evening dinner. What's so unforgettable is that it was the first time that I would hear a basketball game on radio. That night, the seed was planted that would have me becoming a die-hard Kansas State basketball fan from that evening through the mid-1960s. I've had frozen in my left temporal lobe for sixty-four years, the starting five for the Wildcats that January evening. Pachin Vicens, the 5'9" point guard from Puerto Rico, shooting guard Roy Dewitz, forwards Haydon Abbott and Fritz Schneider, and the center, 6'9" Jack Parr who, that season, averaged 17.4 points and fourteen rebounds a game. I must make mention of the point guard Pachin Vicens.

Vicens played at K-State from 1954–1955. After graduating from K-State, Vicens became famous for his performance with the Leones de Ponce of the Puerto Rican National team. During the 1959 FIBA—the International Basketball Federation held in Chile—Vicens was declared to be the best player in the world. While at K-State from 1954–56, Vicens' head coach would become legendary Fred "Tex" Winter. Winter was the mentor of the Hall of Fame pro coach Phil Jackson with the Chicago Bulls and the Los Angeles Lakers. Tex was the innovator of the "triangle offense" which I'll cover later. Vicens, due to cancer, had to have both legs amputated and he passed away on February 18, 2007, at his home in Ponce, Puerto Rico, at the age of seventy-two. Just a special note to my late Uncle Virgil who passed into heaven's pearly gates on July 1, 2017; thank you so much for having that K-State game on radio that bitter January night in 1956. For the next seven years, listening to every K-State basketball game would become so therapeutic for me. I would yell my lungs out for the Wildcats. What a haven of rest and contentment for two hours away from my albatross.

I must share about the first NCAA championship game that I ever listened to on the radio. On March 12, 1956, I was in my bedroom at the parsonage at 204 N.E. seventh with my ears to the radio listening to the San Francisco Dons playing the Iowa Hawkeyes. This championship would become a "signature" for a man who appeared to be playing against boys. Bill Russell had what I recall as an eleven-year-old, the greatest NCAA championship final game by any player in NCAA history. Russell's showcase ended with an unbelievable 26 points, 27 rebounds, and 20 blocks. Really! As an eleven- year-old listening to the commentator, I was simply in "awe" at Russell's historic game. I remember the Iowa Hawkeyes star player Carl Cain who had 17 points and 12 rebounds in that final, and like Russell was a member of the 1956 US Olympic team at Melbourne, Australia. The final score of that 1956 NCAA championship game was the San Francisco Dons, 83; Iowa Hawkeyes, 71. Yes, again a sporting event was a refuse for an emotionally and physically abused boy.

Beginning in the winter of 1956–1957, I would turn onto the 50,000-watt radio station KMOX in St. Louis listening to the St. Louis Hawks Pro Basketball team. My left temporal lobe tells me the starting lineup for that 1956–1957 Hawks team. SG Jack McMahon, PG little Slater Martin, center Bob Petit—my first pro basketball favorite player and the first NBA player to crack the twenty thousand points in a career. SF Cliff Hagen and PF "Easy Ed" Macauley, a local player who played his college ball with the St. Louis Billikens. Macauley would become more famous for the most lopsided draft day deal in NBA history. Prior to the start of the 1955–1956 season, the Hawks sent second overall pick Bill Russell to the Boston Celtics for Cliff Hagan and Ed Macauley and, as the saying goes, the rest is history. Russell's going to Boston would change forever the dynamics of NBA history forever. Year after year, from the mid-1950s to mid-1960s, the NBA finals would pit the Celtics against the Hawks. It was only in 1958 that the St. Louis Hawks would defeat the Boston Celtics for the NBA championship, winning four games to two.

At the age of fourteen I was a diehard St Louis Hawks fan and oh how I despised the Boston Celtics due to their always winning the NBA championship. How that would change in another ten years.

# CHAPTER 46

## Priceless Memories with Grandpa and Grandma Hoover

My parents finally got a TV in the spring of 1956, and once again, Mother had her rules and we had to abide by them or else. There was absolutely to be no touching of the TV, no changing of the channels. If I did, my destination was my prison cellar. I had brunch recently with my brother Chuck. I asked him if he could remember us not being able to touch the TV and he couldn't remember, so in all probability, applied only to me. How cruel Mother could be to me! Mother had to be in control of everything in our home. Her rules were mandatory, meant to be obeyed or else. Mother had bought a 1964 red Valiant and boy did she have her rules. I couldn't even touch the car. This went on for years. Reflecting some sixty-four years later, I've come to the premise that Mother was using me to fill her own unmet emotional needs missing from her own childhood and adolescent years.

My most cherished boyhood memories were those spent at Grandpa's farm. From around 1952–1957, my family one night a week, would drive the ten miles to Grandpa's. These weekly drives would take us right to Grandpa Hoover's kitchen table. Grandpa, Grandma, Daddy, Mother, and I would sit around the kitchen table, listening to Grandpa's storytelling. Like Job in the Bible, Grandpa had his share of travails. Grandpa had experienced so many trials, calamities, loss of family, health issues but Grandpa's faith in his Lord and Savior stood firm. Let me share a couple of what I would like to call Grandpa's fireside chats, like FDR had with the American people, beginning in 1933, to address the fears and concerns of the American people. Grandpa thought so much of his parents-in-law, Samuel and Mary Olive Frey Lady. I can't overemphasize his enduring love for them. Grandpa would tell us of how Mary Olive became like a mother to the five little sisters, ages seven to three months old, standing by her daughter Anna Zelma's last words before she died. "Mama, please take care of my babies."

As I heard Grandpa share of Samuel and Mary Olive's enduring love for the five daughters, it would melt an eleven-year-old's heart. Grandpa had such love for his siblings. Oh how he idolized his fourteen-year older brother Harry, his limbs torn off by a pully belt on the threshing machine. Grandpa's youngest child Harry Dwayne, was named after Harry. Another one of Grandpa's fireside chats would be about his dear brother Ben who had lived a pretty rough life but, toward the end of his life, had a wonderful conversion to Jesus as his personal Savior. I shall never forget another one of Grandpa's fireside chats. It was about a time of trials and hardships for hundreds of farmers. It was the year 1931 in which Grandpa would share with us about the plague of grasshoppers. In July of 1931, Grandpa related of there being a swarm of grasshoppers that hit Nebraska, the Dakotas, and North Central Kansas. I remember Grandpa stating of how thick the swarm of grasshoppers was that in some areas, the sun was blocked out and one could shovel up the grasshoppers with a scoop. Cornstalks were eaten to the ground and left fields completely bare. Grandpa told us of the extreme drought and unusually dry conditions in the years 1931–1932 and the damage to his and other crops. Upon my recalling of Grandpa sharing with us of the drought and dry conditions in 1931–1932, I did a little research on my own. I went to google.com and the head title is "Grasshoppers bring ruin to Midwest." The article states that grasshoppers and locust are insect cousins and among the most-feared pests. A plague of these insects can occur when conditions cause their population to suddenly explode. Usually this happens under drought or very dry conditions since their egg pods are vulnerable to fungus in wet soil. When the soil is very dry, swarms can develop.

I remember Grandpa telling us that the locusts beat against the house, swarming at the windows. At night the insects huddled on train tracks for rest and for warmth. Being sluggish in the cool morning air, they were trampled under the wheels of the passing trains. I recall Grandpa telling us that the oil from the crushed bodies reduced the traction as to stop the train, especially on an upgrade. These weekly sessions sitting around the kitchen table with Grandpa and Grandma Hoover were absolutely the best times of my life. I must add that on our weekly nights visiting Grandpa Hoover's, the radio was always turned on to the *Red Skelton Show* and *People Are Funny*, starring Art Linkletter. Red Skelton would always close his nightly show with the words, "Good night and God bless." *People Are Funny* was hosted by Art Linkletter beginning in 1943 on NBC radio, moving to CBS from 1951–1954, returning to NBC from 1954–1960. Contestants were asked to carry out stunts in order to prove that people are funny. The show seldom had celebrities, focusing instead on everyday people. Red Skelton's radio shows began in 1937 and continued to 1957. Several of the characters that Skelton portrayed were Freddie the Freeloader and Clem Kadiddlehopper. Skelton portraying the hobo Freddie the Freeloader was just hilarious. What special priceless evenings spent with Grandpa and Grandma Hoover!

# CHAPTER 47

## Gillette Friday Night Boxing and Playing Softball in a Cow Pasture

From time to time on a Friday evening, Daddy drove us out to Grandpa's. In the early to mid-1950s, the sport of boxing was incredibly popular as were the Friday night fights sponsored by Gillette on NBC. Grandpa was a huge boxing fan and it was easy to remember his favorite Sugar Ray Robinson, pound for pound regarded by *Ring Magazine* as the number one boxer in the last eighty years of boxing. Sugar Ray's record as an amateur was 85–0. From 1943–1951 as a middleweight, Robinson went on a ninety-one-fight unbeaten streak. Sugar Ray had 108 KOs. Sugar Ray retired in 1952, only to come back two and a half years later and regained the middleweight title in 1955. In 1965 Robinson was broke, having spent the $4 million in earnings that he had made both inside and outside the ring. Sadly Sugar Ray passed away from Alzheimer's disease at the age of sixty-seven on April 12, 1989. Several boxers have passed away from Alzheimer's which could very well be related to continuous hits to the head. I shall forever remember of Grandpa's devotion of being a Sugar Ray fan. Grandpa Hoover added a little icing to the cake as he bought both Chuck and me boxing gloves and Grandpa, Chuck, and I had some great sparring sessions.

Many Sunday afternoons, from mid-April to late fall, we would drive out to Grandpa's and we would have a pickup softball game. Grandpa Hoover had one large front yard. Grandpa was always the pitcher. I would often invite my neighbor friend Larry Minner. Playing in the pickup game would be Daddy, Grandpa, Uncle Harry, and Uncle Virgil Wenger, and before Aunt Delores was married in 1955, she would play as she was quite the athlete and what a throwing arm Aunt Delores had. If it was harvest and the front yard was full of farm implements, we would improvise by going out to the cow pasture. We would gather stones or rocks and use them as bases. Believe me, it really did work.

About three or four times a year, we would have a special treat at Grandpa's with the making of delicious homemade vanilla ice cream. My job was helping in the churning of the ice cream. We would all gather in the washhouse. Grandma would bring out the container she'd filled with all the ingredients. Grandpa would then slide the container into place into the ice cream churner, filled it halfway with ice, a layer of rock salt, more ice, more rock salt, a little more ice, and then cover it with a towel while it churned. I'll always remember Grandpa telling me of how the towel helped to keep the churn cool. Nothing compares to homemade ice cream if it's done just right.

# CHAPTER 48

## The Black Hills

The summer of 1956 had arrived and my family would take our first long road trip since 1953. Our destination the Black Hills in South Dakota, which again would be a fun relaxing time with family with no fighting, arguing, and cursing, far away from my cellar prison. The rugged beauty of the badlands was so spectacular. The badlands are a type of dry terrain where softer sedimentary rocks and clay-rich soil have been extremely eroded by wind and water. My being a lover of US history, Mount Rushmore National Memorial was my trip highlight. Mount Rushmore National Memorial is a massive sculpture carved into Mount Rushmore in the Black Hills region of South Dakota. Under the direction of the Belgian Gutzen Berglum and his son Lincoln, sculpted into the granite of Mount Rushmore sixty-foot-high granite faces of four of the US greatest Presidents: George Washington, Thomas Jefferson, Abraham Lincoln, and the President cowboy, Theodore Roosevelt. I so marveled at this massive sculpture that forty-three years later, in June of 1999, I visited Mount Rushmore a second time. I would love to make it a third time.

Another highlight was attending the Passion Play of the crucifixion and resurrection of Jesus Christ, played and acted out by professional actors. The setting is the Black Hills in Spearfish, South Dakota. The Passion Play ran for nearly seventy years, beginning in May of 1939 and ending on a Sunday, August 31, 2008, and I was so fortunate to attend it twice. We also toured the prosperous mining town of Deadwood where mining was at its peak from the 1860s–1880s. It's in Deadwood on a hillside, where the graves of James Butler "Wild Bill" Hickok and Calamity Jane rest side by side.

What a wonderful vacation it was, how peaceful, what sense of contentment within our family, never an argument, a curse, and best of all, no basement prison. With our trip nearing the end, we visited Terry Peak ski lift with a summit of 7,100 feet. Believe it or not, Terry Peak offers the highest lift service between the Rocky Mountains and the Swiss Alps. We had a really close call while on the lift. Mother and I were on a chairlift, just ahead of Daddy and Chuck. Mother had her purse with her when suddenly, it slipped from her hands, and with my quick reflexes, I snagged it just as it was about to drop tens of feet into the snow below.

Our last stop was at the giant tortoise reptile park. The tortoises were so big that a human could sit on them. Our highlight was visiting the beloved giant tortoise Methuselah who recently passed away on July 9, 2011. It was South Dakota's oldest resident. He was born in 1881 in the Galapagos Islands of Ecuador and weighed six hundred pounds. Let's see, Methuselah would have been 130 years old at the time of its passing. Still the giant tortoise fell 839 years short of its namesake, the biblical figure and patriarch Methuselah who lived to be 969. The biblical patriarch was the son of Enoch and grandfather of Noah. Genesis 5:25–27 tells us that Enoch walked with God and the secret to Enoch's walk with God was his faith (Genesis 24:6–9 and Hebrews 11:5–6. Methuselah, by all accounts, died in the year of the Great Flood).

Something rather humorous happened on our trip home. I remember that we were in a heavy rain while going through a good-size city North Platte, Nebraska. As we were about to leave North Platte, I looked to the left across the street and I couldn't believe what I saw—a sign that said "Musser's Beer Wine and Liquor Store." That was simply hilarious as while living in Abilene, Kansas, my entire boyhood into adolescence, I never knew a person with the last name of Musser. We continued our way home without one argument, no fighting. How our family trips were so therapeutic for both Mother and me.

# CHAPTER 49

## The Frey Family Tree

$A$ family highlight each summer was the annual Frey reunion held every August 14, the birthday of the Frey family patriarch, Adam Frey. Adam Frey was born in Adams County, Pennsylvania, on August 14, 1843. In the autumn of 1864, Adam enlisted in the Army of the North, after serving a few months, he was wounded by a bullet passing through his left elbow. Before he was able to leave the hospital, the end of the war had come.

On January 19, 1869, Adam Frey married Mary Ann Hershey who likewise was born in Adams County, Pennsylvania, on February 20, 1846. As I mentioned earlier, my ancestors on both my paternal and maternal side came from Germany and Switzerland, settling in the Pennsylvania Dutch Country along the Susquehanna River near Marietta, Pennsylvania, in Lancaster County, Pennsylvania, in the Mid-Eighteenth Century. Immediately after Adam and Mary Ann's wedding, they moved to Nachusa, Lee County, Illinois. Adam worked at the shoemaker trade for two and a half years after which they moved with their two daughters, Mary Olive and Emma, to a farm in Decatur County, Iowa, where they resided for five years. Yes, this Ollie was my great-grandmother, born on May 29, 1870, and Emma was born in 1871. On December 29, 1889, Mary Olive Frey married Samuel Jefferson Lady born in Adams County, Pennsylvania, on March 16, 1860.

In Iowa, three sons—Harvey, John, and Rueben—were born. In 1877 the Adam-Frey family moved by prairie schooner (covered wagon) to Dickenson County, Kansas, in North Central Kansas. They left Iowa with two wagons in the month of February and because of rough winter roads, by the time they arrived in Manhattan, Kansas, a horse was so lame that one wagon was temporarily left behind. The family reached Abilene, Kansas, where their five youngest children, Mabel, Jessie, Edith, Christian, and Lawrence, were born. Here the family was brought up in the fear of God and taught the principles of Christian living, at the same time, living with the ravages of grasshoppers, chinch-bugs and drought, and the consequent hard times. By dint of hard work and single good management and the blessing of God, the single quarter grew to several farms and fortune smiled on the family. It was here on the farm that sorrow came to the home with the death of Mother Mary Ann Frey on March 27, 1904. She was the first to break the family circle and be buried in the family lot in the Livingston, now named Union, Cemetery of which Adam Frey and his sons had been the caretakers for a number of years. The Union Cemetery is located ten miles northeast of Abilene. Here you have a family so systematically arranged and so completely rounded out—two girls, three boys, then three girls, and then two boys. There was a twenty-one-year age difference in the children of Adam and Mary Ann Frey, with my great grandmother, Mary Olive Frey, lady being the oldest—born on May 29, 1870—and the youngest, Lawrence, born on May 6, 1891.

In the fall of 1905, Adam Frey had a sale and the old home was broken up. Adam Frey remarried in 1909 to Kate Kugler, also from Adams County, Pennsylvania. After their marriage, they lived in Fairfield, Pennsylvania until her passing in 1917. Adam Frey, for the next ten years, lived with his children in Kansas and then in Upland, California, while living there with his daughter Mabel, passing away on October 12, 1927. Adam was laid to rest next to his beloved Mary Ann in the Union Cemetery, Abilene, Kansas.

# CHAPTER 50

---

## The Annual Frey Reunion

Since the late 1920s, the Frey reunion had been held annually at the at the Abilene City Park now called the Eisenhower Park. In the Years prior, the Frey reunion had been held at Chapman Creek, located about fifteen miles northeast of Abilene. In the 1950s was the height of the popularity and attendance at the Frey reunion. During the '50s, the Frey kin would make the trek to Abilene as far away as South Africa, then Southern Rhodesia, from California and Pennsylvania. The Frey reunion would begin with a delicious family-style dinner. Following the noon meal, there would be a family time of reminiscing, devotions, and several musical numbers. In the afternoon there would be a softball game, usually between the adult men and the younger teenage boys, at the adjacent baseball field, and the Abilene municipal swimming pool was right next to the park. One Frey reunion I'll forever remember: On August 14, 1956, my late nineteen-year-old Uncle Harry Hoover sang and strummed on his guitar the 1956 multimillion-selling single "Young Love," recorded by the Southern gentleman Sonny James. What a beautiful rendition Uncle Harry performed. Regrettably in the last forty years, the Frey reunion has dwindled to just a few members attending. I feel so very blessed that I reached my adolescence in the late 1950s. What a golden era.

Frey Reunion of 1924

The three little girls sitting on the ground from left to right are six-year-old Rozella; the girl in all-white is four-year-old Virgie; the blond-haired girl in partly black dress is three-year-old Faithe, my late mother.

The women in the middle row: in the middle with six ladies on each side of her is my grandmother, Anna Zelma Lady Hoover; Anna is holding baby Eunice; the lady next to Anna to her left holding a baby is my great-aunt Minne, Anna's younger sister; the fourth lady from right with head covering strings is my great-aunt Mildred, the wife of my great-uncle Luther Lady whose home I spent so much time with beginning at age ten. Uncle Luther is two years younger than my grandmother Anna, who burned to death.

The man standing in a row right above the women, the man with the white shirt right behind my grandmother Anna, is my beloved grandfather Irvin Brechbill Hoover, my best friend on God's earth. In the first row of senior people, the lady sixth from the right is my great-grandmother Mary Olive Frey Lady. The man to her left with a beard is my great-grandfather Samuel Lady. Mary Olive and Samuel moved in with Grandpa from 1927 to May 1930 to help my grandpa keep the house after Anna's burning to death. The man standing right behind my aunt Mildred in the back row, third from right, is her husband, my late great-uncle Luther Lady, who took me to Kansas State basketball games. On the first row of adults at far left is my Great

Uncle Chris Frey a younger sibling to my Great Grandmother Mary Olive and beside him his wife Great Aunt Ella. The seventh person from the left in front row is Adam Frey the Frey

Patriarch. At the far right on first row is my Great Uncle Lawrence Frey the youngest of the Frey Siblings and his wife Great Aunt Grace. The 4th person from the right is my Great Aunt Jesse another of the Frey siblings and her husband Great Uncle Sam Ketterman.

Former Pastors and their Wives of the Brethren In Christ Church Abilene, Kansas
Front row left to right-Effie Whisler and husband Rev George Whisler
who began pastoring the Abilene congregation in early 1930's
Back row Esther Snyder and husband Rev Paul Snyder
the pastor from around 1950 to January 1955
Front row far right Faithe Musser and back of her husband Rev David
Musser pastor of the Abilene BIC from January 1955 through 1960

Four-generation photo

My beloved grandfather Irvin Brechbill Hoover. Sitting next to Grandpa is my
great-grandmother Elizabeth Brechbill Hoover, who lived just days from her
hundredth birthday. The woman standing in white is my aunt Virgie, my mother's
older sister. Sitting on my great-grandma's lap is Glenda, the oldest of all thirty-
six of Grandpa's grandchildren from all ten children. Glenda was born in 1941.

Samuel and Mary Olive Frey Lady, my Maternal Great-Grandparents.
The photo is on their wedding day December 29, 1889.

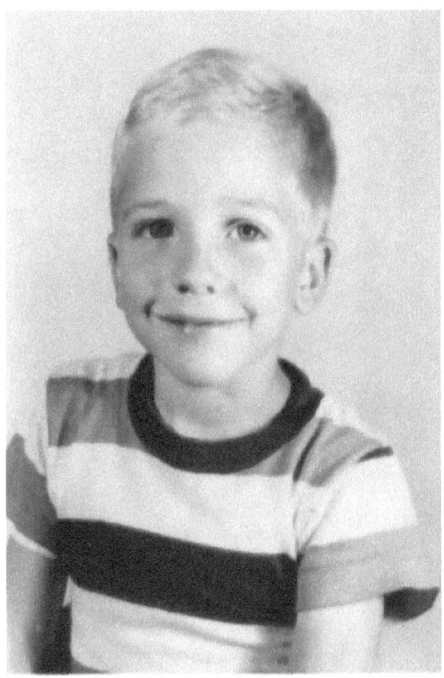

Me Ken Musser age seven

The church that Daddy pastored from 1955–1960 and the boyhood church of the United States 34th President Dwight David Eisenhower at Seventh and Buckeye Street in Abilene, Kansas.

I'm on Daddy's right, and my four-year-old younger brother Charles is on the left. Photo taken in 1957 in front of Eisenhower Museum, which can't be seen.

Summer of 1957. Photo of Grandparents Irvin and Carrie Hoover—the Grandchildren—
front row far left is Marylou Thrush, Janet Eshelman Rozanna Thrush, Connie
Engle, small boy in front Steven Eshelman, fourth boy from left is Vaughn Engle, Ken
Musser "myself" holding bat, Charles Musser boy shirtless Mahlon Thrush The girl
held by Rozanna Thrush unknown and baby held by Grandma Carrie unknown

Photo taken in 1939. Back row: "Eunice" the second youngest of Papa Irvin and Mamma
Anna, and to Grandma Carrie's left to Mary Lou, the youngest of Papa Irvin and Mama
Anna. The boy standing in the back is "Herbert" the oldest of Papa Irvin and Mother
Carrie. To Herbert's front left is Glenn. In the front row are Carol, Harry, and Delores.

# CHAPTER 51

## Street and Smith Magazines Bring Comfort from My Albatross Prison

I would purchase the annual *Street and Smith* year magazines of Major League Baseball and college football and basketball magazines. I remember as though it was yesterday that as a twelve-year-old, I walked into the Banke's drugstore in the three hundred block located on North Broadway. I purchased the 1956 college football magazine. On the cover was a large photo of Jim Swink who led his TCU Horned Frogs to consecutive Southwest Conference championships in 1955–1956. As a result, TCU got to play in the annual New Year Day Cotton Bowl classic in Dallas. Swink's best season was 1955 when against archrival Texas in Austin, Swink rushed fifteen times for 235 yards and scored 26 points in a 47–20 rout of the home team, Texas Longhorns. That fall in 1955, Swink finished second to Howard "Hopalong" Cassidy of the Ohio State Buckeyes in the voting for the Heisman trophy. I would thoroughly read all pages in these magazines while serving my time in my prison basement. Now the anomaly, instead of what would have been an almost-sure star career in the NFL, Swink instead went to medical school. According to the book *June 17, 1967: Battle of Xom Bo II* by David Hearse:

> "The presence of thirty-one-year old Captain James E. Swink, our battalion surgeon was an additional blessing for our wounded men as they were pulled out of the wood line. During battalion size operations, Swink would often

travel with us to the field. He had been assigned to the Black Lions after a five-month stint at the 12th Evacuation Hospital in Cuchi, Vietnam, he was there in the aftermath of the battle helping the medics with the wounded. Fink received a "Purple Heart" and a Bronze Star medal for his outstanding care and doctoring of the wounded in Vietnam."

Swink passed away at his home in Rusk, Texas, due to complications of lymphoma on December 3, 2014. What a true legend and surgeon who sacrificed a sure pro career of stardom in the NFL to be on the battlefield in Vietnam, helping America's wounded soldiers.

The other *Street and Smith's* I purchased annually was the *Major League Baseball* magazine. I purchased the 1956 *Major League Baseball* issue at Bankes drugstore. On the front cover were two of the three Big Apple superstar center fielders in Duke Snider of the Brooklyn Dodgers and the "Comet" from Commerce, Oklahoma, Mickey Mantle. I recall looking through that magazine as I was walking home on North Buckeye Street. The other Big Apple superstar missing on that front cover was the "Say Hey Kid" Willie Mays. I consider Willie Mays the second greatest Major Leaguer ever, the greatest, the Babe. In the first few pages of *Street and Smith's*, there was always baseball records in every category going back to the late 1800s. Listed were major leaguers with the most lifetime hits, home runs, RBIs, stolen bases. Listed were pitching records of players with the most wins, most strikeouts, and shutouts. Yes, the hundreds of hours spent in solitary, my dungeon, my albatross was the beginning of my memorizing literally hundreds of Major League Baseball records, including the all-time winningest pitcher Cy Young with 512 wins, and the "The Big Train" Walter Johnson with 411 wins. Yes, I've had these two records stored in my left temporal lobe for over sixty years. Walter Johnson was one of the few Kansans to play Major League Baseball and he is generally regarded as the greatest pitcher in Major League history.

Let me share about three of the greatest major league baseball players of all time; two centerfielders and a pitcher.

I'll begin with Tris Speaker, "the Grey Eagle" his nickname is due to his prematurely white hair. Tris Speaker is considered one of the greatest offensive and defensive center fielders in baseball history. In my lifetime of baseball research, I consider Tris Speaker the greatest defensive center fielder ever; quite possibly the greatest defensive outfielder period. Tris Speaker has a lifetime batting average of .345 (sixth all-time). When he was still active, there was a saying about the Grey Eagle. "His fielding glove is known as the place where triples go to die." Speaker had 792 doubles. A record that has stood for ninety-two years with Speakers last year of playing MLB in 1928. Defensively, Speaker holds the following records for all outfielders in baseball history; the career record in assists, double plays, and unassisted double plays. Speaker, in fact, turned six unassisted DP's as an outfielder and owns the distinction of making two in one season twice. Speaker played so shallow in the outfield that he was able to execute six career unassisted double plays at second base, catching low line drives on the run, and then beating the runner to second base. Speaker had 3, 514 hits. Ninety-two years after retiring from the majors, he still holds fifth place all-time in total hits. Simply put, Speaker's defensive skills are incomparable. On April 11, 1937, just a week after his 49th birthday, Speaker suffered an accident that nearly killed him. Speaker was working on some flower boxes for his wife, Fran, while standing on a ladder outside their second-story bedroom in the city of Cleveland. With the help of his brother-in-law, Speaker mounted a ladder leaning against a porch railing for support, when the ladder suddenly broke away, and Speaker fell sixteen feet to a walkaway below that was lined with jagged cobblestones. The Cleveland Plain Dealer reported that Speaker glanced off his brother-in-law's shoulder, which broke the fall slightly. However, it didn't prevent Speaker from diving headfirst into the stone walk. The Grey Eagle struck one of the jagged border stones with his face when his left arm, broken by the impact, crumpled under him. Speaker suffered a fractured skull, a aforementioned broken arm, and facial lacerations in the fall. Speaker required one-hundred stitches to close a wound that extended from his eye down to his neck. The Grey Eagle recovered due to his taking care of himself physically during his playing day. The shock over Speaker's accident made many recall his former teammate, Ray Chapman, who had been killed on August 16, 1920 when struck by a pitch ball by Carl Mays of the New York Yankees resulting in a fractured skull. To this day, one-hundred years later, Ray Chapman remains the only major league player to die as a direct result of an open-field injury. At the age of eight, I first read about the Grey Eagle and the Ray Chapman beaning while in my albatross prison and the "Grey Eagle" has long been a favorite player of mine. However, there has been one other on-field death in Major League history. On Major League opening day, April 1, 1996, a second fatality occurred. The first professional baseball team was the Cincinnati Reds Stockings in 1869, baseball's first openly all-professional team with ten salaried players. Due to the city of Cincinnati having the first professional baseball team, the "Reds," for years, always had the opening day Major League game. On that opening day of the year 1996, the home plate empire was John McSherry, a huge man standing six foot two, weighing 328 pounds. After only seven pitches into the game, McSherry motioned to the second base umpire and then immediately collapsed behind home plate dying instantly of a massive heart attack, at the age of fifty-one. Tragically, McSherry was so overweight, and the next day, he was scheduled to see his heart doctor. Cincinnati Reds Manager Ray Knight recalled future Hall-of-Fame Shortstop Barry Larkin who told him quietly and with very much emotion, "Ray, I've had a lot of deaths in my family. In good conscience out of respect for life, I can't go out there." The game was postponed for a day.

My other center fielder, one of my five greatest all-time centerfielders, is Mickey Charles Mantle, named after the great Hall of Fame catcher, Mickey Cochrane, a catcher for both the Detroit Tigers and the Philadelphia Athletics. No major league player ever had more overall physical talent than the "MicK" from Commerce, Oklahoma. Mantle was noted for his ability to hit for both average and power. Mantle hit tape measure home runs, a term that had its origin in a play-by-play announcer on reacting to one of Mantle's 1953 home runs. Mantle spoke warmly of his father and said he was the bravest man he ever knew. "No boy ever loved his father more," he said. Growing up, Mickey batted left-handed against his father who pitched right- handed and Mantle batted right-handed against his grandfather, Charles Mantle, who would pitch left-handed to him. Both Mantle's grandfather and father died young. His grandfather died at the age of sixty in 1944, and his father died of Hodgkin's disease at the age of forty on May 7, 1952. Mantle's father worked in "lead mines" which could have contributed to his young death. Mantle, throughout his adulthood, always feared of dying young. Mantle hands down, is the greatest switch hitter in major league history. No player in major league history has ever been timed faster going from home plate to first base, "Mantle's time is 3.1 seconds. Mantle is the only player to hit 150 home runs from both sides of the plate. Mantle's attempting to steal a base was successful on three out of four attempts. Mantle won the American League Triple Crown in 1956 batting .353, hitting 52 home runs, and 130 runs batted in. Mantle won the (AL) Most Valuable Player three times. When it comes to playoff time, "the cream comes to the top" and so it was with Mantle. Mickey appeared in twelve world Series in which he holds the following World Series records; most home runs (18), RBI's (40), extra-base hits (26), runs (42), walks (43), and 123 total bases. Legendary Hall of Fame manager, Casey Stengel, once stated, "He's got more power from sides than anybody I ever saw, and Casey should know as he managed Mantle."

In the second game of the 1951 World Series, New York Giants rookie Willie Mays hit a fly ball to right-center field. Mantle playing right field, raced for the ball together with center fielder the legendary, Joe DiMaggio, who called for the ball and made the catch. In getting out of DiMaggio's way, Mantle tripped over an exposed drainpipe and severely injured his right knee. Mickey Mantle would play the rest of his "prime" baseball career with a torn ACL which never fully healed. Mantle would play his entire career from 1951-1968 with numerous injuries. In 1960, Mantle hit what was and still is the longest home run in major league history. Mantle's slam went over the right center field roof at Briggs Stadium in Detroit which traveled over 643 feet. As Mantle was winding down his legendary career, more than anything he wanted to end his career with a lifetime batting average of .300 and he fell short with an average of .298. That was Mick's biggest Major League disappointment. Along with his injuries, Mantle lived for the nightlife with best buddies Billy Martin and Whitey Ford staying out until wee hours in the morning drinking. Mickey Mantle had it all, yet he, his wife, Merlyn and their three sons were alcoholic. Mickey was "comet" fast, but his life ran out way too soon due to cancer of the liver, most likely due to his heavy drinking. But glory be to God! Mickey's former teammate Bobby Richardson led Mantle to becoming a believer in Jesus Christ, shared his Christian faith with Mantle and shortly before his death, Mantle made peace with his estranged wife

Merlyn, and at his death on August 13, 1995, Mantle was at peace with his Savior Jesus Christ.

I must share a bit about Bobby Richardson, the Yankees second baseman. Richardson was headed to a sure Hall of Fame career when he abruptly retired at the age of thirty after the 1966 season. In the 1960 World Series against the Pittsburgh Pirates, Richardson set a world series record with 12 RBI's, the first player from a losing team to win the coveted (MVP). Bobby Richardson appeared in five Billy Graham Crusades.

Let me share a bit about who I consider the second greatest pitcher in Major League History, the Man known as "Big Six" and the "Christian Gentleman" and "Matty". Christy Mathewson grew up in Factoryville, Pennsylvania and attended Bucknell University serving as class president while playing on the school's football, basketball, and baseball teams. Mathewson was also a member of Phi Gamma Delta. Mathewson was selected to the Walter Camp all-American football team in 1900 as a "Drop- Kicker"; a kick made by dropping the ball and kicking after it touches the ground. During his seventeen-year major league career, Christy won 373 games and lost 188 for a .665 winning percentage. His career "ERA" of 2.13 and seventy-nine career shutouts are among the best of all-time for a pitcher. Mathewson's 373 career wins are still number one in the National League tied with Grover Cleveland Alexander. Mathewson was highly regarded in the baseball world during his lifetime. His rise to fame brought a better name to the typical ball player who in the early 1900's spent his time gambling, boozing, or womanizing. Mathewson was a devout Christian and never pitched on Sunday. It was a promise he made to his mother that brought him popularity among the more religious New York Giant fans. Mathewson pitched for the New York Giants (1900-1916) and as manager of the Cincinnati Reds (1916-1918). Mathewson enlisted in the US Army during WWI. His wife Jane was very much opposed to the decision but Mathewson insisted on enlisting. He served overseas as a Captain in the newly formed Chemical Service along with the immortal Ty Cobb. When Christy arrived in France, he was accidentally gassed during a chemical training exercise, and subsequently developed tuberculosis which more easily infects lungs that have been damaged by chemical gas. On returning to the States, Mathewson and family moved to the frigid climate of Saranac Lake, New York in the Adirondack Mountains to seek treatment from Edward Livingston Trudeau at his renowned Adirondack Cottage Sanitorium. Mathewson died in 1925 at the early age of forty-five. In 1936, Mathewson was elected into the Baseball Hall of Fame as one of its first five inductees, along with Babe Ruth, Ty Cobb, Walter Johnson, and Honus Wagner. Christy was the only one of the five to be inducted posthumously. In 1999 he ranked number seven on the "Sporting News" list of the one-hundred Greatest Baseball Players the highest-ranking National League pitcher. His plaque at the Baseball Hall of Fame reads, "Greatest of all the great pitchers in the 20$^{th}$ century's first quarter and ends with the statement "Matty was master of them all." On his dying bed Mathews last words to his wife, Jane, "Now, Jane, I want you to go outside and have yourself a good cry. Don't make it a long one, this can't be helped."

# CHAPTER 52

## A Devastating Loss and the Prodigal's Return

The date March 23, 1957, will forever be kept in my left temporal lobe. The setting was the Kansas City Municipal Auditorium in Kansas City, Missouri. At last, Daddy and Mother had gotten a television. It's the final game of the NCAA basketball championship between the North Carolina Tarheels and the Kansas Jayhawks. The multitalented center Wilt Chamberlain from legendary Overbrook High in Philadelphia was a sophomore phenom, playing in his first NCAA championship game. In that era of the 1950s, freshmen couldn't play varsity. The Tarheels were coached by legendary Frank McGuire and KU was coached by Dick Harp who had played under the great tutelage of the master coach, Phog Allen. Harp played on the 1940 KU team coached by Allen which lost in the NCAA championship to Indiana. Wilt's relationship with Coach Harp was one of resentment and disappointment. Chamberlain's biographer, Robert Cherry, has speculated that Wilt would not have chosen Kansas if he had known that Phog Allen was going to retire in 1956. The Tarheels in the one-semi had to go triple overtime to beat Michigan State and their All-American power forward, "Leaping Johnny Green." Green's career Big Ten rebounding average at Michigan State was 16.4 per game, topped by only the Hall of Famer "Incomparable" Jerry Lucas, a devout Christian, whose rebound career Big Ten average was 17.2 rebounds a game. North Carolina was led by their consensus All-American Lennie Rosenbluth who averaged 28 points a game in 1956. The Tarheels came into that 1957 championship game with a 31–0 record yet KU was a slight favorite.

To a boy of twelve who at the time was starving for just a little love and affection, this game was so therapeutic for me as I could let my emotions go. I had to have a refuge and basketball was always there for me, beginning at the age of eight, the start of the double whammy. The halftime score was North Carolina, 29–KU, 22. At the end of regulation time, the score was 46–46. Both teams scored two points in the first OT. In the second OT there was no score. It must be remembered that in that era, there was no shot clock, the reason for such low scores. In the third OT the Tarheels scored six points to the Jayhawks' five. UNC would win 54–53. Wilt Chamberlain took this loss so hard. He was *devastated*. Wilt later would say that this was the most painful loss of his career, both college and pro. Wilt blamed himself for that loss and for the next forty years from 1957–1997, Wilt wouldn't return to Allen Fieldhouse. However, on January 17, 1998, at KU's request, Wilt returned to Allen Fieldhouse and had his jersey number 13, retired up in the rafters at Allen. The prodigal son had returned and, like the father in the Bible, this prodigal son too was accepted back with an overabundance of love. It's a bit ironic as on October 12, 1999, at the still young age of sixty- three, Wilt passed away from congestive heart failure. I'm not sure of the soul of Wilt when he passed into eternity but I feel that God, our Creator, had a say in this prodigal son Wilt's homecoming. I personally took this three- overtime loss so hard. On this March evening in 1957, the seed had been planted in my lifetime love of basketball. The world of sports was truly my safe haven, my Utopia away from the hundreds of hours I would be abandoned and forsaken.

# CHAPTER 53

## *Tragedy Continues in the Lady Family*

There would be so many tragic accidents on both the Hoover and Lady families throughout the years, starting with Great-Grandpa and Great-Grandma Lady losing their beloved daughter Anna Zelma on that fateful New Year's Day of 1927. Let me forward to almost thirty years later in December of 1956 on a Friday evening. My Great-Uncle Luther Lady's son Gerald, a first cousin to my mother, took me to see a high school basketball game at Emporia, Kansas. His son Larry a junior, was already a high school basketball star in the state of Kansas. Abilene High was in the CKL, the Central Kansas League. Emporia was a seventy-mile drive. Yes, this is the same Larry Lady who coached against Daddy in March of 1954 at Abilene City Hall. I recall that evening that Abilene lost a very close game to Emporia. Also making that drive was his daughter Sharon Lady who gave me her green bicycle after our move to Abilene in early 1955. It would be only two months later that tragedy was to again hit the Lady family. Gerald Lady drove a tractor trailer for a local feed company. While driving that February 7, 1957, Gerald was in a fiery crash where he burned to death. My Great- Uncle Luther and Aunt Mildred Lady had already lost a sister and sister-in- law—Anna Zelma on the 1927 New Year's Day—and now to lose their oldest child Gerald, at the young age of thirty-eight must have been so hard on my Great-Uncle Luther's, not only losing a sister to a fiery death and then a son. Their faith in their dear Lord and Savior, Jesus Christ, sustained them through these two terrible losses.

# CHAPTER 54

## Time with Mother and Epic Football Game

At least several Saturdays a month, Mother would drive to Salina, a city of forty-five thousand, located on old Highway 40 West, twenty miles from Abilene. If Daddy wasn't working at JC Penny, he would accompany us. Mother had two favorite department stores: Stieffels and Stevensons, both located on North Santa Fe Avenue, the main north south street in Salina. Almost all the employees at both Stieffels and Stevensons knew Mother. I must give Mother credit where it's due. She had one great personality just like her Papa Irvin. Mother would get almost all her clothes from these two department stores. Also located on North Santa Fe was the local radio station for North Central Kansas, KSAL. One Saturday we visited KSAL, getting to see the disc jockey working the records.

One of these Saturday drives to Salina would become so memorable for me. We were walking past this one television store, and through the window I could see a football game being played. Daddy and Mother continued shopping. One positive I must relate about Mother, she understood my love of sports and my need of it in my life. The game was in the second half and I would watch what would be an historic upset. It was Saturday November 16, 1957. The setting of the game, Owen Field in Norman, Oklahoma, with the Oklahoma Sooners hosting the Notre Dame "Fighting Irish." OU was coached by the late legendary Hall of Famer Charles "Bud" Wilkinson and the Sooners entered that game with a forty-seven-game winning streak. The Fighting Irish was coached by little-known thirty-one-year-old

Terry Brennan. My family continued shopping but I was to witness what would become an iconic upset. That November 16, 1957, saw that forty-seven-game winning streak come a sudden end with the final score Notre Dame 7 OU 0. The Sooners were loaded with super talent including consensus All- Americans, guard Bill Krisher and running back Glendon Thomas. Glendon Thomas would, later in life, serve on the Fellowship of Christian Athletes national board of directors. Thomas summed this game up with the following statement, "I've shaken the hand of every man, woman, and child, who saw Notre Dame end OU's 47-game winning streak. All 63,170 of them saw it come to a sudden end, all wanting to tell me that they were there when the music died." And Thomas continued, "I've probably talked to more than were actually there. Our stadium held so many." I recall as a twelve-year-old, seeing fans crying, looking in a state of total shock. Coach Bud Wilkinson said in the locker room, after the game's conclusion, "There wasn't anything mysterious about it we just got beat." Just another instance of how the world of sports became a refuge, if only for two hours, even if I had to travel twenty miles to find peace and contentment.

# CHAPTER 55

## *Women's Christian Temperance Union*

Back in the early 1950s, a new phenomenon was taking place during daytime television. It was the dawn of the daily soap opera. Mother had a favorite soap, *As the World Turns*, which debuted on April 2, 1956. It ran daily Monday to Friday, noon to 1:00 p.m. CST. I was in sixth grade and I attended the old Abilene High School located right across from our church. The school was located only a block from the parsonage so I could walk home for lunch and would watch the soap with Mother. *As the World Turns* centered around your average American family, the Hughes. Yes, there were those rare occasions that Mother and I could coexist.

With all the years of emotional and physical abuse I suffered at the hands of my mother, I must give her a few kudos. Mother had the talent of memorization, a gene that I inherited from her. During the late 1940s through the late 1950s, Mother was a member of the WCTU, Woman's Christian Temperance Union, a movement that supported the Eighteenth Amendment and its constitution called for the entire prohibition of the manufacture and sale of intoxicating liquor.

Leading up to Mother's talent, Carrie Nation was an American woman who before the time of prohibition, opposed alcohol. She's particularly noteworthy for attacking alcohol establishments with a hatchet. Carrie Nation described herself as a bulldog running along at the feet of Jesus, barking at what the Christ life doesn't like, and she claimed a divine ordination to promote temperance by destroying bars. The Eighteenth Amendment went into effect on January 16, 1920. The Twenty-First Amendment repealed the Eighteenth on December 5, 1933. In over 230 years of the US constitution, the Eighteenth is the only amendment ever repealed.

At the age of forty, Carrie Nation became desperate in her antirum campaign. She became famous for her Bible in one hand and her (hatchet) in the other. Carrie invaded saloons, released the spirits from the bottles, and wreaked general destruction on the nefarious wicked traffic. "Ninety days," the judge said, "for disturbing the peace and destroying private property, you are a mad woman."

"Of course," she said, "I am and for the following reasons, first because I am a woman, second because I am sober, third because I believe it's possible to change the world."

"But, madam, liquor is legal in Chicago," headlined one newspaper. "Poison is never legal," Carrie responded. Strangely enough, the men who had put her into jail helped to have her released. When they saw Carrie going from cell to cell talking to men about their wives and children, they said she should be made queen of the world. She sounded so convincing— so deep was Carrie Nation in her cause, she carried it across the USA, singing the post-Civil War hit song, "When Johnnie Comes Marching Home Again Hurrah Hurrah." To a marked degree, Carrie Nation did change the world. Carrie Nation was born November 25, 1846, and passed away June 9, 1911.

From time to time, the WCTU would have a family night when member families and close friends could attend, and quite often, a member of the WCTU would share her talent. One of these meetings was held at David and Alice Minter's, cousins of mother. This night would belong to Mother. Mother had memorized the entire book of Ruth in the Old Testament. Mother could put so much expression into her delivery. Her speech was just outstanding. I do want to give Mother credit where it's due, but sadly of being a loving mother no.

# CHAPTER 56

## The Left Temporal Lobe and Memorization

$M$y life has had so many downtimes with severe depression, acute anxiety, a low self-esteem, and an inferiority complex. It took my study and writing of my memoir after sixty years, to come to the realization that my lifetime of emotional illness had its seed planted on that fateful New Year's Day, 1927. It's rather ironic that having suffered so much emotional and physical abuse at the hands of my late mother, I've come to inherit a gene of Mother's, that of memorization. Due to my growing up near my Grandpa Hoover and spending so much time on his farm, I've come to memorize so much of Mother's genealogy and birthdates and deaths, namely on her Mama Anna's family. The seed of my exceptional memory was sown on that horrific New Year's Day with the burning to death of my maternal grandmother. However, my exceptional memory took root and developed from my reading of sports magazines, history books, reading the World Almanac from cover to cover, those three years from eight to almost eleven years old when I was locked up for hundreds of hours in that outside cold basement.

I would memorize literally hundreds of birth and death dates of historical figures, sport icons, and celebrities.

Yes, my life has been one of anguish and torment; however, I must say something positive about myself. Let me make mention of the hippocampus part of the brain. It's just so weird that the hippocampus includes the left temporal lobe which lies right under the temple. The left temporal lobe is the part of the brain in which lies the root of emotions, in my case, severe depression and acute anxiety as well as memorization. You could say that my life has been complex, a negative in severe depression and a positive in exceptional memory. As previously stated, studies made with children who suffered PTSD are likely to experience a decrease in the size of the hippocampus. Yes, my mother the innocent five-year-old who was the oldest witness to see her mother on fire, would have one traumatic experience after another from the ages of five to eight. My situation is somewhat unique due to the shrinking of the hippocampus. I've lived with a lifetime of severe depression and acute anxiety; however, from my left temporal lobe, I've been blessed with an exceptional memory. With my sharing my life of severe depression and acute anxiety and with some personal stories I'll be sharing, which I'm certainly not proud of, I feel I owe it to myself to do a little bragging on how the left temporal lobe has given me one exceptional memory and the following will attest to that.

The following dates and facts, both historical and in sports, I've had frozen in my left temporal lobe for well over fifty years. My left temporal lobe tells me that in AD 1066 was the Battle of Hastings, where the Duke of Normandy of France defeated the English at East Sussex in England which began the Norman Conquest of England. For over sixty-five years, my left temporal lobe tells me that both Presidents John Adams and Thomas Jefferson died on the same day, July 4, 1826, fiftieth anniversary of the Declaration of Independence. On John Adams' deathbed, his last words were, "Thomas Jefferson still survives." He was mistaken as Jefferson had died some five hours earlier at the age of eighty-two. Adams lived to a hearty ninety which in the nineteenth century, was unheard of. In fact, John Adams would remain the longest living president for 138 years until Herbert Hoover passed away in 1964, also at age ninety. One of my favorite historical world characters is Queen Victoria for whom the Victorian age is named after. Queen Victoria's reign went from June 20, 1837, until her death on January 22, 1901. During her reign was the demise of rural life as cities rapidly grew and expanded, it brought long and regimented factory hours and the time of Jack the Ripper.

Another one of my favorite characters in world history is Catherine the Great, the Empress of Russia, living from 1729–1796, who reigned from 1762–1796, the country's longest female ruler in history until her death in 1796. Under her rule, Russia was revitalized into one of the great powers of Europe. Catherine the Great's birth and death dates have been in my left temporal lobe for the past fifty years. Yes, my favorite pop singer Karen Carpenter, who died way too young at the age of thirty-three from anorexia in 1983 and how she had a voice like no other. Ben Franklin, 1706–1790; Abraham Lincoln, 1809–1865; FDR 1882–1945; Norma Jean Baker, better known as Marilyn Monroe, 1926–1962.

My all-time favorite actor, Michael Landon, 1935–1991. A bit of trivia about Landon: as a high schooler, he started to let his hair grow long like Samson for strength, and in 1954 Landon threw the javelin 193 feet, 4 inches, the longest throw by a high schooler in 1954; and of course, the rest is history with *Bonanza* and *Little House on the Prairie.* The "Iron Horse" Lou Gehrig, 1903–1941, whose dates I've had frozen in my brain since 1955 when I turned eleven. Both comedians George Burns and Bob Hope lived to exactly one hundred. Burns from 1896–1996 and Hope 1903–2003. The chairman of the board Frank Sinatra, 1915–1988.

A rather interesting character who I've studied about many years of history is General George Custer. Custer met his waterloo on June 25, 1876, at the Battle of the Little Big Horn, also known as Custer's Last Stand. Custer was killed as were two of his brothers, a nephew, and brother-in-law. Custer and his Seventh Cavalry Regiment lost 265 soldiers. The victors were the Lakota, Northern Cheyenne, and Arapaho tribes. General Custer and my son, David, share the following: David was born on June 25, the date of Custer's death, and David was born exactly one hundred years to the day that Custer died, 1976. Custer's wife's name was Elizabeth who never left Custer's side. Despite Custer's Civil War and his post-Civil War in the Dakotas, Elizabeth was always just a hug a way from George. Elizabeth was a woman who, no matter what the danger, almost always traveled with her husband. Elizabeth Custer outlived her husband by fifty-seven years and she lived to just four days short of her ninety-first birthday. Her dates, April 8, 1842–April 4, 1933.

Let me conclude now with James Butler "Wild Bill" Hickok, born in 1837, was a notorious gunfighter and marshal of my native hometown— Abilene, Kansas—the wickedest cowtown in the 1860's-1880's. Wild Bill was shot in the back while playing cards in a saloon in Deadwood, South Dakota, by Jack McCall, known as "Crooked Noose" McCall. The hand of cards which Wild Bill held at the time of his death has come to be known as the dead man's hand: two pairs, aces and eights. Jack McCall was hung. Wild Bill Hickok was killed on August 2, 1876, my birthday is August 2. The lives of two historic women are intertwined, Elizabeth Blackwell and Florence Nightingale. Blackwell, a British physician, was the first woman to receive a medical degree in the US. Florence Nightingale, also from England, was a social reformer, and the founder of modern nursing. During the "Crimean War," a military conflict fought from 1853 to February 1856, Nightingale became an icon of "Victorian Culture," who came to be known as "The Lady with the Lamp," making rounds of wounded soldiers at night. The Crimean War saw Russia losing to an alliance made up of the Ottoman Empire, the United Kingdom, and France. The Allied alliance were victorious with the "Treaty of Paris." What these two ladies shared was birth year and death. Elizabeth Blackwell was born on February 3, 1821, and death was May 31, 1910. Florence Nightingale's birth date was May 12, 1820, and death August 13, 1910. I'm pleased to say that I've also had the privilege to watch a movie on both heroic women and how ironic the coinciding of both birth and death dates that have been stored in my left temporal love for years.

I must not forget about the lady who I've always admired—Helen Keller. It was down in my albatross prison that I first came across the name Helen Keller in a family magazine. Helen was born in Tuscumbia, Alabama, on June 27, 1880, and died on June 1, 1968. I was nine years old when first learning of my most admired woman. At the age of nineteen months, baby Helen became very ill with the result of Helen losing her sight and hearing. Into young Helen's life would be a teacher Anne Sullivan who at the age of five contracted trachoma, an eye disease, which left Anne partially blind and without reading or writing skills became known as the miracle worker. As a last chance before Helen is institutionalized, Anne Sullivan became the "miracle worker." Helen Keller became the first deaf blind person to earn a bachelor of arts degree from Radcliffe College and Harvard University graduating "cum laude" with honors and graduating "Phi Beta Kappa." Helen Keller became an educator, an advocate for the blind and deaf, and co- founder of the ACLU. In Ken Musser's book, Helen Keller was the greatest woman humanitarian of the twentieth century culminating with President Lyndon B. Johnson awarding Keller with the esteemed medal, the Presidential Medal of Freedom.

# CHAPTER 57

## My Dearest Grandma Carrie's Life and Death

I'm so extremely fortunate and so grateful that out of all thirty-six of Grandpa Hoover's grandchildren, including both of Grandpa Hoover's wives, I was that lucky one who was able to spend so many priceless summers at Grandpa and Grandma Hoover's. Yes, I've said it before and I'll say it again, Grandpa Hoover was the best friend I've ever had on God's earth. Four of Grandpa's first five daughters had moved out of state when married. The two oldest daughters, Rozella and Virgie, moved to Pennsylvania; Eunice, the second youngest, moving to California; and the youngest, Mary Lou, married a doctor and lived in Puerto Rico and Missouri. The only daughter of the first five to remain in Kansas was my mother. It's important to remember that of the second five children, only three grandchildren had been born at the time of my grandfather's passing on Tuesday, June 13, 1961. As I referred to earlier, a couple of summers in the early 1950s, Daddy and Mother drove to Dallas Center, Iowa, to hold a monthly Bible school for my Great-Uncle Samuel Lady, a younger brother of my grandmother Anna who had burned to death.

In the fall of 1958, my freshman year in high school, my beloved Step-Grandmother Carrie, who was like a blood Grandma to me, became ill. Grandpa and Grandma had been on a western US trip, traveling by car, with my Uncle Herbert and his wife, Aunt Gladys. One day while driving, Grandma remarked to the three that she had felt something "pop" inside her. Shortly after arriving home, Grandma became very sick and she was driven by ambulance, the 170 miles to the Kansas University Medical Center located at Thirty-Ninth and Rainbow, Kansas City, Kansas. Little did I know at the time that seven years later, I would be working there. My Uncle, Dr. Dale Eshelman, had many professional MD friends and Grandma was able to get the very best treatment. While at the KU Medical Center, Grandma Carrie's body was found to be full of cancer. The diagnosis was a large tumor inside her stomach had burst. My beloved Grandma Carrie passed away on December 15, 1958, at the still young age of sixty-two, dying five days before her sixty-third birthday and Grandma I thought looking much older than her sixty-three years. What a loving wife and wonderful helpmate Grandma had been to Grandpa. Around 11:00 a.m., that Monday, my uncle Darrel Kelly, the husband of my aunt Delores, came to Abilene High to pick me up. Grandma Carrie was such a loving wife, mother, stepmother, and grandmother.

Those many summers while living at Grandpa Hoover's, I was able to see what a tireless worker Grandma was. When I think of my precious beloved Grandma Carrie, I remember her not as a Step-Grandma but as a blood Grandmother. The good Lord had bestowed upon Stepmother Carrie such a selfless heart in the giving of her unsurpassable, unconditional, enduring love to those five young daughters, ages twelve to three years, eight months old. I witnessed my Grandma Carrie, both morning and evening after the milking of the dairy cows, of her cleaning the milking separator and all of its parts. Believe me, this wasn't an easy job by any means. How many times would I see Grandma chasing a chicken down, catching its legs so she could cut off the head. I'll forever cherish our Christmas dinners, sitting around Grandma's dining room table, eating her delicious fried chicken, mashed potatoes and gravy, and to top it off, her delicious apple and cherry pies.

One thing I'll never forget is when Grandma had her head over the kitchen sink, washing her hair with egg white. Yes, I witnessed Grandma washing her hair with egg white numerous times. I can't overemphasize the overwhelming unconditional love that Grandma gave to a young Grandson whose heart was empty and starving for just a little love. Yes, Grandma Carrie's unsurpassable love will forever live in those words, "A tent or a cottage, why should I care?" As I stood before Grandma's casket, I could see the lines on her face. I touched her hands which were rough from her many years of working so hard on the farm and being that perfect Stepmother and mother in her tireless effort in bringing together two families. I remember the lovely blue dress as I gently kissed her forehead, knowing that her Lord and Savior had called her home for an everlasting reward and rest.

The Reverend Savannah Landis from Grandma's home church in Dallas Center, Iowa, officiated at her funeral. I'll forever remember the soloist's beautiful rendition of Grandma's favorite hymn, "Beyond the Sunset." Ironically thirty-nine years later on December 4, 1997, my beloved Uncle Harry had that hymn sung at his funeral as Uncle Harry was laid to rest on his father, Irvin's, birthday. Grandma Carrie was laid to rest in the Livingston Cemetery, now Union, in the same burial plot as Anna where, in less than three years, Grandpa would be put to rest between both wives, waiting for the Second Coming of Christ. That evening, Grandpa's entire family met at his house and I still vividly remember Uncle Dale Eshelman sitting at Grandpa's dining room table, chatting with Reverend Landis, soul-searching for Jesus.

# CHAPTER 58

## A Game That Made the NFL America's Game

In the fall of 1958, I got a job as a newspaper carrier for the hometown, *Abilene Reflector-Chronicle*. I rode my bicycle with a big newspaper bag on the front of my bike. I just happened to be lucky enough that I had the most rundown part of Abilene known as Little Egypt, on Cottage Street on the southeast side of Abilene. It was at about this time that two PKs (preacher's kids), my neighbor Larry, and I, on an autumn evening, decided to do a little experimenting. We went to the back of Larry's garage and leaves were plentiful on the ground. We had some paper and, picking up leaves, we rolled the paper up like cigarettes and begun to puff. Well, as a result, it was a one and done for both of us.

Two pro football games are universally known to be the two greatest ever played and I was right next to the radio for both. The first was the 1958 NFL championship game played on December 28, 1958, at Yankee Stadium. Only eight days earlier, my beloved Grandma Carrie Hoover had been laid to rest on her own birthday, December 20. The 1958 championship game would be the first NFL playoff game to go to sudden death. It was played between the New York Giants and the Baltimore Colts. At the time I was a freshman in high school. I can recall that game as if was yesterday. I was sitting on the kitchen floor with my transistor radio on. Back then having a transistor was almost like having a cell phone today, well, not quite! It would be a three- hour reprieve from my albatross. This game would be the catalyst in marking the beginning of the NFL's popularity surge and eventual rise to the very top of the US sports market. Raymond Berry, a future Hall of Fame receiver, would have the game of his life with twelve receptions for 178 yards and a touchdown. Berry's twelve receptions set a championship record that stood for fifty-five years. With a little over two minutes left in the game, Johnny Unitas engineered one of the most famous drives in football history, a two- minute drill or drive before anyone called it that. As the drive continued, Unitas threw consecutive passes to Berry, moving the ball 62 yards to the Giants' 13-yard line. This set up a 20-yard tying field goal by Steve Myhra with only seven seconds left in the game.

This would set up a sudden death—the first team to score would win the game. The Giants won the coin toss and chose to receive. On the kickoff, future Hall of Famer Don Maynard received the football in which he fumbled but recovered his own fumble. However, the Giants went three and out. On the ensuing drive, the Colts took over on their own twenty-yard line with the future Hall of Famer Unitas at quarterback, working his magic on a thirteen- play drive and the Colts couldn't be stopped. After several key rushes by Alan the "Horse" Ameche and reception by Berry, Ameche scored on a third and goal from the one-yard line to win a game for the ages. Just as Secretary of War Stanton quoted when Abraham Lincoln died, "Now he belongs to the ages."

This game for the ages and the future Hall of Famers in that epic game, for the losing New York Giants: OL Rosey Brown, HB Frank Gifford, LB Sam Huff, DE Andy Robustelli, and DB Emin Tunnell, offensive coordinator Vince Lombardi, and defensive coordinator Tom Landry. The Hall of Famers for the winning Baltimore Colts: WR Raymond Berry, DL Gino Marchetti, RB Lenny Moore, OL Jim Parker who, in my book, is arguably the greatest offensive lineman ever, QB Johnny Unitas, and head coach Weeb Eubank.

This game's legacy, the New York Giants head coach was Jim Lee Howell and he was aided by two coordinators who both would go onto greatness as NFL head coaches, DC Tom Landry and offensive coordinator Vince Lombardi. Landry would become the head coach of the expansion Dallas Cowboys in 1960 and Landry would coach the Cowboys to three Super Bowl wins in his three decades with Dallas. Lombardi would become head coach of the Green Bay Packers. All that Lombardi did was to lead Green Bay to five NFC championships and winning the first two Super Bowl championships and now has the Super Bowl trophy named after him. I consider Vince Lombardi the greatest coach in NFL history with Bill Belichick right behind Lombardi.

Just a note about the Hall of Fame wide receiver Raymond Berry: he is a member of the seventy-fifth anniversary all-time team and in 1999 was ranked fortieth on the Sporting News list of the one hundred greatest football players. However, more important, Barry has been a born-again Christian since 1960 and he considers his faith in Christ as being "a huge part in his life." Raymond Berry will be the first to tell you that he has not followed the Lord perfectly, he has made mistakes. But he is a sinner saved by grace. Berry continues, and as long as God leaves him on this earth, he intends to keep "looking unto Jesus, the author and finisher of our faith" (Hebrews 12:2).

# CHAPTER 59

## Legendary Coach Fred "Tex" Winter

The date is March 13, 1958, and the setting is Allen Field House at Lawrence, Kansas, the home court of the Kansas Jayhawks. It's the semi-finals of the Mid-West regional. At that time there was no March madness like today, but for a thirteen-year-old boy, getting to watch his favorite sports team was maddening. My Kansas State Wildcats were playing the Cincinnati Bearcats with the best player in the nation—the big O, Oscar Robertson. During that 1957–58 season K-State was ranked the number one team in the country for most of the season. The Wildcats were led by Junior consensus All-American 6'8" Bob Boozer and 6'9" Jack Parr, a senior All-American. Oh, what anticipation for a thirteen-year-old getting to see for the first time on television his K-State Wildcats. I was on the edge of the sofa for the second half. The score went back and forth the entire game. This historic game would go into double OT. The Big O had his usual 30 points while the Wildcats had a monster game from Boozer with 24 points and 14 rebounds, and Jack Parr had 17 points and 12 rebounds. The game came down to the final two seconds when Robertson was fouled going to the basket. Robertson calmly swished the first free throw and then for some unknown reason, turned his back to the basket for a second then turned back to the free throw line, and with my eyes shut and hands over my ears, Robertson missed and it was into OT tied at 71–71. Early second OT, Robertson fouled out and the Wildcats held on for a 83–80 win. In the second semi, Oklahoma State defeated Arkansas. The next evening, the big O took out his frustration on the Arkansas Razorbacks by scoring 56 points. My Wildcats were headed to the final four with Seattle, Kentucky, and Temple at Freedom Hall in Louisville, Kentucky.

In the first game K-state played the University of Seattle with their star All-American Elgin Baylor. K-States, star center Jack Parr only scored four points and the final score Seattle 73-K-State 51. And if that wasn't bad enough in the consolation game, my Wildcats were beaten by Temple and its All-American guard Guy Rodgers. There have been numerous stories that K- State's big man Jack Parr was ill throughout the entire NCAA Journey which might have contributed to the Wildcats' poor performance at Louisville's Freedom Hall.

The winning Kentucky Wildcats were led by two all-Americans, forward Johnny Cox and guard Adrian Smith. A thirteen-year-old took these K-State losses so hard. Listening to my K-State Wildcat basketball games from 1956- 1962 was such a refuge from my continual emotional and physical abuse.

Six years later in March of 1964 with legendary Coach Tex Winter still at the helm, K-State once again made the final four. The championship was held at Municipal Auditorium in Kansas City, Missouri. In the semifinals, UCLA defeated K-State 90–82 and Duke defeated Michigan. In the NCAA championship game, UCLA defeated Duke 98–83. K-State was led by their All-American small forward Willie Murrell. This would be the first of UCLA's eleven championships during their run under head coach, the "Wizard of Westwood," Johnny Wooden. Wooden lived just four months and ten days short of his one-hundredth-birthday. And yes, for well over fifty-five years, I'd known that Wooden was born in 1910, passing away in 2010.

Just recently on October 10, 2018, Coach Fred Winter passed away at the age of ninety-six. Winter, when a student at USC, was an All-American pole vaulter in track. At the age of twenty-nine, Winter was the youngest head coach of a major NCAA program at Marquette in Milwaukee. Winter created the triangle offense, also known as the triple post offense. The triangle offense is a continuity basketball offense that combines spacing with a series of actions based on player decisions resulting in a beautiful basketball offensive system.

The following are several quotes from Chicago Bulls stars on their six NBA championships while playing under assistant head coach Winter's innovative triangle offense.

Michael Jordan commenting on Tex, "He was a pioneer and a true student of the game. His triangle offense was a huge part of our six championships with the Bulls."

The following is a quote from Steve Kerr who played on those champion Bull teams. In a statement on October 10, 2018, the day of Coach Winter's passing, Kerr remarked, "I credit Tex for changing my whole life-about the history of the game and the fundamentals of the game than anybody he had ever met in his life."

Kobe Bryant, who played for Tex with the LA Lakers, quoted, "My mentor. I sat with Tex and watched every minute of every game during our first season together. He taught me how to study every detail, he was a basketball genius in every sense of the word. I'll miss him deeply. Thank you, Tex, I wouldn't be where I am today without you. Rest in peace."

Coach Winter was inducted into the Naismith Memorial Basketball Hall of Fame in 2011 which was long overdue. Yes, I'm a sports junkie; and growing up, my transistor was like a smartphone for me, a refuge and safety net from my albatross.

# CHAPTER 60

## Bonding with Daddy

Daddy and I had one special bonding and that was the world of sports. I must share a humorous sidenote about Daddy and I and our love of K-State basketball in the mid-1950s to mid-'60s. With all the talent Daddy had, which shown in his various vocations, it wasn't often that Daddy was home in the evenings to be able to listen to K-State basketball. However, I recall in the winter of 1958, Daddy and I were listening to a K-State game with the K-State legendary announcer Dev Nelson. This one evening the opposing team was getting the best of my Wildcats. I turned the volume down as when by myself, that usually brought me luck.

Well this evening Daddy was with me and did my turning the volume down annoy Daddy. I don't remember of doing that again when Daddy was with me. I'm such an emotional person and I'll share an even greater show of emotion a bit later in my memoir. I can't emphasize enough the importance of the world of sports during my childhood, up through adolescence up to the present day. Unless you've been emotionally traumatized as a boy of eight as I was, you couldn't imagine what a refuge the world of sports and the radio could become. Those years when I was locked up for hours at a time in that cold outdoor cellar, I had no one to talk to. As time went by, this lonely abandoned boy grew up, and he had to find a way to release his emotions, and the world of sports came to be that source of emotional release that this deprived starved for love and affection boy needed, and sports became his source of emotional release into adulthood, even now into his seventies.

Let me for a minute fast-forward some fifty-six years later to the present day in 2020. Yes, I've switched my state of Kansas basketball allegiance from the Kansas State Wildcats to now my beloved Kansas University Jayhawks. I now bleed the crimson and blue. Just recently, in the 2017–2018 season, on February 24, 2018, my Jayhawks won their fourteenth straight Big 12 title under head coach Bill Self, surpassing UCLA's record of thirteen straight league championships. In this era when you have so many five-star players leaving college after only one year and going for the pros, it's amazing what Coach Self has done with a new roll of players year after year. KU is the second all-time winningest NCAA basketball program, right behind the Kentucky Wildcats. Yes, Kentucky is the state where I was born, but there's no love lost between my birth state and me.

However, I'm now in 2020, a die-hard Kansas State football fan. For over half a century K-State football was the losingest NCAA college football program. In 1988 fifty-one-year-old Bill Snyder took over a football program that was "six feet under." Coach Snyder resurrected a program that from 1935–1987 had won only 137 games. From the ages of 12 through 17 on Saturday afternoons, I would be lying on my bed, listening to K-State losing every Saturday from 1955 to 1959 under head coaches Bud Mertes and Doug Weaver. And then comes the football hire of the twentieth century in Bill Snyder. Coach Snyder served as K-State football coach from 1989–2005 and from 2009–2018. Coach Snyder's record over his two tenures is 215, wins- 117 losses-1 tie in his 27 years as head coach. K-State had become the first program in Division 1 to lose 500 games, a winning percentage of .370. Yes, K-State is now a legit college football power and I'm getting one big treat in this wacky fall of 2020 with the coronavirus. Fox Sports and Fox Sports 1 is televising every K-State football game. The most improbable stat is that Coach Bill Snyder was K-State head coach for victories 300, 400, and, yes, 500. Just incredible. Former college Hall-of-Fame Coach Berry Switzer, when asked about Coach Snyder's success, replied with "Bill Snyder isn't the coach of the year. He's the coach of the century!"

# CHAPTER 61

## My Daddy, A Born Trailblazer

My Daddy was a natural-born leader and trailblazer. He wasn't afraid to buck the trend and to go against the establishment. For many generations going back to the 1870s, BIC ministers wore the clerical, the white collar around the neck. In the decade of the 1950s, the BIC Church would gradually be moving to a more liberal dress code. Up until the 1950s, the BIC ministers were still wearing the clerical and most all ladies wore the prayer covering. Well, things were about to change and the leader of an extremely bold movement would be my Daddy. Around the year 1958, the boldness and trailblazing of my Daddy came to light, becoming the first BIC minister to go from wearing the clerical to the tie. Yes, "a bold move it was going from the clerical to the necktie," but then Daddy was a natural-born leader. The most conservative region of the BIC, the Eastern US, including Pennsylvania, New York, Ohio, and Virginia, as well as the Canadian Province of Ontario, took a while longer to make the transition.

A mentor of Daddy's was Alvin Burkholder, the bishop of the BIC Pacific and Central conferences. I remember to this day of Bishop Burkholder saying the following in the mid-1950s about Daddy, "David Musser is one of the most promising young ministers in the BIC Church." I'm almost sure if things would have been different in our family, if Mother wouldn't have had her lifelong mental illness, I'm 99 percent sure that Daddy would have become a Brethren in Christ Bishop. I always looked up to Daddy with reverence in his being a minister. I would annually go through the

BIC conference booklets and I was amazed with how many conference committees Daddy was on. My Daddy would have been a success in any line of work. He was a natural at preaching, a natural at school teaching, a natural at retail administration, and a natural-born salesman, and a bit later, this will be proven.

# CHAPTER 62

## The Years 1959 -1960

Beginning my sophomore year in high school in the fall of 1959, I began a new job as a soda jerk at Trapp's Pharmacy in Abilene. In Abilene for decades, the population has kept right at around seven thousand and still is up to the present day. Can you believe that Abilene in that decade of the '50s, had four drugstores, just unreal! The drugstore with the ever-present soda fountain was the backbone of main street USA during the late 1880s and for much of the twentieth century. Life was so uncomplicated when a nickel or a dime could buy you a Cherry Coke or a root beer—a fountain delight and always included sweet memories.

What's so awesome is that JC Penny was located right next to Trapp's on North Cedar Street. Daddy would come in for coffee at least once on my shift. Daddy's boss, Eldon O'Dell, never failed to get his iced coffee. It could be snowing a blizzard outside and Eldon would still get his iced coffee. The general manager at Trapp's, Francis, was such a hard man to work for and there was a reason. Francis had two sons and a daughter. However in the early 1950s, his one and only daughter was run over by a lady driving—an Abilene schoolteacher—and was killed. Francis I guess, couldn't get over his daughter's death which is completely understandable.

The two most popular drinks I served up were Cherry Coke and a Lime- Aide. Cherry Coke was by far the most popular drink in the 1950s into early '60s. I shall forever remember my first day on the job. A customer had ordered an Orangeade. Well, I did everything right except I forgot the unwritten rule—make sure you put the glass under the slicer. The result was orange juice splattered all over. A friend of both Daddy and mine was

Kimber Zimmerman, a clothing store worker and he never failed to get his Lime-Aide.

Another little tidbit about Daddy as previously mentioned, for decades the population of Dickenson County has stayed at around twenty-one thousand. JC Penny was by far the busiest department store in Dickenson County. People from all corners of Dickenson County would make JC Penny a must stop on their bi-monthly or monthly trip to Abilene. Daddy often told me that he knew 70 percent of the population of Dickenson County and that might just have been a bit of an understatement. Remember, Daddy had taught at three schools, a pastor at two churches, and, for eight years, assistant manager at JC Penny, all in Dickenson County. What's so amazing is that Daddy had done all the above by the age of thirty-one, just remarkable!

I've made mention of my Great-Uncle Luther Lady always on fire for his Lord and Savior Jesus Christ. Great-Uncle Luther, born in 1895, was two years younger than his sister Anna, my grandmother who burned to death. Uncle Luther was a bear of a man, weighing at least 280 pounds. Like myself, Great-Uncle Luther was a die-hard K-State basketball fan. Uncle Luther made the forty-mile trip to the Little Apple Manhattan a good many times. He knew of my love for K-State basketball, and several times he took me with him to watch our Wildcats in Ahearn Field House. One game that I'll never forget while going with Uncle Luther was a game against the Iowa State Cyclones which was always a tough game. It was early 1961 and the visiting Cyclones were taking it to K-State. This wasn't one of K-States banner seasons. K-State was led by junior center Cedric Price and strong forward Wally Frank form Norton, Kansas. The Cyclones were led by forward Henry Whitney and point guard Gary Wheeler.

With 1.40 left in the game, K-State was down by thirteen. Great Uncle Luther and I got up, heading for his car. When getting in the car, we were totally dumbfounded. K-State had made one unbelievable comeback in defeating the Cyclones. I'm sure Uncle Luther never left a game early again. I sure didn't.

# CHAPTER 63

## Eternity in the Balance

It's the summer of 1960, our last summer living at the parsonage. I'm 99.9 percent sure that the reason for Daddy retiring from the ministry at the young age of thirty-nine was due to Mother's mental illness. The following happening will live with me until the day Jesus takes me home to heaven. There was a ringing of the telephone, the call was for Daddy. It was from a middle-age woman who with her children went to our church. Her husband was a lifelong alcoholic and he had been diagnosed with cirrhosis of the liver, normally a terminal cancer. Daddy was preparing to leave when Mother confronted Daddy, slapping him in the face, cursing him, and shouting out the initials NH, NH, NH, NH—of course, the first and middle initial for my paternal grandfather, Noah Harrison. By this time, my insides were being torn up inside.

For years I had wanted Daddy to respond to strike back; he never did. Here you had a life on the line for all eternity and Mother yelling out, "No, I won't let you go." With the grace of God and somehow a miracle, Daddy did make that hospital call that night. Shortly after, the father passed away forever into eternity. If Daddy had one weakness, it's that he was too passive. Please believe me, this wasn't one rare occurrence. This was the norm for our most dysfunctional family. It was shortly after this that Mother told Daddy I did something that I hadn't done. I recall as if it was just yesterday, Daddy took me out of town, just north of old Highway

40 East. It was the last spanking that I ever got from Daddy. In our family, Daddy *never* had a say. In our home, Mother was both judge and jury. I had to live with this constant physical and emotional abuse of Daddy as well as myself from the ages of eight to sixteen. No one—and I mean no one—knew of the hell that was tearing me up inside all those years.

# CHAPTER 64

## *A Country Superstar Finds Jesus*

It was in the fall of 1960 that a special artist was coming to Salina, Kansas, twenty miles west of Abilene. The country artist was Stuart Hamblen, who became one of the radio's first singing cowboys in 1926. Hamblen went on to become a singer, actor, radio show host, and song writer, later undergoing a Christian conversion and a Temperance movement supporter. Hamblen born in 1908, didn't cope well with the pressures of his high-profile career and sought relief in alcohol. Many times his drinking landed him in jail for public brawling and other destructive behavior. Because Hamblen was hugely popular, his radio sponsors regularly bailed him out of jail and smoothed things over. For a while he ventured into horse racing as an owner. Hamblen's drinking and gambling problems severely affected his life and career. In 1949 after years of struggle with alcohol, Hamblen underwent a religious conversion at a Billy Graham crusade in Los Angeles. He was soon fired from his radio program after refusing to do beer commercials. He subsequently gave up gambling and horse racing and entered Christian broadcasting with his radio show *The Cowboy Church of the Air* which ran until 1952.

During a 1953 crusade in Los Angeles, Billy Graham called Hamblen's conversion the "turning point' in the Billy Graham Evangelistic Association ministry" where before Hamblen accepted Christ, the crowds were rather small. Hamblen was the number 1 radio personality in Los Angeles which drew crowds. That night at Salina, Hamblen shared his faith and sung his signature hymn, "It Is No Secret What God Can Do." It was written shortly after his acceptance of Jesus Christ as his personal Savior. Soon after, the actor John Wayne offered Hamblen a drink and Hamblen refused, saying, "It is no secret what the Lord can do." The rest as they say is history. John Wayne said, "You should write a song by that title."

Hamblen's pop hit "This Ole House" was inspired while on a hunting trip in the high Sierras with a friend. The two men came upon what looked like an abandoned shack wherein they found the body of an elderly man, apparently dead of natural causes. Hamblen came up with the lyrics to the song while riding horseback down the mountain and composed the melody within a week. Listen to these lyrics which illustrates the transformed life of Stuart Hamblen.

> This old house once knew my children, This old house once knew my wife.
>
> This old house was home and shelter as we fought the storms of life.
>
> This old house once rang with laughter, This old house heard many shouts.
>
> Now she trembles in the darkness, when the lightnin walks about.
>
> Ain't gonna need this house no longer, Ain't gonna need this house no more.
>
> Ain't got time to fix the shingles, Ain't got time to fix the floor.
>
> Ain't got time to oil the hinges, nor to mend the windowpane. Ain't gonna need this house no longer, I'm ready to meet the saints.
>
> Now my old hound dog lies asleeping, He don't know I'm gonna leave.

Else he'd wake up by the fireplace, and he'd sit there, howl
and grieve.

But my hunting days are over, I ain't gonna hunt the coon
no more.

Gabriel done brought in chariot when the wind blows
down the door.

Here in these lyrics Hamblen compares himself to this old house
which is no longer need as was Hamblen's old life of sin redeemed by
God's saving grace, and the angel Gabriel comes to take Hamblen home
to meet the saints.

"This Ole House: would be recorded by several recording artists
including Rosemary Clooney and the Statler brothers. Yes, the companion
accompanying Hamblen on that hunting trip in the high Sierras was
none other than the actor John Wayne. I remember well in 1954 when
"This Ole House" made its recording debut and it became a favorite of
mine. The original manuscript of the song "It Is No Secret" is buried in
the cornerstone of the Copy Right Building of the Library of Congress.
In 1955 Hamblen had a hit single, "Open Up Your Heart and Let the
Sunshine In." This tune hit number eight on the Billboard Hot 100 pop
charts in 1955. My brother Chuck and I one Sunday morning during
worship service sang this song. Hamblen died on March 8, 1989, in Santa
Monica, California, of brain cancer. This was just another instance of
family fun time which both Mother and I needed. It was in the fall of
1960 while a sophomore, I was getting terrific headaches, some days having
to leave school. Mother's eye doctor, Dr. Cultrone practiced in Salina. I
did need glasses. After the eye appointment, Mother and I did something
special together. For decades in Salina, there's been an ice cream parlor
known for its delicious thick milkshakes. Several times while in Salina my
family would go to this ice cream parlor. About two years ago at a Hoover
family reunion, I chatted with my cousin Mark Hoover who lives in Salina
and Mark told me some fifty-five years later, it's still in business. Mark is
the youngest son of my late beloved Uncle Harry. Yes,
Mother and I did have our fun times.

# CHAPTER 65

## Scars of Childhood Abuse—A Stunning Finding in the Lady Genes

It's the spring of 1961, my junior year at Abilene High, and there was to be a mandatory dress up day. Students were to wear their Sunday best. When I got home that afternoon and told Mother this, she simply went ballistic. She wouldn't even consider letting me wear a suit and tie. I pleaded with Mother to let me wear a suit and tie to no avail. That dress up day Mother made me wear an old tacky blue casual outfit. I would stand out from everyone. The dress up day was here and I was extremely humiliated and self-conscious. Most of my classmates knew that I was a PK, (preacher's kid) and I'm sure they wondered why I was wearing a tacky old outfit. Mother could always find a way to be so extremely cruel to me.

Let's for a moment, revisit my mother at the age of five and her being the oldest witness to her mama's fatal accident. The following is a quote from David Sack MD in an article in *Psychology Today*, "Loss of a parent at an early age has been shown to lead to long term psychological damage in children, especially if that parent is the mother—losing a parent in childhood significantly raises the risk of developing mental health issues."

The following is a quote from goodtherapy.com, "Research indicates that the bereavement rooted in childhood often leaves emotional scars for decades." The following is taken from an article in *The Independent* in the UK, "Physical abuse or intentional use of physical force or implants against a child can delay height growth throughout childhood." Also an article from *Psychology Today* reads, "Emotional abuse can actually stunt a child's growth." Psychologist have known known for some time that children who suffer severe emotional abuse often grow slowly or hardly at all. This statement completely shocks me to the core. My most terrible years of abuse were from the ages of eight to ten. This statement demoralizes me. I always wanted to be a basketball star and it's taken me sixty years later, while doing the research on my life story, to come to the realization that more than likely, my growth was stunted those three years of being locked up for hours in the outside cellar, and to think the seed in all of this was planted on that fateful New Year's Day of 1927.

Epidemiologist Dr. Scott Montgomery and his team of the Royal Free Hospital in London followed up a survey of 1,152 families across the UK which had taken place between 1937 and 1939. Dr. Montgomery states, "It had looked at children's health and lifestyles when they were between ages five and eight; sixty years later 149 members of the same group were tracked down and similar test carried out." Dr. Montgomery continued, "We discovered a significant relationship between parents who had argued and a slower growth rate in their children. Youngsters who live in very stressful situations have been found to have less growth hormones. If they are taken out of this unhappy situation the hormone levels recover." Yes, to say that my entire childhood was stressful is an understatement.

All through my junior high and high school years, I could outshoot, out dribble all the varsity players due to my hundreds and hundreds of hours shooting hoops throughout the years. I was always cut due to my height. I firmly know and believe that I could have been a star basketball player at a major college. Why? The genes are right there in the genealogy of my Great- Grandpa Samuel and my Great-Grandma Mary Olive Frey Lady. Here's my reasoning and the facts—a Grandson and three Great-Grandsons of my Great-Grandpa and Great-Grandma Lady were basketball stars. The Grandson is Wendell Lady, the son of my Great-Uncle Luther Lady. Wendell Lady was a star basketball player at Abilene High and in the 1970s and '80s, went into Kansas State politics, becoming a high-ranking official in the Kansas State House. The three others were high school and college stars, the first is Larry Lady, the Grandson of my Great-Uncle Luther Lady. Yes, this is the same Larry that coached against Daddy in that Dickenson County tournament at the Abilene City Hall in March of 1954. Larry became an all- state basketball player and went to Kansas University on a basketball scholarship. The second star player is Dale Engle, a second cousin of mine and Grandson of my Great-Aunt Minnie Engle, a sister to my Grandmother Anna who burned to death. Dale was a high school basketball star at DCCHS, Chapman, Kansas, and at Messiah College. The third high school star was my first cousin Louis Engle, a son of my Aunt Eunice Engle, two years younger than her sibling, my mother. Louis became a high school basketball star in Southern California. Louis then attended Messiah College, my alma mater, and at Messiah, Louis broke all kind of school scoring records around 1973– 1974.

There you have it, one player a Grandson of my Great-Grandparents and the other three Great-Grandsons of my great-grandparents Samuel and Mary Olive Frey Lady. I would say that my case for having become a basketball star was great. How about it! Just a note about my first cousin Louis Engle, today at the age of sixty-seven, Louis is an American charismatic Christian leader best known for his founding of *The Call*, a national US program that has twelve-hour prayer rallies and his association with prominent members of the Christian right.

# CHAPTER 66

## My Brother, Chuck, and Fun Times at the Abilene Municipal Swimming Pool

Let me share a bit about my younger brother Chuck. His given name is Charles Wesley Musser, four years my junior. He was named after the English Methodist writer of some 6,500 hymns Charles Wesley of the eighteenth century. As previously mentioned, no two brothers could be so different. Chuck was so blessed with the talent of playing the organ. Chuck became the church organist at our BIC Church in Abilene as well as the organist for the Abilene High School chorus. From the second through fifth grade at Talmage Elementary, I took piano lessons from my Daddy's first cousin, Mary Ann Saulman. However when moving to Abilene during my fifth grade, sports took over my life. While at Northern High School in Dillsburg, Pennsylvania, Chuck would meet a lovely young Christian girl, Cara Fissel. Chuck and Cara both attended Messiah College at Grantham, Pennsylvania. They became house parents during their senior year at Messiah. After graduation, they took special schooling in Spanish as they would become missionaries to Nicaragua for eleven years. They would be there during the Somoza dictatorship, and they were caught amid of a lot of civil unrest but weren't harmed. A daughter Charity, was born to them in 1971, and while in Nicaragua, they adopted a year-old Nicaraguan boy named Christian. In the early '70s while home on their first furlough, I often babysat Charity. Chuck for many years, taught Spanish in a state prison and Cara was an RN.

What great memories I have of the summers of swimming at the Abilene municipal pool. I remember the day, July 9, 1957, the summer after my seventh grade, I had my transistor with me. I will forever remember that day as it was the Major League All-Star game played between the National and American Leagues. It was the summer that Cincinnati Red fans stuffed the All-Star ballot box selecting Red players at all but one position. Can you believe that superstars and future Hall of Famers Henry Aaron and Willie Mays weren't even in the starting lineup? Instead Cincy out fielders Wally Post and Gus Bell had been voted in. Baseball Commissioner Ford Frick took care of that. He replaced both Post and Bell with Aaron and Mays. This was the twenty-fourth All-Star game held at Busch Stadium in St. Louis, Missouri. I recall while lying on my beach towel sunning, that in the late innings, the "Splendid Splinter: Ted Williams hit a long drive to deep center field that the "Say Hey Kid" Willie Mays ran down. Previously I mentioned that I have Willie Mays as the second greatest player in Major League history. Here's some stats and records that Mays holds in All-Star games. Mays appeared in a record twenty-four games and holds or shares the following All-Star records: runs scored (20), hits (23), extra base hits (8), stolen bases (6), triples (3), and total bases (40). In the 1963 All-Star game, Mays stole two bases in an inning and, in 1965, led off the game with a home run. Mays was elected as the All-Star game MVP in both 1963 and '68. The American League won that 1957 All-Star game 6–5.

On the second deck was a snack bar and jukebox. It would be in the summer of 1960 while swimming, I would often hear the pop hit "Everybody's Somebody's Fool," recorded by Connie Francis, one of my three favorite pop singers of all time, along with the late Dusty Springfield and Karen Carpenter who passed away too soon. At that time I had a huge crush on a third cousin of mine, and when hearing that song over the pool my heart would melt. Yes, the Abilene pool was a place of refuge, a haven of rest from my basement prison. I still find it hard to believe that Connie Francis isn't in the Rock and Roll Hall of Fame in Cleveland, Ohio.

# CHAPTER 67

## I Lose the Best Friend I Ever Had

It's the summer of 1961 between my junior and senior year of high school. The time was 6:15 p.m., June 12, 1961 a Monday evening, the setting was our family dining table at 1607 North Kuney Street Abilene, Kansas. The special guest was my beloved Grandpa Irvin Brechbill Hoover. The dinner menu was sloppy joes and how Grandpa loved those sloppy joes. After dinner we enjoyed a quiet time of reflection as Grandpa always had a good story or two.

Several notes about my best ever friend on God's earth: I'll forever cherish the memories of riding with Grandpa when he was doing fall plowing, and of the awesome times it was riding on the combine with Grandpa during the summer wheat harvest, and of helping Grandpa and Uncle Harry baling hay. I shall forever cherish Grandpa's tender hugs when he was sitting on his rocker at the corner of the dining room, for I would never get them at home. I shall forever cherish riding with Grandpa in his purple-colored Oldsmobile, and did Grandpa have a heavy foot on the car accelerator. Our drives would often end up on North Cedar Street in Abilene at the General Motors location. Grandpa was known throughout Dickenson County as IB. Grandpa had a saying, "Much obliged," of course a substitute for thank you, and Grandpa only liked two kinds of pies, hot and cold.

Whenever I was with Grandpa he would always be the first to say hi and holding his hand to shake. To this very day that is a trait that I've inherited from Grandpa as I'm always the first to hold out my hand and to say hi.

That Monday evening June 12, 1961, I drove Grandpa the twelve blocks south on Northeast Seventh Street to Uncle Virgil's and Aunt Carol's where Grandpa was living at the time. Both Aunt Carol and Uncle Virgil were to become so very special to me in the coming years. Aunt Carol would become like a second mother to me, even though she's only ten years older than me. The previous couple of days Grandpa had complained about how much his head hurt. You could see it in his face, the pain that he was in. Several months earlier, Grandpa's doctor had told Grandpa that it was time for him to get off the farm due to his diabetes and weak heart. Grandma Carrie had always been so faithful in giving Grandpa his daily insulin shot up to her death in December of 1958.

The next morning, Tuesday, June 13, 1961, Grandpa was driven by Uncle Virgil out to his farm ten miles north of Abilene. Grandpa had always been known as being extremely meticulous with his lawn and the surrounding yard and building areas. Uncle Virgil was mowing the grass, and Grandpa had taken a scythe and was cutting tall weeds and grass. Grandpa must have felt something coming on. Shortly thereafter, Uncle Virgil found Grandpa reclining on a dirt floor in a shed. It had always been Grandpa's desire that when it was his time to die, that God would take him home to heaven while he was on the earth's soil that he so long had toiled on. And what a rejoicing reunion it must have been when entering heaven's pearly gates, where he was reunited with his two loving wives Anna Zelma and Carrie. At last Grandpa had a new body free of all pain, free of traumatic events, and free from natural calamities. And as the Apostle Paul would write in 2 Timothy 4:7–8, Grandpa could say before his Lord and Savior, Jesus Christ, "I have fought the good fight, I have finished the course, I have kept the faith, hence forth there is laid up for me a crown of righteousness which the Lord the righteous Judge shall give me on that day and not to me only, but unto all of them that love his appearing."

I shall forever cherish the loving tender hugs that I received from Grandpa. You know, maybe somehow Grandpa knew of the traumatic abuse I suffered at the hands of my mother, that's not important. What is important is that I did receive those tender hugs from Grandpa which my heart and soul were starving for. I had a very special bond with my precious Grandpa Irvin Brechbill Hoover that I've had with no other person. Reflecting on those cherished memories with them, those summers spent living with Grandpa and Grandma Hoover were my "Paradise on Earth" for a love-starved, abused boy.

However on the day of his funeral I couldn't cry. I recall telling my parents that I really felt sick. Mother then went to my Uncle Dr. Dale Eshelman and told Uncle Dale what the problem was. Uncle Dale got out his doctor bag and gave me a shot and I quickly started to feel better. I was then able to cry during Grandpa's funeral as well as after. Uncle Dale sure knew what I needed. Several days after the funeral Mother couldn't stop crying. Mother and Grandpa had a special relationship due to mother's helping Grandpa Hoover with the wheat harvest. There was the year 1939 that Mother didn't go back for her senior year of high school, instead becoming Grandpa's right-hand man. Several days after the funeral, I was home when Auline Lady the widow of Gerald Lady, son of my Great-Uncle Luther and Aunt Mildred, came to console Mother. Gerald was the Lady who burned to death in his tractor trailer. Auline had such words of comfort for Mother at just the time that she needed it.

# CHAPTER 68

## The Years 1961-1962

Shortly after Grandpa's funeral I was working my soda jerk shift when lo and behold, my Great-Uncle Jesse Lady walked into the drugstore. Great-Uncle Jesse was the second youngest of my Grandma Anna's siblings. Uncle Jesse was in the Abilene area visiting family. We recognized each other instantly. Of the nine children of Great-Grandpa Samuel Lady and Great- Grandma Mary Olive Frey Lady, Great-Uncle Jesse left his mark in the world for his Lord and Savior Jesus Christ. Great-Uncle Jesse's life vocations consisted of the following: a minister, a theologian, a missionary to Africa, and the President of Beulah College in Upland, California, at the young age of thirty-six. Within a week to ten days after Great-Uncle Jesse came into Trapp's pharmacy, none other than my second cousin the basketball star Larry Lady walked in while I was on duty. This was in late summer of 1961. Larry and I had a nice chat and I've never seen Larry again. I couldn't resist bringing up that 1954 championship game at city hall in Abilene, when Larry was filling in as coach for his cousin Myron Lady. We had a good laugh over it. I remember Larry as a man of great character, a friend, and a cousin.

With the mention of my Great-Uncle Jesse Lady, I must share two rather humorous Lady family stories. My late mother told me the following, the family name Lady has been an asset, sometimes a liability. My late great- grandmother Mary Olive Lady shared the following with her granddaughter, my mother. Mother told me the following happening, "My grandfather Samuel Lady was driving along in a horse and buggy when he came upon two women walking. As befitted the kind gentleman he was, he stopped to ask if they would like a ride. The ladies accepted my grandfather's offer. In the course of the conversation, the ladies said their name was Mann. 'Well, isn't that a coincidence,' Grandpa said, 'my name is Lady,' you know like a play on words. The conversation stopped. Grandpa Lady's passengers thought that he was making fun of them. Not until he assured them that his name was really Lady, did the chatted atmosphere return to normal."

Then there was the scandal at Messiah Bible School. My Grandma Anna's older brother Harvey enrolled as a student at Messiah Bible School in 1915. Harvey was taking schooling to become a missionary to Africa. The registrar assigned him to a room with another young man whose name just happened to be Howard Mann. The report went out from the Bible school that a lady was rooming with a man and they weren't even married. Regrettably it wouldn't be so sensational today but it sure was then. Oh, I got to know Howard Mann when attending the Bellvue Park B and C church in Harrisburg, Pennsylvania, in 1969. Yes, it's a small world.

With the coming of my senior year at Abilene High, I had quit the soda jerk job and went to work for an independent grocer. It was a much better- paying job. I would stock shelves and bag groceries. Mother was also employed in the Abilene High cafeteria. She seemed happy and content. Daddy had also begun a new line of work, that of selling Kirby vacuum cleaners while keeping his position at JC Penny. Daddy was so successful with Kirby that he resigned his position at Penny's. Kirby for that era of the early 1960s, was expensive, selling for around $375. What really sold the housewife on the Kirby was it's portable. Daddy would rip the sheet off the bed and would take the lightweight portable to the mattress. The housewife would be in total shock when Daddy emptied that portable bag with an unreal amount of dirt. The housewife was sold right there and then.

Daddy was a natural-born salesman, just as he was when proclaiming and selling the Gospel of Jesus Christ. Within weeks after going full-time with Kirby, Daddy was setting all kinds of record monthly sales. Many months Daddy led the entire Midwest and Pacific Coast in total monthly sales. Often Daddy sold over forty Kirbys, just an astonishing amount considering the Kirby at that time sold for $375!

I must share a humorous side of Daddy. One day Daddy was having an atypical selling day. Daddy knocked on the front door of a house and there was no answer. Daddy then went and knocked on the backdoor. The lady of the house opened the door and Daddy greeted her with this lovely greeting, "I sure hope you aren't as ugly as that lady at the front door." I guess Daddy didn't get that sale but what did Daddy have to lose. Yes, my daddy had a sense of humor.

I would like to share a bit about my social life during my last couple of high school years. My lady friends just happened to live a long distance, cheap of me right! During a three-year period, I corresponded with four girls, two from Oklahoma and two from Iowa. Each summer the BIC conference held a youth camp, Camp King Solomon located six miles west of Abilene. Young people came from Iowa and Oklahoma. The youth camp ran for a week. Two of the girls were sisters from Oklahoma and two were from Iowa. My first crush was my age from Iowa, the next two were the two sisters from Oklahoma, and the last and my most serious crush was on Carol from Iowa, and she just happened to be the youngest of the four girls, three years younger than myself. Ask me what was wrong with the Kansas girls—I really haven't an answer. The setting of Camp King Solomon was beautiful with a swinging bridge over a creek, a nice private setting to spend with a young lady. During the week there was lots of singing, special music groups, Bible study, and plenty of recreation. Dormitory life was awesome with plenty of wrestling matches.

Each spring the BIC conference held a Bible quiz for youth ages twelve to nineteen. Our Midwest conference included the three states of Iowa, Oklahoma, and Abilene. The Bible quiz would be over a book in the New Testament. The quizzing was always held in Abilene due to its central location. Just before my senior year at Abilene High, I had purchased a 1953 green Plymouth. It was late April of 1962 when the church quizzing was held at my home church, the Abilene BIC. I was about to graduate from Abilene High. It's a Saturday evening and I drove Carol out west of Abilene to what's called lovers lane. We just chatted and had a nice time together. Sadly, at about the age of thirty-five, Carol passed away from cancer.

I had mentioned about purchasing a 1953 green Plymouth. Well, I was about ready to find out the hard way to make sure you always have plenty of oil in the car. I was driving south on Highway 15, three miles from Abilene, when my car stopped on me. I found out that the block had broken and my car was history. I've always made sure to have oil in my car since.

It's Wednesday evening, May 23, 1962, time for my high school commencement. After the graduation, we were going to the popular Sunflower Hotel. On what was to have been my special night, Mother upsets the plan. All that I can recall is that I must have done something trivial. A day before the graduation, she told me that I couldn't go to my graduation party. How cruel Mother could be to me? I remember right after graduation of begging Mother to let me go to no avail. The final verdict came in with an emphatic *no*. I had to miss my own graduation party. Another instance of my mother being so very cruel to me.

# CHAPTER 69

## Summer of 1962

I wasn't all that happy at the supermarket so I put an advertisement in the hometown *Reflector Chronicle* for farm work. I was able to get a job with a farmer named Lyle who lived eight miles south of Abilene, who knew my Grandpa Irvin Hoover but then it seemed like everyone in Dickenson County, Kansas knew Grandpa Hoover. Well, this summer I was about to let Grandpa down. I would stay with his family Monday through Thursday evenings and either Daddy or Mother would pick me up for the weekend. My first job that summer for Lyle was to paint a long wooden fence that extended around the entire front yard. Here I was a Tom Sawyer, only I had a transistor radio. Having a transistor in the 1960s was almost like having a smartphone today, well, not quite but I couldn't have been without mine.

So often today when hearing a golden oldie from the 1950s–1960s, I will associate it with a certain period of my life. It was while painting that fence white, that I heard for the first time, what would become a million-dollar selling record, "I Can't Stop Loving You," recorded by Ray Charles. I had never heard of Ray Charles, and for years, I didn't know that he was blind. Charles started to lose his sight at the age of four or five and was blind by the age of seven, apparently as a result of glaucoma. That song has become one of my all-time favorites.

Another one of my duties was driving a truck for the wheat harvesting. However, I had a problem—I just wasn't and never have been mechanically inclined. Well, this one late June day of '62, things hadn't been going so well for me and Lyle told me to my face in these exact words, which I'll never forget, "You aren't anything like your grandfather IB Hoover," which I'll admit, without any hesitation, was the truth. Many people around Dickenson County called Grandpa by his first and middle name initials. Just to let you know how well known my Grandpa Hoover was, Grandpa's farm was a good twenty-five miles from Lyle's farm. And that was my last week working for Lyle.

Beginning the second week of July '62, I landed a job that I really liked. It was working on an asphalt crew. The owner, Jewel Bach, was an acquaintance of Daddy. The work was done in Junction City, Kansas, a town twenty miles east of Abilene on Highway 40. One morning as we were on our thirty-minute drive to Junction City, a new hit came on the radio, "Roses Are Red," sung by Bobby Vinton. Listen to that song on YouTube, it's a beautiful rendition.

The date was Monday August 6, 1962. It was noon and time for dinner. There was a nice family restaurant that we frequented. I got hold of a newspaper and was shocked to see that the glamorous actress Marilyn Monroe had passed away on Sunday, August 5. I read where the cause of death appeared to be an overdose of sleeping pills, however, that has never been made certain. Marilyn's given birth name was Norma Jean Baker. Every week for twenty years, Marilyn's ex-husband and the great "Yankee Clipper," Baseball Hall of Famer Joe DiMaggio, had flowers sent weekly to Marilyn's grave. Both Monroe's and DiMaggio's birth and death dates have been stored in my left temporal lobe for twenty years—Monroe's birth in 1926 and death in 1962 and Jo DiMaggio's birth in 1914 and death in 1999. I spent much of my work on top of the asphalt truck where the heat could reach 125°F. I did wear out several pairs of shoes but the excellent pay was worth it and it was a job with no anxiety—and believe me, as you continue reading my memoir, you'll come to find that I've lived with acute anxiety my entire life. I don't wish it on anyone.

# CHAPTER 70

## Fall of 1962 — My Freshman Year at Messiah

It's a Thursday evening August 30, 1962, about 6:00 p.m., and I was leaving on a Greyhound bus, destination 1,200 miles away at Grantham, Pennsylvania, and two nights on the bus. I was to meet my cousin from Oklahoma, Stanley Eyster, in St. Louis but his bus was behind schedule. I met this nice young lady about my age, a Moravian, headed for Bethlehem, Pennsylvania. It was in Bethlehem, in 1741, where the first successful community was established by German Moravians. The Moravians are possibly the oldest Protestant denomination in the world. The Moravians were started by Jesuits in early fifteenth-century Bohemia who objected to some of the practices of the Catholic Church. I remember one evening, my Moravian friend was cold and I gave her my jacket to keep her warm.

On my arrival at the Harrisburg, Pennsylvania, bus depot on that Saturday September 1, 1962, I recall it being unseasonably cool for that time of year. I took a taxi for the ten-mile ride to Grantham, Pennsylvania, the location of Messiah College. Upon my arrival at Messiah, hardly any students had yet to arrive. What's so nice was that my mother's two older sisters, Aunt Rozella and Aunt Virgie, both lived an hour and a half from Grantham, Pennsylvania. As a freshman at Messiah in the fall of 1962, Messiah's enrollment was 150. Today fifty-seven years later, Messiah's enrollment is over 3,500. Messiah was founded in 1909 by the Brethren in Christ Church under the Presidency of S. R. Smith, a church leader and

Harrisburg, Pennsylvania, businessman. Today in 2020, almost every faith in the world is represented at Messiah.

Being one of the first students to have arrived on campus, where else would I go but to the school's gymnasium? Only one other person was in the gym, a young girl of about twelve. I was about to find out what a small world it was. Her name was Carolyn Feese, and after chatting for a short time, I found out that her mother was in the BIC Church home mission work in Kentucky with my parents in 1944, the year that I was born. About seven or eight years later, I would have a major crush on Carolyn. We had several dates but nothing came of it.

# CHAPTER 71

## *Thanksgiving and Christmas of 1962*

What a wonderful Thanksgiving I had on November 22, 1962, at my Aunt Rozella's and Uncle John Thrush's. Their son Irvin had picked me up at Messiah. Irvin was their second oldest child. Aunt Rozella was the oldest child of my grandparent's Irvin and Anna Zelma Lady Hoover, my grandmother who burned to death. I had so much fun with my Thrush cousins that Thanksgiving, Johnny, Irvin, Rozanna, Mahlon, and Mary Lou, the youngest at thirteen. Yes, this was the same home where twelve years earlier on July 12, 1950, my cousin Janet Eshelman would celebrate her third birthday, blowing out her birthday cake candles on Uncle John's large front lawn. Sadly in the upcoming years, tragedy would come to haunt Aunt Rozella's family of which I'll share a bit later.

My freshman year at Messiah I would play junior varsity basketball and tennis. Soon it came time for Christmas vacation and I had no ride home to Kansas. At the last moment, I was able to get a ride with a science professor at Messiah, also named Ken, and he was a native Kansan. No sooner had I gotten home that I headed for my home away from home for years, the Abilene Public Library. I recall having to do some research for a hymnology class. I also got to play some pickup basketball games at Abilene City Hall where, eight years earlier, Daddy had coached the East Buckeye School to a county basketball championship. On the last of my two Sundays home, I was able to preach the evening message. Some fifty-seven years later, I remember the title, "Why the Church Never Gives Up."

I was making many new friends at Messiah and was even dating a little. I got to be a real close friend to a man about six years older than myself. His name was Mark and we both took Spanish class together. Mark and I would stay up until 1:30 a.m., memorizing Spanish vocabulary. Yes, both Mark and I aced the class with straight A's. However, there was one class that I simply felt overwhelmed, the course was The Life of Christ, and the professor was an Oxford scholar, Dr. Robert Sider. In this class were fifth-year theology students. To this day, I have no idea how I got in this class. Luckily I was able to pull a D.

# CHAPTER 72

## Fun Summer of 1963

After my freshman year at Messiah, I spent the summer living with my Aunt Rozella and Uncle John Thrush. In early June of '63, the BIC annual conference was held in Fort Erie, Ontario. It happened that a carload of men from Mount Rock BIC, Uncle John's home church, were driving up to Ontario, Canada. Along in the car besides Uncle John and me, were four other men. Fort Erie is located right next to Niagara Falls. This was my first time of seeing the honeymoon for lovers. How breathtakingly beautiful was the falls at night when all the colored lights came on, making the setting so spectacular.

That summer of 1963 I got a lucky break. A new Highway 81 was starting construction. Highway 81 was to become a main corridor from the US northeast down through Tennessee. As soon as I got back from Canada, the work had just started. It just happened that the new highway was to cut through part of Uncle John's farm for which he would be reimbursed. I worked at the batch plant located a quarter-mile from Uncle John's. My work was standing on a platform, helping in the mixing of the cement. The pay was excellent. Everything just broke right for me that summer, truly one of the very best summers of my life with no anxiety.

The summer of '63, I had a huge crush on a girl three years younger than I. Her name was Dena who just happened to be the very best friend of my cousin Rozanna, Aunt Rozella's oldest daughter. I had several dates with Dena and even slept overnight once at her home—not in her bedroom.

However I would soon be a sophomore in college and Dena would only be a junior in high school. For some unknown reason, I seemed to have had a not- so lucky crush on girls three years younger than me.

What great memories I have of that summer of 1963. Next to my precious memories of those summers spent at Grandpa Hoover and Grandma Hoover's, I would put this summer of '63 right up there. Uncle John's had a basketball goal put up in the barn in the area where the hay was kept. In that barn my cousin Irvin Thrush and I had some great one-on-one games. It was a summer with no anxiety whatsoever which was such a blessing. The summer of 1963 will forever be remembered as the summer of such great pop music hits. There was Little Miss Peggy March, the fifteen-year-old 4'10" pack of dynamite with her megahit "I Will Follow Him" which not only reached number 1 in the US but also in Australia, New Zealand, South Africa, Japan, and Scandinavia. However, for some unknown reason, it failed to chart in the UK. The Chiffons with "He's so Fine," Kyu Sakamoto, a Japanese singer, with his international hit song "Ue o Muite Aruko," sung in Japanese and sold over 13 million records. Sadly, Sakamoto along with 519 on board Japanese Airlines flight 123, on August 12, 1985, crashed, the deadliest single aircraft accident to date. His number 1 hit song lyrics translated to "happiness lies beyond the clouds" and "happiness lies above the sky." It's a bit ironic that Kyu's death came above the skies.

Leslie Gore with "It's My Party" and "You Don't Own Me," the Beach Boys, "Surfin Usa," "Catch a Wave," and "Little Deuce Coupe." Claude King had his one-hit wonder, "Woolverton Mountain," my late cousin Mahlon Thrush's favorite. The Crystals with their megahit "Da Do Ron," my favorite hit that summer of '63 was "I Love You Because" recorded by Al Martino. When hearing that song, warm thoughts of Dena crossed my heart. "Blame It on the Bossa Nova" by Edie Gorme, the Cascades' "Rhythm of the Rain." Lastly in May of '63, George Hamilton IV had one very special hit, "Abilene." Hamilton visited my hometown Abilene, Kansas, and was given the keys to the town. Whenever I hear these golden oldies, the fun summer of 1963 always comes to mind. The following are the lyrics to the song "Abilene."

Abilene, Abilene
Prettiest town I've ever seen
Women there don't treat you mean
In Abilene, my Abilene
I sit alone most every night
Watch those trains pull out of sight
Don't I wish they were carryin' me
Back to Abilene, my Abilene
Crowded city, there ain't nothin' free
Nothin' in this town for me
Wish to the Lord that I could be
In Abilene, sweet Abilene

I'll forever cherish those games of hide-and-seek with my Thrush cousins. I'll never forget Camp Roxbury, the beautiful music, the evangelistic services, and recreation playing softball. Aunt Rozella was like a mother to me that summer of '63. However, I think that I might have taken advantage of her, I would get up in the middle of the night, and would snack on raw cabbage. Crazy, right! One night my Thrush cousins pulled a prank on me. Earlier in my memoir, I had written about my fear of mice which was sown in that basement prison, left all alone, forsaken. As a boy of three I was playing around some garbage cans when I was bitten by a rat. I did get a tetanus shot for it. About the prank, one late summer night my cousins took me out to the barn where the dairy cattle were milked. Upon the turning on of the light, lo and behold to my horror, rats were running wild. I screamed and I couldn't get out of that barn fast enough.

# CHAPTER 73

## Fall of 1963

Upon my return to Messiah as a sophomore in September of '63, I had a new roommate, Vernon Martin from Ohio. Vernon was from a family of singers, the Martin family. His family would sing at church camps throughout the US during the summers. Through my high school years, I had gotten to know Vernon, and during our freshman year at Messiah College in 1962 to 1963, we became good friends.

The day of the week was Friday the twenty-second, the month was November, and the year 1963. The setting, my biology class at Messiah, the time, 1:30 p.m. EST. When coming over the school intercom came the shocking announcement that left you stunned and dumbfounded. JFK had been shot riding in a presidential motorcade in Dearly Plaza in Dallas, Texas, by former US marine Lee Harvey Oswald. It was either a Sunday or Monday evening that a carload of us boys drove down to Washington, DC. We would wait in line for hours to get into the capitol rotunda to pass by JFK's closed coffin. It was an extremely solemn setting. I'm forever grateful that I was able to get there for the viewing.

By my sophomore year I was still undecided on a major. I guess it was either history or religion. I was on the JV basketball team as the point guard. During that winter of 1963–1964, our basketball team made one unforgettable trip to New York State. It was in early December while on our road trip on the Pennsylvania Turnpike that I first heard the new megapop hit "Forget Him," sung by Bobby Rydell. This would become one of my all-time favorite hits. Some forty-four years later, I got to see the trio of Golden Boys in person, Fabian, Frankie Avalon, and Bobby Rydell, at the American Music Theatre in Lancaster, Pennsylvania. This trio of boys all grew up in the city of brotherly love, Philadelphia. On this road trip we would play games against Nyack College from Nyack, New York, Houghton College from Houghton, New York. These two schools are both located close to the Army at West Point, New York. I recall our star point guard Howie Landis scoring 46 points against Nyack, at the time a Messiah record for points scored in a game. The buildings at West Point, with the elements of Gothic, Victorian, and Tudor architecture and the granite-gray buildings, is just spectacular. West Point, near the Hudson River, is the oldest continuously occupied military post in North America.

# CHAPTER 74

## An Excruciating Case of Acute Anxiety

I'm sure if you're a classic movie lover like myself of the 1930s–1950s, your familiar with the 1946 suspense thriller *The Spiral Staircase*. It stars Dorothy McQuire and George Brent. The movie is about a young deaf mute woman who is working in a New England mansion as a domestic worker, being terrorized by a maniac who is killing off people with disabilities. After being warned of the danger to her personal safety, she plans to leave the dark old house but it's too late. The maniac is in the house and she is his prey. Well, getting close to Christmas vacation in 1963, Ken Musser, age nineteen, was soon to be heading down a spiral staircase of his own with an attack of acute anxiety that I wish on no one.

It's a week before Christmas 1963. A carload of us students from Abilene, Kansas were driving home for the seventeen-day Christmas break. On leaving Ohio I needed a restroom break. However when entering the restroom I simply couldn't void. We continued our drive through the states of Indiana and Illinois. At numerous stops I entered the men's room, flushing the toilet, trying to block out any noise, and then put my hand in the water, hoping that would work like I was in my own little world with no one else around. I was having the most excruciating acute anxiety a human could experience, a shy bladder syndrome. After driving through the states of Indiana and Illinois, I still couldn't void and it felt like my bladder was about to burst. We were soon to enter Missouri and had driven through two states, a part of Ohio, a seven-hour-period. I was now in agony. I whispered to the driver that he had to stop. About twenty miles into Missouri we exited at Warrentown. As I entered the commode

I was praying to God, "Please help me to go." Again I flushed the toilet, going through my routine of putting my hand in the water, and at last, I relieved myself. I recall saying, "Thank you, Jesus, thank you, Jesus." It was six-plus hours of pure agony. Some fifty-six years later, I've come to accept the fact that my lifelong acute anxiety was sown on that fatal New Year's Day of 1927, when an innocent five-year-old saw her mama on fire, burning to death, and that the root of my lifelong acute anxiety gave nourishment and water on those three years of being abandoned, locked up for hours in my albatross. I've lived with acute anxiety my entire life but thank the Lord I've never had to relive that agonizing six-plus hours that I lived through on that 1963 Christmas road trip.

In early 1964 Messiah held a free throw shooting contest and I immediately signed up. As a pure shooter I had so much confidence that I could either win or come in second. Reflecting fifty-five years later, I've come to believe that the shooting contest should have been off limits to the basketball players. The overall winner was our varsity point guard Howie, who made ninety one out of a one hundred, and I came in second, making eighty-eight out of a one hundred. I always looked forward to Friday nights in the gym as a good number of Messiah faculty and students would play volleyball and the games could really get heated up.

Many times in my teen years into early 40's I would shoot hoops on the far left corner of the basketball court. I would often shoot 20 straight shots and the basketball went swish finding nothing but netting. Why could I swish all the shots in a row finding nothing but netting; as a 9-10-year old I would shoot baskets hours on end in a blanket of snow.

# CHAPTER 75

## *The Most Depressive Summer of 1964*

I'm now to get into a rather sensitive subject but it's so important that I share this with you as the following all had its roots in those years of traumatization by my mother from ages eight to eleven. Year after year my insides were being torn apart by the double whammy of both Daddy's abuse and mine. As I reflect on my life as an emotionally and physically abused boy, I gave no thought to my being abused and how it would later impact my life. It was watching my Daddy continually being cursed at and my mother's yelling the initials NH NH NH NH that was tearing my insides apart. I gave no thought at all to what my mother's traumatic abuse to me was doing to my insides, and the long-term mental damage it was doing to me. In my entire childhood into adolescence, the word *sex* was never mentioned nor would I ever get a loving hug from my parents, and never did I hear those three little magic words that every child needs to hear, *I love you*.

One spring day in 1964, while a sophomore at Messiah, I started out hitchhiking the ten miles to Harrisburg. I had my left thumb out hitching a ride. The first person to stop of all people, was an acquaintance, a fifth-year theology student. Buddy asked me where I was going. I told him that I needed a break from my studies. However the truth be known, I knew of my destination, God knew, and I'm sure that the evil tempter Lucifer did too. A few times during my two years at Messiah, some buddies and I would drive on a Friday night to Castiglios on North Third Street, well-known for their delicious steaks. You just couldn't get that delicious taste at the Messiah kitchen. I was heading for a corner outside newsstand, located a block north of Market Square on North Second Street. One couldn't miss seeing this newsstand. After purchasing the girlie magazine, I walked over the Harvey Taylor Bridge named after the late Pennsylvania senator. A nice lady picked me up after I had crossed the bridge and she drove me the eight miles south on Highway 15 to the Grantham exit. I do remember that as soon as I got back to my room, I had to hide it from my roommate.

I've always been known to be a nice guy, sensitive, never wanting to criticize. However I must admit that I had a bit of mischievous side to me. Toward the end of my sophomore year, a buddy and I got hold of a whole lot of toilet tissue and we decorated the south side of Old Main with toilet tissue. I was also in on another prank; a number of my buddies and I picked up a college professor's Volkswagen, carrying the VW up the steps of Old Main to the its center, and no, I was never found out for either of those pranks. I do recall it was about this time, the invasion of the of the Beetles to the US.

With my having completed my sophomore year of college, I had no idea where my life was headed. There would be no highway construction in the summer of '64 as there was in the summer of '63. Quite unexpectedly, my parents had moved to Little Rock, Arkansas, in the spring of 1964. Daddy had been out of the ministry for four years and had outstanding success as a Kirby salesman. The Midwest headquarters for Kirby were in Little Rock. The Kirby company gave my parents an expense-free move to Little Rock. I lived at Uncle John Thrush's for three weeks helping with the harvesting with no success of having found a job. Daddy was thinking that I could be a success like he was but it wasn't in the cards. What would lie ahead of me that summer of 1964 would become one hell of a nightmare.

Aunt Rozella dropped me off at the Shippensburg, Pennsylvania, Greyhound bus depot and I was heading for a summer—the worst in my life. It started out on a positive note with Mother picking me up and taking me out for lunch. The world of sports has always been my heaven on earth, and while eating lunch with Mother, I was reading the sports section of the Little Rock newspaper, the *Arkansas Democrat-Gazette*. It was the weekend of the 1964 US Open professional golf championship being at Congressional Country Club in Bethesda, Maryland. The 1964 Open was won by the late Ken Venturi. I would be living with my parents for only a week when all hell broke out. Mother was constantly berating and calling me a failure.

Mother kicked me out after only a week and my destination was the Little Rock YMCA. Little did I know that for the next five years, the YMCA would become my home. My living quarters was a small room with no kitchen facilities, living mostly on fast food. I was also trying to sell a most expensive vacuum cleaner for that era of $375. My entire life was one of acute anxiety. While doing my sales presentations, I would stutter which was so humiliating and embarrassing. I previously shared a classroom experience twelve years earlier; as a second grader, while reading in front of the class, I had a most humiliating stuttering experience. Somehow I did sell around thirteen cleaners in about a five-week period. It just happened that I got into the home of a thirty-eight-year-old divorced lady. During my sales presentation, I stuttered terribly which was so humiliating. After my sales presentation, I would find the following happening a bit weird. She took me around her entire home, the bedroom, the bathroom. She did tell me that she had a master's in speech therapy and she invited me to a speech seminar which I attended with her which, I remember, I got nothing out of. Miraculously I did sell her a cleaner. Reflecting fifty-five years later, I've come to the premise that we were two lonely people seeking a little friendship and love. I never saw her again.

What a lonely cruel world and wasted summer of 1964. I've mentioned numerous times, of how when listening to a special pop hit song, it always takes me back to a period of my life. That summer there were two megahits which I'll always associate to that summer of '64, "Wishin' and Hopin'" by Dusty Springfield and "Rag Doll," recorded by Franki Valli and the Four Seasons. Dusty Springfield passed away from cancer in 1999, only fourteen days before what would have been her sixtieth birthday. Yes, I've had Dusty Springfield's birth year, 1939, and death frozen in my left temporal love for over twenty-one years.

During that summer of '64 when I spent seven weeks in Little Rock, I was in my parents' living room only once. It was a Saturday evening and miraculously Mother had me over for Saturday evening dinner. I remember that evening, fifty-six years ago, that Pennsylvania Governor Bill Scranton was on TV being interviewed as he was running for the 1964 Republican presidential ticket. Ultra Conservative Barry Goldwater won the Republican nomination for president, and of course history tells us that Goldwater got swamped 486 electoral votes to 52 electoral votes with LBJ doing the swamping. That summer of 1964 I felt completely estranged from my family. Ken's lonely cruel world had now begun which would run from late August 1964–1970. Yes, I'm back on a Greyhound bound for another Y in Harrisburg, Pennsylvania. Often I've wondered why I didn't take that Greyhound to my hometown of Abilene, Kansas. For what would lie ahead of me the next six years, *I wish on no one*, meaning that with emphasis. Upon my arrival at the Harrisburg bus depot it felt like it was 100 degrees out. I remember of walking the thirteen long blocks in the sweltering heat with all my luggage. By the time I reached the Y I was dying of thirst. In mid-to-late August of 1964, two more pop hits were recorded which I'll always associate with that summer of '64, "Downtown," recorded by the UK's Petula Clark, and "The Boardwalk" by the Drifters.

The Harrisburg Y was located on the corner of Front and North Street right adjacent from the beautiful Susquehanna River. Frequently I would walk up and down Front Street with my transistor, either listening to pop hits or to Philadelphia Phillies' baseball games. Being late summer many boats were out on the water. Front Street was lined with park benches. There would be times when I would sit by myself up to a couple hours at a time. I was a twenty-year-old with no mission, no purpose in life, without a friend. I landed a job at an Italian restaurant on North Second Street, located five blocks from the Y. Ken's world was a lonely cruel world. I was barely existing day to day. My job was a dishwasher which really didn't help my self-esteem. I did get one free meal on a shift. I did love their halibut fish. To this day, fifty-six years later, it remains the best halibut I've ever eaten. I lasted only ten days there.

# CHAPTER 76

## The Fall of 1964

And then there came a glimmer of hope. My Aunt Faith, my Daddy's younger sister, lived in Palmyra, Pennsylvania, a thirty-minute drive from Harrisburg. Uncle Glenn and Aunt Faith were a devout Christian couple. Uncle Glenn was an MD, and with his professional contacts, he helped me to land a job at a local shoe factory, the J Landis shoe factory in Palmyra. I worked on an assembly line putting and tacking soles to shoes. I did have an accident when I got a tack into my finger and had to get a tetanus shot. What was so nice was that my one-room second-floor apartment was only a ten- minute walk to Aunt Faith's on Green Street. Aunt Faith was one awesome cook. I was able to eat all my nightly meals at Uncle Glenn's. Her specialty was cooking a delicious Chinese meal with rice, noodles, and Chinese food.

By the fall of 1964 Uncle Glenn's had a two-year-old daughter Marta, and twin sons, Thomas and David, not quite a year old. Aunt Faith would also give birth to a daughter, Kristen, and a son, Andy. Uncle Glenn's would adopt a beautiful Korean girl named Kim Sue. What's so nice was that Kim Sue and Kristen were the same age. For a good number of years, Kim Sue and her husband David, have been missionaries to the Ukraine. Sadly Uncle Glenn passed away from pancreatic cancer in 1993; however, he lived long enough to walk the new bride Kim Sue down the wedding aisle.

My parents only lived in Little Rock for about nine months. During their time living in Little Rock they attended a Church of the Nazarene. They weren't all that happy in Little Rock and decided to move to South

Central, Pennsylvania at Christmas 1964. I think that they missed having close friends and the BIC Church. They bought a one-floor ranch-style house near Mechanicsburg, Pennsylvania, and their home was only three miles from Grantham. Daddy and Mother are buried in the Grantham cemetery. Daddy started up his own Kirby business in Uptown Harrisburg, eight miles east of their home. Daddy was a success as he was able to get appointments as far away as Carlisle, a forty-five-minute drive from Harrisburg.

# CHAPTER 77

## Ken's Unstable Life, Coast to Coast in 1965

Daddy and I were forever bonded by our sharing our love of sports. From the late 1960s into the early '70s, Daddy and I would meet at least twice a week at a Dunkin Donut located just off 32nd Street in Camp Hill, Pennsylvania, located about halfway between Harrisburg and my parents' home. We would chat about our beloved Boston Celtic basketball and our love for the KC Royal Major League Baseball team, our love of Penn State football and Coach Joe Paterno. Often I would drive with Daddy to his sales appointments in Carlisle, a forty-minute drive; and many times we would tune in to the radio station in Boston, WBZ, listening to the late Celtic broadcaster, the legendary Johnny Most. At that time, in the late 1960s, the Celtic greats still playing were; the legendary Bill Russell, the Jones boys, KC and Sam, one of the Celtic all-time greats in "Hondo" jersey 17 John Havlicek, and my all-time favorite Celtic "Dynamite" Don Nelson, the sixth man off the bench and a pure shooter.

My crazy and unstable life would continue into the summer and fall of 1965. I had quit the shoe factory job and it's the second week of June 1965, and once again I'm on a Greyhound bound for the Golden State. My destination some 2,700 miles away in Upland, California, four nights on the bus with hardly any sleep. I was going to try and get work in California while living with my paternal grandparents, Noah and Vesta Musser. Mother's younger sister Eunice and her husband and family lived in Upland, a suburb of LA, forty miles to the east. Aunt Eunice's husband was Gordon Engle and they had a daughter, Connie, a son, Vaughn, and twins, Louis and Lucille. I would get to spend some premium time with Aunt Eunice and family.

Like Daddy and I, Uncle Gordon's were a sports nut family. It just happened that Connie was graduating from high school and I got to attend her graduation. Uncle Gordon like Daddy was a teacher and a coach. A highlight of that trip West was Uncle Gordon taking me to an LA Dodgers game to see the Dodgers play the Philadelphia Phillies. I only lived seventy miles from Philadelphia and I rooted for the Phillies. Yes, the Brooklyn Dodgers had been my boyhood team, but when they moved to LA in 1958, I lost my love for them. It happened that the Phillies' ace southpaw lefty Chris Short was pitching that night. The Phillies' other ace was Jim Bunning, a future Hall of Famer and future state of Kentucky congressman. I wished that I could have seen my favorite Major League player that night, future Hall of Famer jersey 32, Sandy Koufax, but it wasn't to be. The Phillies won the game that night.

Another highlight was going to Uncle Gordon's for dinner. Uncle Gordon had a basketball pole up in their driveway. Uncle Gordon, sons Vaughn, Louis, and I had a couple of great pickup basketball games. I recall that entire trip of being depressed, my heart wasn't in staying in Upland. Reflecting fifty-five years later, I've come to accept the fact that I was living with severe depression without knowing it and the sad fact is that I would live with it for twenty-five more years before being put on my wonder drug, Prozac. That June of 1965, the BIC was holding its annual conference in Upland, California. It happened that the couple David and Emma Wenger, who took the pastorate of the Abilene, Kansas, BIC Church in 1960 after my daddy's retirement were at the conference. I was able to get a ride back to Abilene with them.

Upon my arrival in my native Abilene in late June of 1965, I would take up lodging with my second family, Uncle Virgil and Aunt Carol Wenger. I did land a temporary position with Morton's transfer moving company. I then spent three weeks helping a first cousin of my mother's, Mahlon Engle, plowing corn. Reflecting fifty-five years later, I've come to the conclusion that the summers of '64–'65 were just a complete waste for me. My aunt Francis, my daddy's older sister was vacationing in Abilene visiting relatives; she was driving to Pennsylvania and I was able to get a ride with her.

Shortly after arriving back in Pennsylvania, I got a call from Uncle Sam to get a physical for the armed forces. What's so ironic was that I failed my physical due to a slight heart murmur. Since that physical in late summer of 1965, no doctor or specialist has found a trace of a heart murmur. I had been thinking of doing some volunteer service as many Mennonite, Church of the Brethren, and BIC had an alternate service called 1W. It was a two-year volunteer service which took the place of serving in the armed forces. However since failing my physical, it wasn't necessary for me to do that. I had written some months earlier to Aunt Mary Lou in Kansas City, Missouri, that I might like to do some voluntary service. However my world was so chaotic, so unstable with a fear of failure. I owe that unstableness to my mother who I now know ruined my life in those eight to ten years locked up in that basement prison.

I hadn't notified Aunt Mary Lou when I might be coming back to KC. Daddy saw me off at the Harrisburg, Pennsylvania bus depot and I was back on the road again. Upon arriving at the Kansas City, Missouri, bus depot, I didn't call Aunt Mary Lou up. I would take up residence at the KC YMCA— sounds familiar. It was in the mid-to-late '40s that Uncle Dale had done his residency in training toward his MD degree at the Kansas University Medical Center. I spent five nights at the KC Y without calling Aunt Mary Lou. I then checked out of the KC Y and took a Trailways bus seventy miles west to the state capital in Topeka. I took a city bus around Topeka, applying at several places without success.

You know the saying, "it's a small world?" Not far from the Topeka YMCA is the hospital Stormont Vail. As I was walking one night, I came upon two nurses waiting for a city bus. I recognized the one young lady right away, her name being Wava from my Talmage Elementary days. With no self-esteem or confidence, I walked on. I've regretted many times over the years of not chatting or saying hi to her. I heard years later that she had passed away at about age sixty. Again I was on a bus heading back to the KCY. I had spent nine days at the YMCA's before calling Aunt Mary Lou. That tells you a bit about my mental state. My cousin Jan who had turned eighteen that July, picked me up at the KC Y, the same Janet who blew out her three birthday candles on Aunt Rozella's large front yard fifteen years earlier on July 11, 1950.

I had such a happy reunion with Aunt Mary Lou and family. Their children were Jan, age eighteen; Steven, age twelve; and David, who was born in Puerto Rico, was ten. Uncle Dale's had a ping-pong table in their basement as well as a pool table. Jan, Steven, and I had some great ping-pong matches. I spent two days at Aunt Mary Lou's. Uncle Dale helped me to get a position at the KU Medical Center at Thirty-Ninth and Rainbow in Kansas City, Kansas. My work was in the ER. I would have my own desk and would give directions to visitors to the ER. There was a time that I was in the delivery room for a mother who was having a hard time giving birth. Uncle Dale helped me in finding a real nice basement efficiency apartment, and no, this wasn't an albatross. My apartment was in Missouri and I would walk the ten long blocks to work in Kansas every day. I had a very nice landlord, Mrs. McCaffery, who would let me watch some sports. On Wednesday, September 8, 1965, I would have my transistor on as this would be a very special night for a Kansas City A's baseball player. Shortstop Bert Campaneris, the all- time hits leader for both the Kansas City A's and the Oakland A's franchises, would play all nine positions that evening. Bert retired with 649 stolen bases, seventh most all-time, and retired with 2,249 hits, and was fifth in all-time games played 2,097.

# CHAPTER 78

## The Remarkable Left Hand of God

At that time I had just turned twenty-one, and although it had been eleven years since my dungeon prison in the country and five years since the parsonage cellar, the world of sports never failed me in my place of refuge. The very next evening on September 9, 1965, my favorite Major League player number 32, Lefty Sandy Koufax who I consider one of the three greatest Major League players still living, along with the "Say Hey Kid" Willie Mays and Henry Aaron at the present day in January of 2020, was pitching for the LA Dodgers. On this September 9 Koufax would pitch a perfect game against the Chicago Cubs, and just to think only three months earlier, I had been at Dodger Stadium. This would be the legend's fourth career no-hitter which at that time would be a Major League record. He would retire all twenty-seven Cubbies that night. Koufax's baseball career peaked from 1961–1966 before arthritis in his throwing left elbow ended his storied career prematurely at the young age of thirty. Sandy in those years was on another planet. Sandy Koufax has often been called the left hand of God. It's the greatest six consecutive years pitching in Major League history. Sandy won three Cy Young awards in 1963, 1965, and 1966 as Major League's best pitcher and Sandy is the only pitcher to win the Cy Young award three times when the award was given to just one pitcher, including both the National and American League. That's quite the achievement. Koufax was unanimously elected to the Hall of Fame on the first ballot at the age of thirty-six, the youngest player ever elected to the Baseball Hall of Fame. Just an added note, the Cy Young award is named for the legendary pitcher Denton True "Cy" Young who won 512 games in his legendary career, debuting in 1890.

What I consider Sandy Koufax's greatest living legacy is due for its own paragraph. On October 6, 1965, was the first scheduled game of the 1965 World Series between the LA Dodgers and the Minnesota Twins. Not only was Koufax the most dominant pitcher in baseball, but also the most prominent Jewish athlete of his generation. October 6, 1965, was the most important holiday among Jews Yom Kippur, the Jewish Day of Atonement. Koufax chose faith over the needs of his team. While Koufax spent that October 6 in a Minneapolis synagogue, his Dodgers lost that first game 8–2 with the Dodgers' other ace and future Hall of Famer Don Drysdale pitching. Koufax came back to throw two shutouts in that 1965 World Series, capped off by a decisive game 7 with Sandy pitching his third start in eight days, truly remarkable! By the beginning of the 1965 World Series, Koufax knew that the next season would be his last. Traumatic arthritis in his left elbow required a regimen of cortisone shots, codeine, along with anti-inflammatory medicine sickened Koufax and slowed his reaction time. Unfortunately Koufax lived before laparoscopic surgery could have fixed his arm and kept him pitching for years. The two-series shutouts gave him a total of 29 complete games and 10 shutouts for the 1965 season. In 360 innings, he had struck out 411 batters and walked only 76 while going 28–9 with an unreal era of 1.93. Yes, no matter what the time or where I was living, the World of Sports and my transistor radio would always be my place of refuge, peace, and contentment.

My cousin Janet who over the years I've became so very close with, as mentioned earlier, had just turned eighteen, recently getting her driver's license. On a day off from the ER, Jan drove me to downtown Kansas City, Missouri, to the KC Public Library where I was in library heaven. My junior high, throughout my high school years, the Abilene Public Library was my home away from home. One Saturday evening Jan and I went to watch a premier of the *Sound of Music*, starring Julie Andrews as Maria Von Trapp. On a good number of my off days at the medical center, I would take a city bus across town to Aunt Mary Lou's home in Raytown, Missouri. If it was a Saturday, there would be some intense ping-pong games with my cousins. Incidentally Steven, the middle child of Aunt Mary Lou, graduated from high school as the class valedictorian out of a graduating class of 450. Steven would go on to become a renowned psychiatrist, located in the Little Apple, Manhattan, Kansas. Jan has a wonderful husband, Roger Fielder, children, and grandchildren. Aunt Mary Lou's youngest child David never married, but in recent years, lives at home caring for his mother, Aunt Mary Lou who recently turned ninety-four. Yes, the three-month-old infant in her upstairs crib on that fateful New Year's Day of 1927 with her mama burning to death. On some of my days off during the week, I would take a bus to Raytown and Aunt Mary Lou and I would bond as we would watch the game show *Jeopardy*, then hosted by the late Art Fleming.

My apartment was only a fifteen-minute walk from the famed Country Club Plaza, consisting of eighteen separate buildings. The Country Club Plaza was the first shopping center in the world designed to accommodate shoppers arriving by automobile. The plaza opened in 1923 to immediate success and the longest life of any planned shopping center in the history of the entire world.

# CHAPTER 79

## *The Spring and Summer of 1966*

My time of working at the medical center was brief, it wasn't a bit challenging. Another example of it's a small world: I was working at my ER desk when I noticed a familiar face, his name was David Byers from Brown County, Kansas, located near the Nebraska border. There is a BIC Church in Brown County. At about the age of thirteen, my parents drove up to Brown County with Daddy giving the Sunday morning message, and afterward, the Byers had us for Sunday dinner. I could have said hello to David, however, with no self-esteem and an inferiority complex, I passed that up.

About mid-January 1966, Uncle Dale drove me to a nice used car lot that he was familiar with. I bought a Nash Rambler. I was so tired of all the bus riding which I had done in both '64 and '65. I longed for my independence, once again driving in the wide open spaces of beautiful America. I recall while driving through Ohio, when I first heard the pop hit "Ballad of the Green Beret," recorded by Staff Sargent Barry Sadler himself a Green Beret. This hit would reach number 1 for five weeks on the pop Billboard chart in the spring of 1966. Upon my return to Pennsylvania in January of 1966, I enrolled in several courses at Messiah but I was a long way from graduating. The sixty-four-thousand-dollar question was— could Mother and I coexist? The answer—an emphatic no. Over and over I would hear the words from Mother, *failure*. Again I'm back at a most familiar setting, the Harrisburg Y.

I finally got my lucky break in late spring of 1966. The US Postal Service had a new work opportunity for low-income college students called YOP, which stood for youth opportunity postal. It was part-time work, four hours a night with excellent pay. It was while employed at the Harrisburg Post Office that I refined my ping-pong skills. Every day I would arrive at work early to compete in pickup ping-pong games. I had perfected an almost nonreturnable serve with English on it. Out of the top twenty-five players, I would reach the top three. This postal income also allowed me to buy a nice used red Volkswagen.

The summer of 1966 would have its highs and lows. While employed at the postal service, I got to know a beautiful young lady named Kathy. I had a huge crush on her. On our first date we went to see the newly released movie *The Agony and the Ecstasy*, starring Charlton Heston as Michelangelo, a sixteenth-century Italian sculptor, painter, and architect. I guess we could have chosen a movie a bit more romantic. What are the odds; that we discovered our shared birthday on August 2. However the odds seemed to be against us in having a physical relationship, as she was a devout Catholic and I couldn't say at the time that I was a devout Protestant. I have Catholic friends who I'll meet in heaven. Kathy and I remained good friends.

One early August morning in 1966, I began itching all over my body—in my hair, my underarms, and my pubic area. I called my Uncle Dr. Glenn Hoffman about my symptoms. He told me to drive down to Palmyra at once. It didn't take Uncle Glenn long for his diagnosis—I had one terrible case of lice. I still recall seeing the lice under Uncle Glenn's microscope. Uncle Glenn immediately put me on an antibiotic and he told me never to go back to that apartment. I told my landlady what happened and I checked out of 929 North Second Street in Harrisburg, and I was once again back at a very familiar setting, the Harrisburg Y.

# CHAPTER 80

## My Demons of Addiction

I now must come to share the most difficult part of my life story and that's of my own dark demons of sexual addiction. The lonely cruel life of Ken was in progression. It's a Saturday in my lonely life in the fall of 1966, and I'm on a Trailways bus to New York City. Upon my arrival in Lower Manhattan, I immediately got a room at the local YMCA in the Big Apple. I'd never been on a subway, and I'd heard so much about Coney Island, a residential Brooklyn neighborhood known for its beaches and amusement parks. In this era every July 4, Coney Island is host to the Big Nathan hot dog ten-minute eat off. In recent years, a young man, Joey Chestnut, has held the world record by eating seventy hot dogs in ten minutes. This past July 2019, Joey Chestnut broke his own world record by eating seventy-four hot dogs. You've got to be kidding!

I was now on the subway headed for Coney Island. Upon arriving at the Coney Island exit, I had absolutely no idea where I was. There wasn't a beach nor an amusement park in sight. I thought that maybe there was more than one Coney Island exit. Seeing no beaches or amusement parks, my innermost sordid thoughts came at hoping to find a lady of the night. Perhaps that was my intention all along in taking the subway to Coney Island. I literally walked for blocks, even into the most darkened areas, hoping that I might find a lady for a quick fix. After several hours of walking not meeting a soul, I got back on the subway, headed back for Lower Manhattan. Remember, I had just turned twenty-two and I was so ignorant of the consequences or the risk factor I had just taken. I did tour one historical landmark at 350 Fifth Avenue, the Empire State Building.

The Empire State Building stood as the world's tallest building until the completion of the World Trade Center North Tower in Lower Manhattan in 1972, and then again was the tallest building in the world until the new One World Trade Center surpassed it while under construction in April of 2012. The tallest building in the world now with its tower, is the Burj Khalifa skyscraper in Dubai, United Arab Emirates, with its tower of 2,722 feet to the top. Also it has the world's fastest elevator, whizzing up to the 124th floor in just thirty- five seconds. Reflecting fifty-three years later, would I take that same trip to the Big Apple and get on the subway for Coney Island? No way! I've come to realize that God had his guardian angel protecting me on that September day of 1966.

Shortly after my trip to the Big Apple, I hopped on a Trailways bus for the short trip down 83 South to downtown Baltimore. I had heard about a notorious area called the block. It was known for its vice and prostitution. I walked in and out of several adult shops not spending a penny. I must be honest in admitting that my sole purpose in taking that trip to the block was to watch X-rated movies or to find sex. Yes, I must admit, I was a bit embarrassed going in and out of Satan's dwelling. I returned to Harrisburg again having not spent a penny.

I was constantly preoccupied with sex. A small section in Uptown Harrisburg at Broad Street and Third in the 1960s to early '70s was known for its vice and prostitution. I would drive my VW up to Broad and Third Street and park for up to three to four hours at a time. I might not find a lady of the night, yet I got what's called the thrill one gets when night after night, going through the same ritual. This nightly ritual went on for well over two years. From time to time I would pick up a lady, getting my quick fix; and at the end of the night, I was ridden with guilt. I hit rock bottom one night when a lady I'd picked up stole seventy dollars from under my front seat. Why was a twenty-two-year-old so preoccupied with sex? The sad truth is my family was truly dysfunctional. My family life was one big lie. Was I physically abused? I can't put enough emphasis on this question? When an eight to nine- year-old is forced to spend up to three hours locked up in a darkened outside cellar and totally abandoned, and not getting nature's vitamin D sunshine that God created in the growing process, yes, that's physical abuse. My lonely aching heart was starving for love, just a little hug, a little affection, it never came.

# CHAPTER 81

## *My Mental Illness and Its Torment*

What's the purpose of my writing my life story, sharing about consequences that I certainly can't be proud of? It's being written for the therapeutic purpose with the emphasis on mental illness. It's my hope that my life story of having suffered from both double whammies, both of witnessing abuse and of myself being traumatically abused, can be of help and therapeutic to those who have suffered as I have. And there is hope for all who have been abused. I've come to accept the fact that experiencing the darkness of one's suffering is the first step in your recovery from traumatic abuse. In all sincerity, in all my adult years, I was unaware that I was emotionally and physically abused. It's taken me sixty-six years to realize the traumatic abuse I suffered. It took me writing my memoir, these many years later, to accept the fact that I was emotionally and physically abused. I've come to accept the fact that my mental illness was sown on the horrific New Year's Day of 1927.

The following is from an article called *Good Therapy* by Angela Nickerson of New South Wales in Sydney, Australia. "When a child experiences the death of a parent the emotional trauma can be devastating." Nickerson and her colleagues analyzed data from 820 adults who had experienced the death of a parent during childhood. In their studies, they found the younger a child was at the time of the loss, the more likely they were to develop health problems, including anxiety and substance abuse. In my case history of mental illness, it's been acute anxiety and severe depression that has tormented me for a lifetime.

In my research on mental illness, I've come to find that if a parent is missing in a young child's life, it's impossible to replace him or her no matter how good the other parent is, the void loss of the deceased parent will always be felt. No matter how young or old you are when this traumatic event happens, nothing can prepare you for the loss of a parent and there's nothing that can help you get over the pain or loss of a mama who has loved you unconditionally. When my mother witnessed her own mama burning to death, that had to have left a gaping black hole in little five-year-old Faithe's heart and life as she was the oldest witness on the scene at only five.

What's unconditional love? Webster tells us it's known as "affection without any limitations," or love without conditions. Papa Irvin no matter how great the trauma and hurt he suffered due to the loss of his dearest Anna Zelma, his unconditional love for whom he called his five little angels would continue. Riches couldn't break up his family with the offer from the rich young couple who wanted to adopt three-month-old Mary Lou. Dr. Bob Murray PhD, states, "Nearly every researcher agrees that early childhood trauma, those that happen before the age of six is the root of most long-term depression, anxiety and every emotional and psychological illness." So it was with my mother.

Please believe me, I witnessed this all firsthand—my mother's long-term depression, her mental illness, and believe me, as a young boy beginning at age eight and being emotionally and physically abused by Mother and my witnessing this long-term abuse on Daddy, the result is my own life of severe depression and acute anxiety. I've been there, done that, and believe me it's not fun. Nothing can fill that void of unconditional love.

My mother had all kinds of odds going against her in that the most severe trauma of witnessing her mother burning to death, the brain needs an environment where there can be a safe time for the brain's process of recovery. My mother didn't have this chance for her brain to begin its process of recovery from seeing her mama put in what she called that big black hole. Why didn't young Faithe have this chance? Simply put, there wasn't the time. Her papa suffered one traumatic event after another in his young adult life and Faithe was there to witness all of Papa's traumas. In a three-year period, Faithe witnessed her mama Anna burning to death, she being the oldest witness, her uncle Harry being killed instantly, having his limbs torn off by a pulley belt of a threshing machine, and a cyclone leveling there house and all its farm buildings. These three tragic events took place from January 1, 1927, to mid-April 1930. There simply was no safety net for Mother's brain to begin the healing and recovery process. Also Faithe didn't have access to the mental health resources of today. An innocent five-year- old witnessing her mama's most horrific death has been linked to the next generation to her son Ken and his life of acute anxiety and severe depression, with the chain link continuing to his own children's generation. Yes, I've more love for my mother than I've ever had due to my research on her lifelong mental illness. However guilt and shame can travel from generation to generation, in this family's case history, to four generations.

# CHAPTER 82

## Ken Musser's Tender Love

Today as I'm writing my memoir in January of 2020, you will not find a more tender loving, more huggable gentleman on God's earth than Ken Musser. I truly sincerely feel and know that what I'm about to express may be the most important part of my true story. In the last number of years, almost always when texting, speaking on the phone, or in person, I'll say those special three words to my three children, *I love you*, and my children replies back, "I love you, Dad."

Many times they're the first ones to say those four magic words. I have eleven wonderful grandchildren, the two oldest are boys, ages twenty-one and nineteen. Both will tell me in person, "I love you, Pop." This past week, the nineteen-year-old brought food around to me and we hugged and he said, "I love you, Pop."

Even my third oldest grandchild, my sixteen-year-old princess says those three magic words in person and when texting on the phone, "I love you, Pop." Even several of my younger grandchildren are telling me in person, "I love you, Pop." And how did this all begin—with me saying those three magical words, *I love you*. Missing out on all that loving tenderness when I was growing up has just overwhelmed my heart with an abundance of giving tender loving hugs. Ken's well of giving tender loving hugs will never run dry. I'm so grateful that as an abused boy I did receive those tender loving hugs from my Grandpa Hoover which I shall forever cherish. As a young boy, with Grandpa in his rocker, he would take me in his arms, squeezing me with tender loving hugs. Papa's love for his five young daughters was an enduring limitless unconditional love.

Early in July of 1966, while employed by the US Postal service, I was driving a US mail van, collecting mail from the US blue postal mail containers, when I began getting sharp pains in my groin and lower back area. I was in such excruciating pain that I drove straight to the ER at Harrisburg General Hospital and was immediately admitted. The diagnosis was a kidney stone. I would be in Harrisburg General for three days and nights before passing the stone. A little sidenote from my hospital stay: Numerous times, I've referred to my exceptional memory. I was in my hospital bed on July 30, 1966, listening to the legendary WCMB radio announcer Pete Wambach who, on this day, was celebrating his fiftieth birthday. Wambach's signature greeting every morning was, "It's a beautiful day in Central Pennsylvania." Wambach was born on July 30, 1916, and passed away on May 17, 2008, at age ninety-one.

# CHAPTER 83

## Super Bowl 1

On January 15, 1967, what would soon come to be known as the Super Bowl took place at the Los Angeles Memorial Coliseum with the Green Bay Packers representing the (NFL), playing against the Kansas City Chiefs representing the(AFL), the new league founded by the late Lamar Hunt and the future president and owner of the Kansas City Chiefs. What's so amazing about this, I was watching this game at Daddy's and Mother's home at 409 Berkshire Road, Mechanicsburg PA. It's the only time I would ever watch a sporting event in their home where they lived for thirty-four years. The National Football League Packers were a heavy favorite with the NFL being the established league. Each team was led by two future Hall of Fame quarterbacks, the Packers Bart Star, and the Chiefs Len Dawson. To this day it remains the only Super Bowl to have been simulcast in the US by two networks. NBC held the rights to nationally televise AFL games while CBS had the rights to broadcast NFL games. Daddy and I watched NBC with their talented duo with legendary Hall-of-Fame announcer Curt Goudy doing the play-by-play and the Hall of Fame University quarterback at Missouri Paul Christman doing the color commentary.

The first half of Super Bowl 1 was competitive as the Chiefs outgained the Packers in total yards 181–164 with the Packers leading at half-time 14–10. However early in the third quarter, Green Bay safety Willie Wood intercepted a pass and returned it 50 yards to the Chiefs 5-yard line and the route was on with the Packers scoring 21 unanswered points in the second half. Packers quarterback Bart Starr completed 16 of 23 passes for 250 yards and two touchdowns with 1 interception and was named the MVP. The final score was 38–10 Green Bay. It just happened that these were my two favorite teams so I couldn't lose, and it's one of the few championship games that I didn't have to get emotional. Yes, I'm an extremely emotional person. What a list of future Hall of Famers who played in this first Super bowl; the KC Chiefs future Hall of Famers: Lamar Hunt, owner; Hank Stram, coach; players Bobby Bell, Buck Buchanon, Len Dawson, Johnny Robinson, Emmitt Thomas. Green Bay Packers future Hall of Famers: Vince Lombardi, head coach; players Herb Adderly, Willie Davis, Forest Gregg, Paul Hornung, Henry Jordon, Jerry Kramer, Ray Nitschke, Dave Robinson, Bart Star, Jim Taylor, Willie Wood. With these two teams, you could say it's a who's who of Hall of Famers.

Superstar quarterback of the KC Chiefs Len Dawson was the first great quarterback from the college known to be the cradle of quarterbacks— Purdue University. The following are all former All-American quarterbacks at Purdue: Len Dawson, 1953–1956; Bob Griese, 1964–1966; Mike Phipps, 1967–1969; Gary Danielson, 1970–1972; Jim Everett, 1981–1985; Kyle Orton, 2001–2004; and last but the greatest, a sure first-ballot Hall of Famer, Drew Brees, 1997–2001. Yes, this was one of those fun and happy days with Daddy who I truly bonded with through our love of sports.

# CHAPTER 84

## The Incomparable Bob Gibson

Sadly the YOP postal came to an end in late summer of 1967. In September of 1967, I began work at Sears and Roebuck in the Colonial Park area of Harrisburg. I was a stocker at Sears and the date was October 12, 1967, the seventh and final game of the World Series between the St. Louis Cardinals and the Boston Red Sox. I'm in the stock area with a radio being on. This would be the World Series that the great Bob Gibson from Omaha, Nebraska, cemented his reputation as an unhittable post-season pitcher. Gibson allowed only three total runs over three complete games, just an unreal accomplishment! One more little tidbit from the 1967 World Series: the late Ken Bret, older brother of Hall of Famer George, became the youngest pitcher in World Series' history at age nineteen years, twenty days, when he pitched one-third of an inning. Just another illustration of how the world of sports was such a comfort for me, my solid rock to lean on through my years of suffering emotional abuse.

# CHAPTER 85

## *The Ice Bowl*

It's a Sunday December 31, 1967, the setting, my small room at the Harrisburg, Pennsylvania, YMCA at North and Front Street. I was listening on my transistor to what has become known as the Ice Bowl. It's the National Football League championship between America's team the Dallas Cowboys and the Green Bay Packers, Ken Musser's team. It's considered one of the two greatest football games ever played, along with the NFL championship sudden death overtime game of 1958, won by the Baltimore Colts over the New York Giants. The Ice Bowl game was coached by two future Hall of Fame coaches Vince Lombardi of the Packers and Tom Landry of the Cowboys.

The Ice Bowl was played at frosty Lambeau Field in Green Bay, Wisconsin, with a game time temperature, a balmy -15 degrees with a wind chill at -48 degrees. Near the game's end the thermometer read -20. With 4.50 left in the game and Dallas leading 20–17, the Packers last offensive possession has come to be known as "the drive." At the time the wind chill was -70 degrees. The future Hall of Fame quarterback Bart Starr took possession on his thirty-two-yard line with running back Donny Anderson and full back Chuck Mercein picking up rushing yards on the icy field; Mercein ran out of bounds to stop the clock. Starr dropped straight back on first down and fired a thirteen-yard pass to Boyd Dowler over the middle. Cornell Green's tackle slammed Dowler's helmet off the icy turf and Max McGee replaced Dowler. Starr then flipped a pass to Mecein who ran out of bounds with 1:11 to play. Following a block by left tackle Bob Skoronski, Mercein shot through the hole to the three-yard line. Running back Anderson carried on the next play to the one-yard line for a first down. Twice Anderson attempted to run the ball into the end zone, but both times, he slipped on the icy field when taking the hand off, and was tackled inside the one-yard line. By then the thermometer read -20°F and the Packers called their last time- out. With the Packers at the Dallas two-foot-line with 11 seconds remaining, Starr goes to the sidelines and said to Lombardi, "Coach, the linemen can get their footing for the wedge." A very simple blocking scheme. Bart Starr then told Lombardi, "I can shuffle my feet and lunge in."

Lombardi told Starr, "Run it and let's get the hell out of here."

And now the block, the following is a radio replay of the Packers third down and inches with Packer radio announcer Ted Moore calling the game's final play, "Here are the Packers, third down, inches to go to pay dirt 17–14 Cowboys out in front; Packers trying for the go-ahead score. Starr begins the count, takes the snap, He's got the quarterback sneak and he's in for the touchdown and the Packers are out in front 20–17 and the crowds going wild with 13 seconds left."

On that final play, Starr kept the ball and offensive future Hall of Famer Jerry Kramer and center Ken Bowman executed a post-drive (double team) on left defensive tackle Jethro Pugh. And yes, I simply went crazy, yelling so loudly I'm surprised I didn't get kicked out of the Y.

## Ice Bowl: The Aftermath

The aftermath—emotionally both the Packers and Cowboys were spent. In the Packer's locker area the players openly wept. Just how cold was this game for the ages—referee Norm Schacter blew his whistle to signal the start of play and it froze on his lips. As he attempted to free the whistle from his lips, the skin ripped off and his lips began to bleed. The games conditions were so hostile that instead of forming a scab, the blood simply froze to Schachter's face. Future Hall of Fame linebacker Ray Nitschke developed frostbite in his feet and his toes turned purple. At one point during the Ice Bowl, CBS radio announcer and football Hall of Famer Frank Gifford said on air, "I'm going to take a bite of my coffee." Linebacker Dave Robinson had to flag down a random passing motorist for a ride to frosty Lambeau Field. Many Green Bay Packer players were unable to start their cars in the freezing weather, forcing them to make alternate travel arrangements. Dallas wide receiver Lance Rentzel later remarked that on the team flight home to Dallas, "Not one word was spoken on the flight."

Just another illustration from the world of sports as being a place of refuge for me even in this tiny YMCA room. Here I was, all alone with no friends, for three and a half hours where the world of sports brought a peace and comfort to a young man who just a few years earlier, had been forsaken abandoned in that dark locked up outside cellar.

# CHAPTER 86

## *What a Cruel Lonely Life*

The date was April 4, 1968, a day that would become fatal and dark in US history. I was driving over the south bridge in Harrisburg, Pennsylvania, when over the car radio, came the shocking news that Martin Luther King Jr. was fatally shot at 6:00 p.m. CST while standing on the balcony outside his second-story room at the Lorraine Motel in Memphis, Tennessee. King would die at 7:05 p.m. The assassin was a fugitive, James Earl Ray. Almost three months later to the day, I was walking on North Third Street in Harrisburg with my transistor on, when the chilling shocking announcement came that Robert F. Kennedy, while campaigning for the Democratic nomination for president of the US, had been mortally wounded shortly after midnight and he was pronounced dead at 1:44 a.m. PST on June 6, about twenty-six hours after he had been shot.

My lonely cruel life continued into the late 1960s into early '70s. There was a small chain of restaurants in the city of Harrisburg—three to be exact—called Davenports. These were restaurants catered to seniors and to the poor. I would go into a Davenports usually ordering a coffee or soda. Their food wasn't all that great due to the clientele. I would sit there for a couple of hours at a time while reading a newspaper or a book. I would be surrounded with sickly-looking senior citizens, although not all were seniors. I was now drifting further and further away from my peers.

Let me forward to October 25, 1971. I'm sitting in a Davenports on the two-hundred-block East Market Street which had become like a home to me for two to three years. Yes, sadly this was my daily routine for several years. Reflecting on researching mental illness; I see an eight to ten-year old boy locked up in that outdoor basement for three hours at a time, yes that eight- year-old locked up in the outside cellar, forsaken, abandoned, without God's vitamin D sunshine, are one and the same as the twenty-seven-year-old young man, sitting all alone in that restaurant away from his peers, not knowing how to love or how to receive love. Oh how this young man longed to be sitting on his grandfather's lap, getting tender loving hugs, his Grandpa Hoover always being his safe harbor.

On that October day while sitting in Davenports, I was reading the Monday sports section of the *Harrisburg Patriot News*, getting the scores of Sunday's NFL games, when my eyes came upon a story that read, "An NFL Wide Receiver Dies on the Football Field," the article about Chuck Hughes, a wide receiver for the Detroit Lions NFL team. Hughes was returning to the team huddle when suddenly, he dropped to the turf, clutching his chest, collapsing on the field near the Chicago Bears future Hall of Famer Dick Butkus. Hughes died from a coronary thrombosis, one of Hughes coronary arteries was found to be 75 percent blocked, dying of a massive heart attack, the only player to have died on a football field up to that time in 1971. That continued up to the present day in January of 2020. Hughes story is so sad yet remarkable in that the NFL began in 1920; so on the one hundredth anniversary of the NFL with only one death on an NFL football field is quite remarkable. Although on August 1, 2001, Korey Stringer, an offensive tackle for the Minnesota Vikings died from a heatstroke while in training camp. I remember that day as I was in the city of Columbia, Pennsylvania, eating my noon lunch when over my transistor came the shocking news of Stringer's passing. The irony of Chuck Hughes' death is that he was born on March 2, my daughter Carrie's birthday, and passed away on October 24, my late mother's birthday. Again just another illustration of how the world of sports and radio have been there a lifetime for me in what was, for so many years, a cold, lonely, cruel world for me.

My lonely cruel life continued as many nights I would walk into the Harrisburg, Pennsylvania, Train and Bus Depot, spending up to two to three hours sitting all alone on a bench, usually with a newspaper or book. The date was July 19, 1969, and I was sitting on a bench about twelve midnight. I began reading the Harrisburg *Patriot-News*. On the front-page headline was a photo of a young twenty-eight-year-old school teacher, Mary Jo Kopechne. Kopechne was in a car driven by Senator Ted Kennedy on Chappaquiddick Island, near Martha's Vineyard, Massachuetts. While driving on a narrow unlit bridge without guardrails, Kennedy drove his car into Poncha Pond, with the car landing on its roof. Kennedy extricated himself from the vehicle, saving his life, but failed to report the accident until the next day. Kopechne drowned, with the death certificate listing the cause of death as accidental drowning, and for all practical purposes, this accident coverup would forever put an end to Senator Kennedy's presidential aspirations.

# CHAPTER 87

## Bob Gibson's Encore

By 1968 the furthest thing from my mind was continuing my education. What a talented waste of a young man with so much talent for history, whose life was slowly wasting away. In May of 1968 I got a job working with the city of Harrisburg. It was better pay than Sears and it was outdoor work where I seemed to thrive, just as was that six-week asphalt job in the mid-to- late summer of 1962. I worked on a road crew as well as painting fire hydrants. A black man on my construction crew had his transistor on for the 1968 World Series between the Detroit Tigers and the reigning World Series Champs, the St. Louis Cardinals.

The 1968 Major League season will forever be remembered as the year of the pitcher. If Bob Gibson's 1967 World Series heroics weren't enough, how about an encore in 1968. The ace right hander had a Major League season for the ages. Gibson the future Hall of Famer, had a ridiculously low era of 1.12, the third best mark since 1900 and the lowest era in a season not played in the dead ball era which ended around 1920. We were working on East Market Street in Harrisburg and I can recall the exact same spot we were working at when we heard Bob Gibson breaking Sandy Koufax's record of fifteen strikeouts in 1963 with his seventeenth strikeout. The dead ball period ended in 1919, the year that Babe Ruth hit a then-record of twenty-nine home runs. The dead ball period ran from 1900–1920. During the dead ball era there was a lack of home runs and very low scoring games. Even more remarkable was Gibson's throwing an astronomical thirteen shutouts, only three fewer than Grover Cleveland Alexander's Major League record of sixteen shutouts in 1916 in the dead ball era which makes Gibson's feat of thirteen shutouts even more remarkable. In that 1968 season for the ages, Gibson pitched a record live ball three-hundred-plus innings; and in Gibson's twelve starts in June and July, Gibson pitched a complete game in every start including an unheard of eight shutouts in those twelve starts. Really! You've got to be kidding! It's the greatest one-year pitching record ever.

The Detroit Tigers had their own pitching star in Denny McLain who won thirty-one, the most games won by any pitcher in a season since the thirty games won by Jerome Hannah "Dizzy" Dean in 1934. No one has won thirty games since McLain's 1968 season. The star of the 1968 series was lefty "Southpaw" Mickey Lolich who won three games. And what did the future hold for both McLain and Gibson? McLain was charged with embezzlement with organized crime and served prison time. Bob Gibson was not only elected to the Baseball Hall of Fame in 1981, but also named to the All- Century team in 1999; and as for McLain, it should have been election to the Hall of Shame.

With my immense knowledge of Major League baseball, I put Bob Gibson, Bob Feller, Denton "True" Cy Young and Christy Mathewson, as four of the greatest right-handed pitchers behind "The Big Train" Walter Johnson in a league by himself, as the greatest right hander in Major League history. The Detroit Tigers won that sixty-eighth World Series four games to three. Here's a humorous story about Dizzy Dean. Dizzy's younger brother Paul, was a rookie in 1934 when Dizzy was in his prime. As a rookie Paul won nineteen games, including a no-hitter against the Brooklyn Dodgers in the second game of a double header. Dizzy pitched a three-hitter in the first game. After that three-hitter, Dizzy said, "If I'd known Paul was going to pitch a no-hitter, I'd have pitched one too." Dizzy boasted before the 1934 World Series that "me and Paul would win two games each." Dizzy made good on that prediction as Dizzy won the opener and the seventh while Paul won the third and sixth.

In November of 1968 I would finally get out of the city of Harrisburg and move six miles west to Mechanicsburg, Pennsylvania which in a way, felt like I was returning to my native Abilene as both were about the same in population and size. I began work at the Book of the Month Club in Mechanicsburg. It was a nice change-of-pace job of picking books in a warehouse for subscribers. I'll always remember at noon break we would have a touch football game. I had gotten a nice first floor one-room apartment with kitchen privileges in Mechanicsburg.

# CHAPTER 88

## Therapeutic Wonder of Penn State Football

On my move to Mechanicsburg in the fall of 1968 was when I started to follow Penn State football. For the last fifty years, Penn State football has helped me to keep my sanity. The lonely depressive years of 1968–1974 had me always turning on the radio to Penn State football. In the last fifty years I've never missed a Penn State football game whether on radio or television. The three Penn State play-by-play broadcasters from 1968 to the present are the late Tom Bender, the late Fran Fischer, and the present broadcasting crew of play-by-play voice of Steve Jones and colorman Jack Ham who's the only Penn State player in both the college and pro Football Halls of Fame.

In listening to Penn State football over the years has been so therapeutic for me. During many times of suffering from depression during the last fifty years, I've turned on Penn State football for solace and comfort. Being completely honest, I'm not sure if I would be here today on God's earth if it wasn't for Penn State football. Often when suffering from severe depression and thoughts of suicide, I turned to Penn State football radio broadcast for refuge and safe harbor. It was in the fall of 1966 that the future legendary coach Joe Paterno would succeed his former coach Charles "Rip" Engle for whom he had played quarterback for at the prestigious Ivy League school Brown as Penn State head coach. Penn State football on fall Saturdays would become the most important part of the week for me. This is why and my purpose of writing so much about Penn State football as I've had two rocks to lean on for the past fifty years, my Christian faith and Penn State football.

In years 1968–1970, Penn State would begin its glory years and dominance of Eastern US NCAA division 1 football. In 1968 the Nittany Lions would go 11–0 yet Penn State in the final AP poll, finished behind 9–0 Ohio State and 9–0–1 Southern California. In 1969 Penn State again finished 11–0, but once again the Lions got no respect and no national championship. President Nixon said that he would consider the winner of the December 6 match between the Texas Longhorns and the Arkansas Razorbacks, who at the time in 1969, were ranked number 1 and number 2 respectively as national champions and both were still in the Southwest Conference. During this era in NCAA football, the national champion was selected before the Bowl games. I'll forever remember those words that Coach Paterno was quoted as saying at the 1973 Penn State commencement, "I'd like to know how could the President know so little about Watergate and so much about football." Then Pennsylvania Governor Raymond Shafer appealed to the White House to give the Lions some respect for their back-to-back undefeated seasons. A White House assistant then called Paterno up to invite him and the team to the White House to receive a trophy.

Result: Joe Pa responded with, "You can tell the President to take that trophy and shove it."

Ken Musser says, "Shame on you President Nixon. You were a benchwarmer at Whittier College. You should have at least learned a little about football.

A bit of shocking Penn State "football" trivia: running back Charley Pittman was a member of Joe Paterno's first Penn State recruiting class, an All-American in 1969. Charley Pittman never lost a game he started in high school and neither he nor son Tony, ever lost a game they started at Penn State. Their combined college records are 45–0–1. In the sports world, that is almost a miraculous number. While at Penn State, both Charlie and Tony were academic All-Americans. New York Giants general manager Ernie Accorsi, who spent decades guiding NFL teams, notes, "It's unprecedented; it's hard to believe, that record of father and son at the same university—and the son played in the 'Big Ten'—That is something mind boggling."

A Penn State Bowl game I'll forever cherish is the 1969 Orange Bowl between the Nittany Lions and my native state Kansas Jayhawks. I had a second-floor apartment in Mechanicsburg. I was alone, without a friend in the world. Once again, listening to a Penn State game on radio would bring peace and comfort to my soul, even if just for three hours. This would be the game that would enhance Penn State's national respect as a football power. With a minute to go in the game and trailing by seven, Penn State blocked a KU punt and took over at midfield. Quarterback Chuck Burkhardt completed a deep pass to Bobby Campbell who was knocked out at the three-yard line. Campbell scored on a TD plunge to make it 14–13, pending the conversion attempt. The Nittany Lions went for the two-point conversion to win, however, Burkhardt's pass was incomplete but the Lions were still alive as KU had twelve men on the field. On their second attempt, Campbell scored to give the Nittany Lions the one-point win. Hall of Fame running back John Riggins scored a TD for KU in the game. This game was played at the Orange Bowl in Miami, and yes, my loyalty was with the Nittany Lions.

I can't leave out the 1987 NCAA championship game between the Miami Hurricanes and Penn State. This game is often considered the most memorable championship in all of college football history. Miami had demolished every single opponent in the fall of 1986 arriving at the Fiesta Bowl in Tempe, Arizona, on January 2, 1987, wearing army fatigues, trying their best to psych Penn State out. Penn State consensus All-American linebacker Shane Conlan had a game for the ages with two interceptions and eight tackles. The most memorable interception was his second, returning it to the Hurricanes' five-yard line which set up DJ Dozier's game winning TD.

In closing Penn State football, I must give mention to the Nittany Lions which over the last fifty years, has come to be known as Linebacker U. The Nittany Lions have just had a remarkable number of All-American linebackers like the Louisville slugger factory putting out bats. The following are Ken Musser's ten all-time top Penn State linebackers. Please believe me, all ten of these linebackers could easily be another Division 1 top linebacker. Ken Musser's 10 Greatest Penn State Linebackers: Counting from # 10 to #1 the Greatest

Starting with:

(10) Brandon Short, 1996–1999. His fifty-one tackles for loss is second in program history, ten more than the next linebacker Shane Conlon. Short and La Var Arrington were the first teammates to be named finalists (Butkus Award) given to the country's top linebacker. Any other year, Short most likely wins the award.

(9) Navarro Bowman, 2007–2009. Career stats: 215 tackles, 36 tackles for loss, 8 sacks, 3 interceptions. In his sophomore season, in the absence of the injured Sean Lee, Bowman had 106 tackles, 16.5 tackles for loss, and 4 sacks as a red shirt sophomore. Bowman was a two-time All-Big Ten first team and All-Pro first team four times.

(8) Sean Lee, 2007–2009. Career stats: 325 tackles, 29.5 tackles for loss, 11 sacks. Joe Paterno labeled Lee "as one of the best kids" he ever coached. But it's Lee's perseverance that endured him to Penn State fans. Lee tore the ACL in his right knee before his senior year and was named captain and guided the defense from the sidelines. All Lee did upon his return in 2009 was to record 86 tackles and 11 tackles for loss. Let me add a personal note. I've never been a Dallas Cowboy fan, but when I see number 50 Lee playing LB for Dallas, I always root for Lee. Lee has often been out with injuries as a pro, but still, his stats are outstanding with a total of 695 career tackles, 3 sacks, 2 forced fumbles, 4 fumble recoveries, 3 interceptions, and 2 defensive touchdowns.

(7) Dan Connor, 2004–2007. While not generally held in the same regard as Jack Ham, Arrington, or Conlan, Connor is Penn State all-time leading tackler with 419, 35 tackles for loss, and 14 sacks. Connor has 47 more tackles than former teammate Paul Posluszny. And I only have Connor at number 7. I sincerely apologize, Dan.

(6) Greg Buttle, 1973–1969. On any other NCAA team, Buttle's stats could make him number 1 linebacker. For almost three decades, Buttle was Penn State's all-time leading tackler with 343, which is just unreal! A consensus All-American in 1975.

(5)    Dennis Onkotz, 1967–1969. His name is not as familiar as the Hams, Arringtons, Conlans. However, Onkotz, along with David Robinson, were truly the two linebackers who made Penn State Linebacker U. Although a linebacker and because of his speed, Onkotz held the unlikely position of punt returner with an impressive average of over thirteen yards per return. Fifty-two years after graduation, first in school history for interceptions by a linebacker; 11 interceptions by a linebacker—just incredible! Onkotz, drafted by the New York Jets in the 1970 draft, suffered a broken leg just nine games into his career. One of my two all-time favorite Nittany Lions.

(4)    Lavar Arrington, 1997–1999. Known for the Lavar leap against Illinois in 1999. Arrington's 1999 a "season for the ages," 20 tackles for loss, 9 sacks, 2 fumble recoveries, 2 blocked kicks, and 1 interception while being a two-time- All-American and winning the Butkus, Bednarik, and Lambert awards all in one season. How the Heisman trophy voters only made Arrington number 9 in 1999 is "beyond disbelief."

(3)    Jack Ham, 1968–1970. Accolades galore for Ham: In 1970, his senior year at Penn State, Ham had 91 tackles and 4 interceptions. Ham had 3 blocked punts in 1968, a school record not tied until 1989. On December 11, 2014, the Big Ten network included Ham on the Mount Rushmore of Penn State football along with John Cappelletti, who surprisingly is Penn State's only Heisman winner, Lavar Arrington and Shane Conlan. Ham was even better in the NFL, a six-time All-Pro first team. Former teammate and Hall of Fame Coach Tony Dungy wrote, "I have never seen anyone play the outside linebacker position better than Ham. Fundamental, technique, awareness, and athleticism were all exceptional. He was the total package."

(2)    Shane Conlan, 1984–1986. A two-time consensus All American, defensive MVP of the 1987 national championship win over Miami. His career Penn State stats, 274 tackles, 25 tackles for loss, and 16 sacks. Conlan became the sixth two-time Penn State All-American and on the Mount Rushmore of Penn State football.

(1)  Paul Posluszny, 2003–2006. Not Shane Conlan, not even Arrington, not even himself, no, Jack Ham calls Paul Posluszny "best ever linebacker at Penn State. After not missing a Penn State football game on either radio or telecast the past fifty-two years, I agree with Ham. Several of Posluszny's achievement—two-time consensus All- American, two-time Chuck Bednarik Award winner—given annually to the nation's best defensive player. Only current Northwestern Coach Pat Fitzgerald has won that award twice. Posluszny won the Dick Butkus award in 2005 as the country's top linebacker, and the first Nittany Lion to lead his team in tackles for three straight seasons. Paul could very well be on Penn State Mount Rushmore.

# CHAPTER 89

## The Incredible NBA Championship Final of Number 44 Jerry West

I'm in my bedroom on my second-floor apartment in Mechanicsburg, Pennsylvania, on May 5, 1969, watching a classic national basketball championship between the heavily favored Los Angeles Lakers and my beloved Boston Celtics. The Lakers with future Hall of Famers Wilt Chamberlain, Elgin Baylor, and jersey 44 Jerry West were heavy favorites. The aging Celtics were led by their player coach Bill Russell, arguably on the short list of the greatest NBA centers of all time. Several historic facts about this seven-game series: Jerry West, known as "Mr. Clutch," with a series average of 38 points a game, won the finals MVP award despite being on a losing team. This was the first year that a finals MVP award was given to a player on a losing team and it remains so fifty years later. It also marked the first time in history that a road team, the Celtics, won a final game 7, defeating LA 108–106. Zeke from Cabin Creek, West Virginia, had the championship of a lifetime, Cabin Creek being Jerry West's hometown. In game 1, a two-point win for the Lakers, West scored 52 points, and in game 7, West had 42 points, 13 rebounds, and 12 assists. Just a side note: it's Jerry West's silhouette that's on NBA jerseys.

Three months after the Celtics won the 1969 championship, Bill Russell officially announced his retirement. The Celtic dynasty was over, at least the Bill Russell part of it. It's just incredible what the Celtics did during Russell's legendary career, winning eleven titles in thirteen years, a string unmatched by any team in any major sport. An unsung hero in that '69 finals was my all- time favorite Celtic player, Don Nelson, the best sixth man in the game during his era, and Nelson was a pure shooter. The late legendary Celtic broadcaster Johnny Most pinned the nickname "Dynamite Don" to Nelson. Nelson would go on to a Hall of Fame career as a coach with a record 1,335 wins in NBA history. Both Daddy and I loved our Celtics.

# CHAPTER 90

## Meeting a Lovely Lady and the Game of the Century

In late August of 1970, positive happenings began for me. I got the nicest apartment in Mechanicsburg. It was a lovely second floor efficiency apartment. In September of 1970, I resumed my studies at Messiah College, commuting as a part-time student for the next three years. Also I would land the perfect job for the next three years, that of being a full-time night custodian in the Cumberland Valley school district near Mechanicsburg, Pennsylvania. It was a position at the Middlesex Elementary School. The hours were from 3:30 p.m.–11:00 p.m. Reflecting some fifty years later, this would be the perfect job for me due to my acute anxiety, working by myself.

Shortly after beginning work at Middlesex in the fall of 1970 I became acquainted with a second grade teacher named Roxanne. She was a year older than me. Roxanne and I dated off and on for about three years. Roxanne invited me to go with her to a Methodist Church youth group in the Pocono Mountains between Christmas 1970 to New Year's Day 1971. I led in devotions with the boys in their dormitory. I was a huge Nebraska Cornhusker football fan, and that New Year's evening, January 1, 1971, Nebraska played in the Orange Bowl against number 5 LSU. Earlier that New Year's Day, both top ranked Texas and number 2 Ohio State had lost their bowl games; and that New Year's evening, Nebraska's 17–12 win over fifth rank LSU gave the Cornhuskers their first national championship under legendary Coach Bob Devaney. Tom Osborne in his second season as offensive coordinator, would earn legendary status himself, winning three national championships at Lincoln for the Big Red.

Roxanne and I had a nice relationship, however she was living at home with her parents and she was hesitant about getting serious. Also I just couldn't seem to handle a long-term relationship with a lady. Reflecting now almost fifty years later, after doing my research and writing my memoir, I've come to realize that it was due to my late mother's having me locked up in that outside albatross for three years, all alone, forsaken in complete solitary. How cruel my mother was to me, robbing me of my childhood, my stunted growth without sunshine.

I was in my second floor lovely apartment on Thursday November 25, 1971, when a game which has come to be known as college football's game of the century, was being played at Owen Field in Norman, Oklahoma. The game pitted number 1 Nebraska versus number 2 Oklahoma, played before a televised record of 55 million homes. It was a battle of wills, the Cornhuskers top-ranked defense against the nation's most productive offense with OU's wishbone offense, averaging over 472 rushing yards per game—an NCAA record. The *Sports Illustrated* magazine had on its cover Nebraska linebacker Bob Terrio and Oklahoma running back Greg Pruitt nose to nose beneath the headline, "Irresistible Oklahoma Meet Immoveable Nebraska." Nebraska had a defense for the ages with consensus All-Americans and two Outland trophy winners in defensive tackle Larry Jacobson and middle nose guard Rich Glover, along with two-time defensive end All-American Willie Harper. The Huskers' offense was led by superlative junior flanker Johnny Rodgers, a future Heisman trophy winner, and quarterback Jerry Tagge, along with bullish tailback Jeff Kinney. The Sooners had their own All-American in QB Jack Mildren, who rushed for over 1,000 yards that season, and Heisman candidate HB Greg Pruitt who that season averaged a stunning 9.5 yards, rushing a carry just an unbelievable stat.

The Cornhuskers struck first with lightning Johnny Rodgers, shocking the Sooners with a 70-yard punt return for a TD. In the second half, Jack Mildren led the Sooners with a pair of rushing TDs, and with 7:05 left in the game, OU was up 31–28. The Cornhuskers got the ball back on their own 26-yard line. Then on the OU 48-yard line Huskers QB Jerry Tagge threw to the magnificent Rodgers who broke tackle after tackle and ran to the 15-yard line. I remember Jeff Kinney carrying four consecutive times, the last resulting in his fourth TD of the game, regaining the lead 35–31 and Cornhuskers sacks of Mildren on third and fourth down gave the Cornhuskers the win. Would you believe that in that final AP poll for the 1971 season; Nebraska, Oklahoma, and Colorado, all from the Big 8 conference, ended up first, second, and third? The top two teams in NCAA history had never been from the same league, let alone three teams.

The sporting news in 1988 named the 1971 Cornhusker team as the greatest team of the twentieth century. I shall forever remember this being the greatest college game that I ever watched. At game's end, I was simply going crazy on my recliner. Just another instance of how the world of sports, if only for three and a half hours, helped me to let my emotions go and enabled the severe depression and acute anxiety to leave.

# CHAPTER 91

## Graduation and the Break of a Lifetime

One evening in the summer of 1972 while in my second floor apartment, I began to get contortions in my face. It's like my face was going into convulsions with my having no control of the contractions of the facial muscles. I called Uncle Glenn Hoffman up from a pay phone on West Market Street in Mechanicsburg. I was hardly able to speak to Uncle Glenn. Uncle Glenn called in a prescription to Daniel's Pharmacy which went to work almost instantly for me. Uncle Glenn was always there for me, a best friend. In the years to come, I would find out the hard way about the risk of taking different meds at the same time. That will come up later. Uncle Glenn and I just had one difference of opinion on an NFL subject. He loved his Dallas Cowboys, partly due to their head coach Tom Landry who was a devout Christian. There has never been love lost between the Dallas Cowboys and me. I shall forever cherish Uncle Glenn and my intense ping-pong games. Uncle Glenn was sixteen years my senior and we almost always battled to a draw in our games. Uncle Glenn passed away too soon in 1994 from pancreatic cancer. Uncle Glenn was always there for me.

June 14, 1972, would go down in history as an historic weather day in the Southern and Eastern US. Hurricane Agnes moved slowly across the Yucatan Peninsula. The damage Agnes caused in Mexico is unknown. There were twenty-six confirmed twisters in both Florida and Georgia. The hardest-hit state with damage done by Agnes was Pennsylvania. On June 21 and 22, Agnes would drop eighteen inches of rain on Harrisburg. Overall Agnes caused 128 fatalities and nearly 43 billion in damage, and

I was living right in the center of this one horrific storm in South Central Pennsylvania.

After eleven years, I finally graduated from Messiah on May 5, 1973, with a degree in religious education and was only two history courses short of a double major. Daddy and Mother did make my graduation, of which I was grateful, and took me out for dinner. Sitting next to me at the commencement was Phil Musser, a nephew of Uncle Virgil Wenger, and we shared August 2 birthdays. I was still leading a lonely life. I shall ever remember where I ended up that late afternoon on the day of my graduation. Yes, I would walk into the Davenport restaurant on East Market in Harrisburg and my lonely life went on what should have been a celebratory day. I would continue working at Middlesex Elementary that summer of 1973, and then in early September of '73, my break of a lifetime came.

I had recently applied with the US Postal Service for training on what was called an LSM machine. It was a three-week intensive training period. It was a letter-sorting machine involving zip codes of the entire US. LSM operators would use some twenty keyboards to type in two or three numbers of the zip code, with the result of the mail being sent into one of 277 or more bins representing sections of the country. As an operator I sorted mail at the rate of sixty letters a minute. It was an extremely tough three-week training, but on the last day, I prevailed and was now officially employed by the United States Postal Service. The money was great as were the benefits. However by spring of '74, the LSM was driving me crazy, so very stressful, and my production was off. I did have a chance of becoming a letter carrier. However, I was having difficulty concentrating, and at the time, I had no idea that my life was that of severe depression and acute anxiety.

# CHAPTER 92

## The Most Depressive Summer of 1974

For several months I had been in contact with the Brown Memorial Home located in my beloved native Abilene, Kansas. The home is a senior retirement center with its setting on a beautiful hill just south of Abilene. I had been in touch with the superintendent of the home, the Reverend Harold Correll. Harold via our correspondence, had told me that he and his wife Letha would welcome me to their staff at Brown's. Incidentally I had a good connection with Harold in that his brother Frank Correll, was superintendent of Dickenson County Public Schools from the mid-1940s to mid-1950s at the time of Daddy's teaching. I had accepted the position at Brown's before having notified the postal service. I had absolutely no idea of what was to become the most depressive summer of my entire life. That depressive summer in 1964 at Little Rock would pale in what lay ahead in the summer of '74. Yes, the summer of 1974 was to become the darkest period of my life. Reflecting years later, I was completely in the dark of what a state of depression I was in on my move to Kansas. The chance to return to my beloved hometown was too irresistible, too compelling. It would be a decision that would leave me torn up inside of leaving a secure government job. I was soon to find out that the right place for me at that time in my life wasn't to be Abilene. I've come to understand forty-five years later, that I wasn't ready for such a drastic move. There's a saying that one can never return to his hometown and I was about to find that out, particularly when I had no idea of the severe depression I had at the time of the move.

To this very day I'm still mystified in the fact that I took a Greyhound to Abilene instead of driving my red Volkswagen since I've always enjoyed driving so much. My dearest Aunt Carol was there to pick me up at the Abilene Greyhound depot, the same depot where almost twelve years earlier, I had departed for Messiah College in Grantham, Pennsylvania. Upon my arrival at Brown's home, I would find my living quarters to be in the basement where other residents also had rooms. My room was small and carpeted. My duties were to lead Sunday morning chapel service, drive residents to their doctor appointments, to their bank, and to the drugstore to get their meds. I would also when needed would wash the dishes in the kitchen. In the basement was a pool table. I would pick up a lot of games with the residents which helped me to keep my sanity.

If there was a positive during this most depressing summer, it was that my two Aunts Carol and Delores, and my Uncle Harry all lived in Abilene but I seldom visited them. Uncle Harry was one of those rare individuals who could do it all with his hands: a carpenter, an electrician, and a mechanic. Uncle Harry for years was a lineman and supervisor for Kansas Power and Light.

I'll forever remember that twenty-two years earlier as a boy of eight, Uncle Harry made me that basketball backboard that would become my field of dreams, an escape from the hundreds of hours of being locked up in my outdoor albatross. This one Saturday Uncle Harry and his wife, Aunt Carolyn had me over for the day. Uncle Harry ever busy, was building an addition to his house. I was doing my best to help Uncle Harry out. While hammering I got my right index finger caught between the hammer and the stake. I was bleeding profusely. Uncle Harry made the ten-minute drive to the Abilene General Hospital in five minutes. I had some thirty stitches to my index finger, which up to the present day is deformed. That Saturday evening Aunt Carolyn had one delicious supper. To this day, the fried chicken dinner Aunt Carolyn had prepared is still the most delicious chicken dinner I've ever eaten.

My first couple of weeks at Brown's Home went well. One evening a close boyhood friend Ron, drove out to Brown's where Ron and I had a great time throwing football on Brown's large beautiful front lawn. Tragically six years later in 1980, Ron would be killed in a fiery car truck accident while driving in Western Kansas. While at Brown's in my free time, I would spend it alone in my "little corner of the world," as Anita Bryant's song goes. I was shut off from the rest of the world, a world of severe depression.

Easing my depression temporarily, I would listen to Kansas City Royals baseball games. That summer of 1974, the Royals had a young rookie third baseman phenom George Brett. Brett would go on to have a storied Hall of Fame career. It was in 1980 when the Royals won the American League Pennant that Brett would hit for a batting average of .390, the highest average since the remarkable 1941 season of the "Splendid Splinter" Ted Williams who hit the magical .406. What's so remarkable about Williams' feat is that going into the final day of the season, he was batting .39955, rounding out to .400. Williams could have rested on his laurels, instead "Teddy Ball game" played in the final day, double header at Shibe Park in Philadelphia, the home of Connie Macks, Philadelphia Athletics. All Williams did in that double header was to bat 6 for 8 rounding out to a .406 batting average. And at the age of thirty-nine in 1957, Williams was generally regarded as the greatest hitter who ever lived batted .388.

Ted Williams magical 1941 season is just one of the many hundreds of facts, birthdates, and deaths of famous people from all walks of life, that I've come to memorize beginning as an eight-year-old in 1952, locked up in my albatross prison reading sports and history books. I was so depressed and longed to return to Pennsylvania. I had requested a conference with Harold Correll and he told me that he could tell of my unhappiness. We mutually agreed it best that I return to Pennsylvania.

To let you know the state of my mind, I had no sooner arrived back in Harrisburg that I longed to go back to Brown's. Without my realizing it, depression had taken over my life. I'm sure by now the reader is aware of the exceptional memory that the good Lord has blessed me with. Yet forty-five years later I can't remember of staying a night in Pennsylvania. I only remember calling Harold Correll up and asking if I could come back. Harold was sympathetic and his answer was yes. The sixty-four-thousand-dollar question was—would it work out a second time? Reflecting forty-five years later, I can now see how depression had taken over my life. I couldn't think straight; I couldn't even remember of staying a night in Pennsylvania. It's like that part of my life has been blocked out. I don't even remember of getting back on a Greyhound. Did I stay in Pennsylvania several nights and what about my car? Why didn't I drive it back, as by this time I was really beginning to dislike riding the bus. Again I'm back on a Greyhound, destination Brown Memorial Home. Both Harold and his wife, Letha welcomed me back with Christian love. I so wanted to keep positive, but when your entire being is wrecked with depression that's impossible. Night time couldn't come fast enough for me so I could sleep.

It was during my first week back at Brown's when I was driving several residents into town. That afternoon I drove two residents, one to her medical appointment and the other lady to the Citizen's Bank. Upon arriving at the bank, I helped the lady walk with her stroller into the bank. Upon entering the bank, lo and behold, I saw a familiar face sitting at a desk to my right, an old elementary and high school friend, Gary, a year younger than myself. To once again point out my exceptional memory, at recess one day, while in the fourth grade, we had a softball game going. As I was stepping up to home plate to bat, this same Gary asked me, "Kenny, are you Catholic?" Gary must have thought that I crossed myself when getting into the batter's box. I also remember of Gary having an emergency appendectomy while attending Talmage Elementary. I was soon to find out that at the age of twenty-nine, Gary was vice president of the Citizen's Bank. Well, about now, my self-esteem and inferiority had hit rock bottom.

One of the few positives during that most depressive summer of 1974 was that during the summer and fall months, the Abilene orchestra would hold a weekly concert at the band pavilion at Eisenhower Park. I've always enjoyed listening to the big band music era of the 1940s: the Glenn Miller Band, Jimmy and Tommy Dorsey, and Duke Ellington. I would drive residents to the concert which would become a temporary refreshing change for me. One other fun time was playing a one-on-one basketball game at the city park with a twenty-one or twenty-two-year-old man named Stanley. Stan attended the Abilene BIC Church when Daddy was pastor from 1955–1960. Stanley son of a minister, would go to seminary, later becoming Pastor of the same church but not the same building, the Abilene B&C church.

To let you know of my depressed state, I can't remember visiting my Aunt Delores Kelly and family that entire summer. Harold's hobby was fishing, and this one afternoon Harold wanted me to walk along with him to a small creek just east of Brown's. I'd hardly ever fished in my entire life, and this afternoon, I was extremely depressed. I know that I disappointed Harold but my heart wasn't into fishing that day.

The crises came one late July afternoon. I was in the basement at Brown's on the telephone with Aunt Carol. I cried and I couldn't stop crying. Aunt Carol now realized that I was sick and needed help. She knew of an outstanding psychiatric hospital located about an hour and fifteen minutes southwest of Abilene. I was evaluated and the diagnosis was severe depression. I could have been admitted that day, but with no health insurance I wasn't but probably should have been. How many times that summer of '74 did Aunt Carol come through for me? I was so overwhelmed with depression. I was missing my VW and needing my freedom. I was longing for the wide open spaces. Again Aunt Carol would come through for me. She had heard that a first cousin of my mother's was coming back to visit immediate family in the Abilene area and Martha needed transportation. Martha agreed to drive my car back. Aunt Carol wanted to surprise me as Martha was on the road driving my VW. What a morale booster it was, having my car.

The date was August 9, 1974, and I was relaxing in the social room at Brown's while watching television and the resignation of president of the US, Richard Milhous Nixon. These were my last days at Brown Memorial Home. Again Aunt Carol was there for me. A senior-age man, David Engle, who I knew from Daddy's pastorate at the Bethel BIC Church was seeking a ride to visit family in Ohio. This would give me some gas money and as the Willy Nelson song goes, "I was back on the road again."

Arriving back in Harrisburg, Daddy had gotten me a temporary room as I had called him, letting him know of my coming back and driving his friend David Engle back to Ohio. To let you know of my state of mind, several days after I had gotten back, I was at a phone booth in Uptown Harrisburg, placed a call to Harold Correll, requesting to come back; and this time, the answer was no. Shortly after, I had to go back to the US Postal Service to see if I could be reinstated and the answer was no. I remember, when leaving the Harrisburg Post Office, I felt like I was in the valley of death. Without knowing it at the time, in the third week of August of 1974, my being emotionally and physically abused by my mother had now come full circle. This traumatic abuse, having lied dormant for twenty-two years, had now left me as a very lonely man with no hope for the future. In the upcoming years, this abuse would take fruition in my relationship with my three children and my wife.

Letha Correll lived a long godly life. She was born in 1906 and passed away in 2012 at the age of 106. Two brothers Frank and Harold Correll married the two sisters, Letha and her sister.

# CHAPTER 93

## A Young Lady Named Carol

The last place on God's earth that I would want to work would be in the kitchen of my alma mater, Messiah College. However, I needed a job and there was a part-time position working mornings in the kitchen. In the fall of 1974 shortly after returning from my ill-fated Abilene summer, I accepted that position in Messiah's kitchen, while at the same time, getting a nice second floor apartment which had previously been Messiah's music building, Hill View. Due to my excellent work in the Cumberland Valley school district, from 1971–1973, I got a part-time second-shift position at the Good Hope Middle School, Mechanicsburg, Pennsylvania. While working in Messiah's kitchen, I met a lovely young Christian Lady named Carol. Carol from Pottsville, Pennsylvania, a Messiah graduate, had come back toward getting her elementary teaching degree. Carol and I really hit it off, and every day Carol would pack me a bag lunch for my evening custodial job. Meanwhile I had applied for a sales position at a snack food company located near Chambersburg, Pennsylvania. I did get the position in sales with Nibble with Gibbles beginning the first week in January of 1975.

Once again Aunt Rozella and Uncle John Thrush were back in my life. I had lived with them that most delightful summer of 1963 between my freshman and sophomore years at Messiah. Uncle Johns lived on a farm outside of Shippensbug, Pennsylvania, and the snack company was located about fourteen miles away near Chambersburg. I moved in with Uncle John's after New Years and my first day at work with the snack company was Monday January 6, 1975. I had no idea of what was to lie ahead of me, that of acute anxiety. There was a three-week training in which my immediate supervisor Shannon, rode with me. Everything went well those first three weeks. However there was a negative—my sales area was in Lancaster, Pennsylvania, a one-hour-fifty-minute drive to my first stop. On top of that, the company had the governor set at fifty-two-miles-per-hour on the diesel. That came to almost four hours on the road each day just coming and going.

# CHAPTER 94

## *Acute Anxiety*

Most mornings driving to Lancaster, I had a Gospel preacher and singer on WDAC Lancaster, Pennsylvania. About six weeks into the job, I got a new sales supervisor Trent. Each evening after getting back from my daily run, I would load up the van with chips and pretzels for the next-day run and fuel up. If Trent would come up to me and ask me what time I was leaving in the morning, my heart would sink with a hollow pale feeling. That night would be a sleepless one. One morning when Trent was going with me, I drove the fourteen miles to the plant and then turned right around and drove the fourteen miles back to Uncle John's. That entire day I would be ridden with guilt. I would feel so worthless, my entire being was overwhelmed with acute anxiety. Reflecting some forty-four years later and after doing research on my memoir, I've come to the conclusion that my being locked up for those two and a half years in that outdoor locked up prison cellar for up to three hours at a time, abandoned, forsaken, was the root of my anxiety. The seed of my depression and anxiety was sown on that fateful New Year's Day of 1927, and the root continued to grow in that cellar my albatross. I've always had a fear of being one-on-one with another man for a long duration, especially a man who has authority over me in a working environment. I'm an extra sensitive man and I've always had a hard time of both giving and receiving criticism. Anyone who has never lived with acute anxiety doesn't know the hell of living through it.

I've shared with you that morning of driving fourteen miles to the plant and then driving right back the fourteen miles to Uncle John's, that's acute anxiety. Another instance of how acute anxiety overwhelmed and dominated my life: if I knew that my supervisor was going with me on Monday morning, I would drive the fifty-five miles to the Acme food market in Middletown, Pennsylvania, to make sure that no potato chips were out of date. Yes, driving over one hundred miles just to check to see if one snack bag is out of date, that's acute anxiety. Believe me, I did that Saturday drive more than once. Living with acute anxiety you have no self-esteem, no self- confidence, always thinking of failure. It's extremely important that I express for years and years, I wasn't aware of that second double whammy. Yes I knew of Daddy's years of being emotionally traumatized, abused, but I wasn't aware of the second double whammy—that of my being abused.

# CHAPTER 95

## Courting and Marriage

What would keep my spirits up was Carol's driving the fifty-five miles one night during the week, and we had our weekends together. Carol and I had our favorite spots: the South Mountain where we had our privacy, and Wolf's Diner in Dillsburg, about four miles south of Messiah College at Grantham. Wolf's Diner had at each booth a jukebox, where you could put a quarter in and hear your favorite song. We had our favorites: the Carpenters, Olivia Newton John, and Captain and Tennille. Oh how we loved Olivia Newton John's "Have You Never Been Mellow," the Carpenters, my favorite dou, of brother and sister Richard and Karen Carpenter. My favorite Carpenters hits "Top of the World," "Solitaire," "We've Only Just Begun." Carol's favorite dou was Captain and Tennille's and thier hit "Love Will Keep Us Together." Kenny Rogers and Dolly Parton's "Islands in the Stream Carol's favorite." Karen Carpenter, my all-time favorite pop singer, had a one-in-a-million voice. When you heard her singing, you instantly knew whose voice that was. Tragically Karen passed on way to soon. Karen was thirty-three days short of her thirty-third birthday, passing away from anorexia. When Karen Carpenter died, the world lost one of its "greatest treasures." The following are quotes from Pop Superstars about the voice of Karen Carpenter; the legendary Sir Paul McCartney said the following about Karen Carpenter, "She has the best female voice in the world, melody, tuneful, and distinctive". Sir Elton John says of Karen, "She has one of the greatest voices of our lifetime". Madonna says the following, "Karen Carpenter had the clearest, purest voice". With a distinctive three-octave contralto vocal range, Karen was praised by her peers as one of the greatest singers ever. Karen Carpenter had that rare ability while singing to go to what Karen called her "basement". Karen's voice tended toward the melancholy such as her singing of "Solitaire". Author Jim Farfaglia shares of the comfortable melancholy singing range of Karen in her million dollar hit "Solitaire"

Solitaire

There was a man
A lonely man
Who lost his love
Through his indifference

A heart that cared
That went unshared
Until it died
Within his silence

And Solitaire's the only game in town
And every road that takes him down
And by himself it's easy to pretend
He'll never Love again.

Millions and millions like me could identify
with Karen Carpenter's hits

On August 23, 1975, Carol Ann Fisher and Kenneth David Musser were united in marriage at the Dillsburg, Pennsylvania, BIC Church with the groom's Daddy David Musser, officiating, assisted by the Reverend George Kimber, a religious professor at Messiah College. My best man was my late cousin Mahlon Thrush, the groomsmen were my Uncle Dr. Glenn Hoffman and Carol's brother, Kenny. Carol and I moved into a nice clean trailer park just north of Chambersburg. The trailer park was located only eight miles from my work. For the first time in years I was content and at peace.

In late September of 1975, my paternal grandparents, Noah and Vesta Musser, visited us from California. It would be the last time that I would see Grandpa as he went home to glory in 1977. It was Saturday, October 11, 1975, and I was looking forward to watching the World Series between the Boston Red Sox and the Cincinnati Reds. However the weather was so beautiful that at the last minute, we packed up and decided to take a day trip to Skyline Drive, and it was nearing the peak of the fall foliage. Skyline Drive is a historic 105-mile drive along Virginia's Blue Ridge Mountains and the scenery and foliage are breathtakingly beautiful. Oh, and about that 1975 World Series, the Cincinnati Reds won that series four games to three, and in 2003 it was ranked by ESPN as the second greatest World Series ever. It was the perfect World Series, complete with five one-run games and the most famous extra inning game in World Series history which came in game 6, ending with Carlton Fisk's down-the-line blast. I can still recall Fisk hammering a long drive down the left field line and the question was—would it just stay inside the left field foul pole? I remember Fisk waving frantically at the ball, willing it to stay just inside the foul pole and it did. This was an elimination game for the Red Sox so they lived to play another day, however getting beat in the seventh and final game. The Red Sox would have to wait another twenty-nine years (2004) before winning their first World Series since 1918.

On September 16, 1975, I was on the way home from work and had picked up the Pittsburgh Pirate flagship station KDKA. On that Tuesday afternoon, the Pirates were playing at Wrigley Field. A Panamanian, Reggie Stennett, would have a game for the ages. That day, Stennett would have seven hits in a nine-inning game to become the only player in the twentieth century to accomplish that feat. Ironically Stennett's first hit in that game came off Cub starter Rick Reuschel and his seventh hit came off Rick's brother, Paul. What would the odds be for that! In 1977 Stennett was batting .336 for the season and on pace for a possible Hall of Fame career, when he broke his right leg sliding into second base and he never recovered from that. Here's a little bit of baseball trivia: Reggie Stennett was a member of the Pittsburgh Pirates who took the field on September 1, 1971, with the first all- black lineup in baseball history. Just another illustration of my exceptional memory being stored in the left temporal lobe and how the world of sports has come to define my life.

# CHAPTER 96

## Another Trailer Park, Acute Anxiety, and Beautiful Colonial Williamsburg

About a month after Carol and I had moved into the trailer park, my acute anxiety would rise about 100 percent. It so happened that my supervisor Trent and his wife Bobbi, moved into our trailer park, and on top of that, just three trailers from ours. Every night I barely had stepped into our trailer that there was the ringing of the telephone and yes it was Trent. I told Carol that I had to get out of that trailer park. Up to the present day, if I don't recognize a phone number, I will not answer. I've a ringing of the phone phobia going back forty-six years.

Carol in September of 1975 had gotten a substitute position with the West Shore school district near Mechanicsburg, Pennsylvania. It would be a daily hour-fifteen-minute commute. Luckily we were able to find a nice trailer park only three miles from my work. Our new address was St. Thomas, Pennsylvania, located four miles west of Chambersburg.

A famous St. Thomas native was the late Baseball Hall of Famer Nelson Fox, a second baseman for the Chicago White Sox in the late 1940s–1950s. Fox's best Major League season came in 1959 when he was the American League MVP, when the White Sox played and lost in the World Series to the LA Dodgers. The 1954 and 1959 season were the only two years between '49 and '59 that the Yankees didn't win the American League pennant. The other year that the Yankees didn't win the American league pennant was that magical 1954 Cleveland Indian team that won a record 111 games in the still 154-game schedule. Nellie Fox was the third hardest player in Major League history to strike out. Now for a little bit of baseball trivia: in 1951 with the White Sox Fox hit 12 triples and he struck out only 11 times, an incredible stat; and even more incredible, Fox struck out only 216 times in his career, an average of one every 42.7 at bats, just incredible! Fox was also a great fielding second baseman, becoming the first Major League Gold Glove award winner in 1957 and 1958–1959. How many men have played in the Major Leagues? Beginning in 1871 to the present day of 2019, 18,918 players have played Major League baseball. Fox after retiring from baseball was diagnosed with skin cancer and treated for lymphatic cancer. Fox passed away on December 1, 1975, at the still-young age of forty-seven. I do remember watching Fox play on TV and he was a lifelong tobacco chewer. Fox is buried at the St. Thomas Cemetery at St. Thomas, Pennsylvania.

It's early 1976, the US bicentennial, and every morning and evening on my hour-and-fifty-minute drive, several released pop hits would keep me company: (1) the megahit by Sir Elton John, "Philadelphia Freedom," what an appropriate song for the two hundredth birthday of the US. (2) "I'm Not Lisa, My Name Is Julie," recorded by Jessi Coulter, a devout Christian. Jessi Coulter is the widow of the late cowboy outlaw singer Waylon Jennings. This song is a bit different but it's catchy. Go to YouTube to listen to it. (3) Olivia Newton John, "Have You Never Been Mellow." (4) Don Williams, "Till the Rivers All Run Dry." (5) The Bellamy Brothers, "Let Your Love Flow."

In mid-April of 1976 with Carol going on seven months pregnant, we took a trip to Colonial Williamsburg and its cobblestone streets. As a history buff I fell in love with this historic town. What a highlight it was for me to tour the college of William and Mary, founded in 1693 by letters patent issued by King William III and Queen Mary II. It's the second oldest institution of higher education in the US after Harvard University, founded in 1636. American Presidents Thomas Jefferson, James Monroe, and John Tyler were all educated at William and Mary as well as possibly the greatest chief justice of the US Supreme Court John Marshall. I'll forever remember the pink beautiful azaleas at Williamsburg that spring of 1976. And being a history lover, we couldn't pass up seeing historic Jamestown, founded in 1607 by John Smith.

# CHAPTER 97

## *A Fourth Generation Begins*

Carol and I thought we had the possibility of having a bicentennial baby on July 4, 1976. However on Friday, June 25, 1976, at 1:30 p.m., Carol gave birth to a boy David Kenneth Musser at the Chambersburg Hospital. On Saturday Mother and Daddy drove to Chambersburg, Pennsylvania, to see baby David and then took me out for dinner. When David was about a year old, a special guest was coming to the nearby Chambersburg mall. He was none other than Brooks Robinson, known as "The Human Vacuum Cleaner." Robinson along with Michael Jack Smith are generally acknowledged as the two greatest third basemen in Major League Baseball history, although Eddie Mathews and George Bret could make an argument. Certainly Robinson is one of the two greatest fielding third baseman ever along with Michael Jack Smith, although Pie Traynor who played from 1920–1938, is acknowledged as the greatest up to WWII.

David got to meet Brooks and to this day David has a baseball signed by Robinson. The 1970 World Series would bring legendary status to Robinson in the Baltimore Orioles World Series victory over the Big Red Machine, the Cincinnati Reds and their great power hitters. The Reds were led in 1970 by future Hall of Famers Johnny Bench, 45 home runs, 148 RBIs, .293 batting average; Tony Perez, 40 home runs, 129 RBIs; plus another Hall of Famer Joe Morgan, and Pete Rose the all-time-hits leader at the time. Oh, and there's George Foster a 3-time RBI leader and 2-time Home Run leader. Foster hit 52 home runs in 1977 and National League MVP. What a lineup! In addition, the 1970 World Series would be a matchup of two Hall of Fame managers in Earl Weaver of the Orioles and

George "Sparky Anderson" of the Reds. In that 1970 World Series, Brooks Robinson, never known for his hitting prowess, batted .429 with 2 home runs. However it was Brooks' defensive play, making one remarkable play after another. This was the World Series that Brooks got the nickname "The Human Vacuum Cleaner." Robinson's defensive wizardry left Red manager Sparky Anderson saying, "I'm beginning to see Brooks in my sleep. If I dropped this paper plate, he'd pick it up on one hop and throw me out at first." At the time of Robinson's retirement in 1977, his .971 fielding average was the highest ever for a third baseman. Robinson's performance in the 1970 World Series won him the World Series MVP award, presented by *Sport Magazine*, as well as the Hickock Belt as top professional athlete of the year. Ken Musser's top five third basemen of all time: (1) Michael Jack Schmidt, (2) Brooks Robinson, (3) Eddie Mathews, (4) Pie Traynor, (5) George Brett.

Located not far from St. Thomas is the beautiful state park Cowan's Gap. Cowan's Gap was on the western frontier of the original thirteen colonies and stretched back to the French and Indian War (1756–1763). Cowan's Gap includes a beautiful lake with a lovely spacious picnic area. Located only about eight miles from St. Thomas, Carol and I often took a picnic lunch and then we would take one-year-old David for a boat ride on the peaceful calm lake. Cowan's Gap State Park was so much fun, so relaxing, and peaceful, far away from my chronic anxiety.

During the summer of 1977, Carol, David, and I drove out to my beloved hometown Abilene, Kansas, to attend my fifteenth high school reunion. To this day it's the only high school reunion I've attended. We lodged at my Aunt Carol and Uncle Virgil Wenger's home. It was in the spare bedroom at Uncle Virgil's where our second child would be conceived. On our way home we took a southern route. My being a history buff, we visited the log house in which our sixteenth president of the US Abraham Lincoln was born at Hodgenville, Kentucky, on February 12, 1809. Yes, I've had that date memorized in my left temporal lobe since the age of eight. Abraham Lincoln is my personal hero in all of US history. Not far from Hodgenville, Kentucky is the site of the Mammoth Cave National Park, a long cave system of chambers and subterranean passageways. The highlight for both Carol and me was the frozen Niagara section, known for waterfall-like flowstone formations.

Shortly after arriving home in mid-August of 1977 I was to learn that Gibbles was moving a distribution center to Lancaster County, Pennsylvania, where sales of potato chips and pretzels were off the charts. In late September of 1977, we relocated to Mount Joy, Pennsylvania in Lancaster County. Our new home was a nineteenth-century stone farmhouse. We would share one- half of the house with another young couple, Jim and Cindy Yeaglin. Carol and I would begin attending Mount Pleasant BIC Church in Mount Joy. Carol and I would become involved in the church ministry.

# CHAPTER 98

## *Our Children's Early Years*

On Thursday, March 2, 1978, Carol and I welcomed a new baby daughter, Carrie Joy Musser, into our home. Carrie was born at St. Joseph Hospital in Lancaster, Pennsylvania. The day of the week was Wednesday, March 28, 1979. The setting was Three Mile Island Nuclear Power Plant, Middletown, Pennsylvania. An accident had occurred in reactor 2. It was the most significant accident in US commercial nuclear history. Pennsylvania Governor Dick Thornburg had advised evacuation of pregnant woman and preschool-age children who lived within a twenty-mile radius of the island due to the radioactive releases. David wasn't yet three and Carrie earlier that month had turned one. Our house as the bird flies, was located only eight miles from TMI. Carol immediately drove to her home, Pottsville, Pennsylvania, a sixty-mile drive, with David and Carrie.

On Monday, June 9, 1980, Carol and I were blessed with a third child, Maribeth Ruth Musser. All three of our children were towheads, all blond hair. Maribeth was born at the Lancaster General Hospital. That summer of 1980 I planted a garden. I borrowed a rototiller from a friend and I went to work cultivating. The good Lord blessed us with a nice harvest of potatoes, tomatoes, corn, and peas.

In mid-September of 1980 Carol, Maribeth, and I took a trip to Niagara Falls. These family trips were always fun times and a respite of seven days from the acute anxiety from work. We dropped David and Carrie off at Carol's parents in Pottsville, Pennsylvania, and we continued our drive up 81 North to 95 West to Buffalo, New York. What a breathtaking site is Niagara Falls. Carol, three-month-old Maribeth, and I took a boat ride on the famed Maid of the Mist which takes you right under the rainbow bridge, over to the Canadian side, and ending at the Maid of the Mist on the US. side. We also visited the Skylon Tower which we took up seventy-seven feet to the tower observation deck where you could enjoy a panoramic view of the falls. We also took the walking tour under the falls, just as was in the classic movie of 1953, *Niagara*, starring Marilyn Monroe, Joseph Cotton, and Jean Peters. The highlight of Niagara Falls for me was the sight of the rainbow colors at night lighting up the falls majestically.

Our three children went to Grandview Elementary in Mount Joy. All three had a wonderful kindergarten teacher Mrs. Bailey. What a wonderful teacher she was and such a sweet lady. Carol and I were both actively involved at the Mount Pleasant BIC Church in Mount Joy. I was elected Sunday school superintendent for several terms and I also taught Sunday school. For several years, both Carol and I directed the young people church quiz team. The quiz was on a book or books of the New Testament. There were the local quizzes and then the regional finals were held with the winners of the regionals going to the BIC General Church Conference. Carol was also a teacher and heavily involved in the church prayer ministry. Located several blocks from our house was the Mount Joy Park. Carol and I would walk the children to the park. We spent valuable family time there. On one occasion two-year-old David was going down the slipper side when somehow, in a freaky accident, he broke his leg. When Carrie was about ten and Maribeth eight, both were riding their bicycles when wrecking into each other, Carrie suffered a broken clavicle which connects the breastbone and shoulder.

# CHAPTER 99

## Wonderful Family Time on Our Longest Trip

By June of 1982 I'd been with the snack company long enough to get a paid two-week vacation and we used it wisely. These family trips were so therapeutic for me, far away from the daily anxiety of the job, even if just for fourteen days. Our first stop would be at the Gateway Arch in St. Louis, Missouri, the crossroad of the West. The Gateway Arch is located right along the mighty west banks of the Mississippi. The Arch was built at the very location where the founding of St. Louis took place on February 15, 1764 by the French. The Gateway Arch is a 630 feet high monument, clad in stainless steel. It's the world's tallest arch and the tallest man-made monument in the Western hemisphere. What a breathtaking view from the top of the arch.

Our next destination would be in Raytown, Missouri, a suburb of East Kansas City, Missouri. My dearest cousin Jan and her husband Roger Fielder live here. It was Jan, her mother Mary Lou, and my mother and I who took the Greyhound bus to Pennsylvania in the summer of 1950. Their home was located close to a lake, just a beautiful setting. David and Carrie had such a wonderful time wading in the lake with their cousins. We spent a night at Jan's and resumed our travel the next day to my native hometown Abilene, Kansas. We spent a night at my dearest Aunt Carol and Uncle Virgil Wenger's. What lingers in my mind thirty-seven years later was our drive on Highway 10 West from La Junta to Walsenburg, Colorado. Driving for miles, there was a flashing lightning to our south that went on for well over an hour. I've always been mystified by it. It was like a July 4 fireworks. Our initial stop in the Rocky Mountain State was the Great Sand Dunes National Park in Southern Colorado. What fun we all had climbing the highest Sand Dunes in North America, rising to 750 feet with the beauty of rugged fourteen thousand peaks in the Sangre de Cristo mountains in the distance.

From the Great Sand Dunes National Park, I drove north to Canon City, Colorado, to the site of the magnificent Royal Gorge which up to that time in 1982, was the highest suspension bridge at 955 feet in the world. In 2003, the Beipan River Guanxing Bridge in China became the world's highest suspension bridge at 1,214 feet. In the 1950s a miniature railroad was built by the edge of the gorge and an aerial tram was opened in 1969 which our family took advantage of. We got to jump aboard an aerial gondola to glide 2,200 feet across the gorge, 1,200 feet above the river.

We continued north to Colorado Springs, Colorado, where my Uncle Herbert and family lived. Uncle Herbert was the oldest child of my Step-Grandmother Carrie and my Grandpa Irvin Hoover. Uncle Herbert's first wife Aunt Gladys passed away in 1972 from cancer. Born to this union was a daughter Cindy, and sons Greg and Doug. Uncle Herbert would then meet a lovely Christian lady from Ohio named Dawn. Born to this union was a daughter Karen. Uncle Herbert had hoped to take over the farm from my Grandpa Hoover. However, early in life, Uncle Herbert came down with asthma, a chronic disease that inflames and narrows the airways of the lungs. Colorado Springs was the perfect location for an asthmatic person to live with its low pollen and its air quality. Uncle Herbert for years worked for a dairy, had a horse and did David and Carrie have fun riding.

Located right to the west of Colorado Springs is Pikes Peak. The mountain is named in honor of American explorer Zebulon Pike who was unable to reach the summit in early November of 1806. The summit of Pikes Peak is 14,115 feet, higher than any point in the US, east of its longitude. Uncle Herbert's sixteen-year-old son Doug accompanied us on our driving up Pikes Peak. About halfway up Pikes Peak, our car got a vapor lock which is quite common as there are park rangers stationed at various locations and they helped us to get going again. The view at the summit is simply majestic. Located forty miles north of Colorado Springs is the Air Force Academy with its magnificent triangular-shaped chapel which stands 150 feet high. We also got to set foot on the Air Force football field, located near the bottom of the Rocky Mountains. What a spectacular setting is the Air Force Academy. Upon arriving home we were in for a shock. Our landlord Lloyd Melhorn, was going to make an antique business out of our house. Luckily we were able to find another farmhouse only two miles from our house.

# CHAPTER 100

## Demons and Addictions Rule My Life

Shortly after moving in the fall of 1982, the roots of my childhood abuse and trauma which had lain dormant for years, had begun to take over my life. This childhood abuse had taken thirty years to come full circle. My being locked in the outside cellar started in 1952 and now we're in 1982. I began to throw objects around the house breaking things. I wasn't yet on antidepressant meds and it would be another eight years before that would happen. I should have been on antidepressants years earlier. Sadly and regrettably, sexual addiction was taking over my life as I got into watching pornography which wasn't just a recent happening. In my hometown of Abilene, Kansas, in the 1950s into the '60s, was a store located on West Third Street, the arcade run by, Mr. Dobkins. At around the age of sixteen, I would coyly walk into the arcade, and when Mr. Dobkins wasn't looking, I would take a look at a magazine. However I was too shy or too embarrassed to purchase the magazine and I probably was too young to purchase one.

I'm certainly not proud of what I'm about to share but I must be candid and forthright. As previously mentioned, my purpose in writing my life story is twofold: First to share about my being a survivor of emotional and physical abuse as a child, and of witnessing physical and emotional abuse of my Daddy which as a result, has led to a lifetime of sexual addiction. Secondly my purpose in writing is meant to be therapeutic not only for myself but hopefully to others reading my life story who have also suffered traumatic abuse and physical trauma as children. Believe me, there is hope for all who have been abused at the end of the corner. Spending hours writing my life story and doing research on mental health has been so therapeutic for me.

I would continue to be haunted by my demons of acute anxiety. Acute anxiety ruled, dominated, playing havoc on my life. I lived with it twenty-four hours a day. At the end of the work day, if my supervisor would come up to me and ask, "What time are we leaving in the morning?" A hollow pale empty feeling would pierce my heart. How I dreaded being one on one with another man for an entire day, especially a supervisor. I would take this home with me, telling Carol about his going with me the next day. That evening every minute of every hour, I would be thinking about the next day. I would withdraw into a shell that evening, in what should have been valued family time. The demons of acute anxiety dominated my life. I've come to the realization that being locked up in that outside albatross has come to define my life. It took away my self-esteem, took away my self-confidence, left me in constant fear of failure like beginning a new job. It's taken sixty-seven years to accept the following facts: those years 1952–1954, robbed me of my childhood. Spending those two to three hours locked up, abandoned, has come to define my life, an eight to ten-year child, forsaken, missing out on God's vitamin D sunshine. Yes, it's taken the writing of my memoir and doing research on mental illness to fully understand the physical and emotional damage that was done for life to that eight to ten-year-old. Please remember my writing that I never got a hug from either parent, never heard the three magical words that a child needs to hear—*I love you*. It shouldn't be that hard to say those three words. Without hearing those three words and never getting a hug leaves the child with an empty heart. It's why I've become one of the most tender people on God's earth. After all these years, I'm giving back double, triple of what I never received.

# CHAPTER 101

## *Another Tragedy in the Hoover-Lady Lineage*

As if there hadn't been enough tragedy in the Hoover Lady Lineage, yet another was to happen on August 2, 1982. On that day the oldest child of Uncle John and Aunt Rozella Thrush would have a fatal accident. The son was Johnny and for years, both Aunt Rozella and Uncle John had prayed for Johnny's conversion to Jesus Christ. Wonderfully and to God be the glory, Johnny's life was transformed with his having been born-again and as a result was his daily witnessing for his Lord and Savior, Jesus Christ. On that fateful Monday, August 2, 1982, Johnny was working under his car when suddenly the jack slipped, crushing Johnny, killing him instantly. Johnny, a most recent newborn in his belief in his Lord and Savior Jesus Christ, would enter into heaven's pearly gates for all eternity. Johnny would leave behind a loving wife Mary, and a daughter, Laloni. Sadly Johnny was killed on his parents' forty-first wedding anniversary, his great-grandmother's Elizabeth Brechbill Hoover's birthday, who lived to age ninety-nine, and on my own birthday, August 2. Aunt Rozella was a believer in fervent prayer, a prayer warrior, as was Johnny's younger sister, Rozanna. James 5:16 tells us, "The effectual prayer of a righteousness man availeth much." First John 1:9 states, "If we confess our sins, he is faithful and just and will forgive us our sins and purify us from all unrighteousness." Because of a mother, father, and sisters enduring love and prayer, Johnny is celebrating with his best friend and Savior Jesus Christ, for all eternity.

# CHAPTER 102

## In the Blink of an Eye

It's late summer of 1983 and Gibbles snacks was having their annual picnic near Chambersburg, Pennsylvania. On awaking that Saturday I had an upset stomach. However I ended up driving to the picnic. I exited off Highway 81 South which would take us the two miles to Uncle John's farm. David was seven, Carrie five, and Maribeth three. My cousin Mahlon a best friend had a motorcycle. Mahlon took each of the three children for a short motorcycle ride in the nearby field. Well sometimes Ken does the craziest things and this instance was no different. I got on the motorcycle and I just froze and panicked, not realizing what lay straight ahead of me—a farm disc. In an instant, in the blink of an eye, I could have been in eternity as I was thrown from the motorcycle, hitting the disc, taking a deep nasty gash just below my left knee almost down to the bone. I was bleeding profusely. Carol drove ninety miles an hour to the Chambersburg Hospital's ER twelve miles away. I would require some fifty stitches. This was the same hospital that David was born in. I've had a nasty scar in the left leg for years and I've never been on a motorcycle since, and no, I didn't have to make that picnic.

# CHAPTER 103

## Traumatic Child Abuse Finds Refuge in Letting My Emotions Go

It's the 1984 NBA championship matchup between two bitter archrivals, the LA Lakers and the Boston Celtics. Game 5 at the Boston Garden will forever be remembered as the heat game as it was played under 97°F. The Celtics didn't warm up with their sweatpants due to extreme heat and an oxygen tank was provided to give air to an aging Kareem Abdul-Jabbar. Referee Hugh Evans became dehydrated and fainted at one point in the first half. Evans worked the entire first half but was replaced by John Vanak for the second half. The Celtics would win this fifth game with Larry Bird scoring 34 points in the intense heat. It was a championship of future Hall of Famers. The Lakers Hall of Famers: Kareem Abdul Jabbar, Magic Johnson, Bob McAdoo, Jamal Wilkes, and James Worthy. The Celtic future Hall of Famers: Larry Bird, jersey number 33, the incomparable small forward; Kevin McHale, jersey number 32, the gangly strong forward; Robert Parish, 00, the chief; and the late Dennis Johnson, the point guard also known as DJ, my favorite Celtic on that team. The other pure shooting guard on that Celtic team was Danny Ainge, now the present-day president of the Celtics. My Celtics would win the seventh and final game 111-102 at Boston Garden with Larry "Legend Bird" winning the (MVP) award averaging 27 points, and 14 rebounds a game. Larry Bird also won that season's (MVP).

On this Tuesday evening June 12, 1984, I had to let my emotions go. It was going around 11:30 p.m. and I went running outside, screaming my lungs out and simply going crazy. The tenant who lived in the other side of the house Abby, thought that something dreadful had happened. Yes with my favorite sports teams, I get extremely emotional, the world of sports has always been there for me, when at the ages eight to ten, all forsaken, locked up, I had no way of letting emotions go. Yes, those three years, all alone in my little world, plus the years up to seventeen, would come to define my life. Sports would become a lifeline for me, along with Grandpa Hoover's farm, the Abilene Public Library, and the study of history along with our family trips. Ironically both legends Larry Bird and Irvin "Magic" Johnson's storied careers would mirror each other.

Let's backtrack five years. It was March 26, 1979 that Irvin "Magic" Johnson and his Michigan State Spartans would defeat Larry Bird and his Indiana State Sycamores 75–64 to win the NCAA championship. Through the years that they met in the NBA finals and played against each other, both men had the utmost respect for the other. I must share a bit about one of my three all-time favorite Celtics Dennis Johnson known as DJ. As a senior in high school, Johnson warmed the bench and only got two scholarships to play college basketball, to Pepperdine in Malibu and Azusa Pacific. During junior college DJ grew seven inches and Larry Bird not known for lightly tossing around compliments, called Johnson "the best I've ever played with." Sadly on February 22, 2007, yes the birthday of our first President which I've had stored in my left temporal lobe since eight years old, Dennis Johnson died from cardiac arrest at the young age of fifty-two. Dennis Johnson was truly one of the greatest defensive guards in NBA history.

Dennis Johnson was inducted posthumously in 2010 to the Naismith Memoria Basketball Hall-of-Fame. D J, as he came to be known, made the NBA All-Defensive First Team six times and the second team three times. Dennis Johnson's number 3 has been retired by the Celtics.

I must share with you two of the youngest Superstar guards in the NBA when I was a freshman at Abilene High. The two are Jerry West, known as Zeke from Cabin Creek, West Virginia, and The Big O, Oscar Robinson from Indianapolis by way of the University of Cincinnati. I feel that with today's media and the televising of so many NBA games and much "adu" about Michael Jordan and LeBron James, I resent that Jerry West and The Big O don't get the respect of their true greatness.

In my mind at 6'2", West was the first elite combo guard ever. At 6'2" West punished smaller defenders and sped by big guards. West's range was unlimited. West was named to 10 All- NBA first teams. West NBA playoff games are ridiculous, on another planet as before mentioned in that 1969 playoffs with the Boston Celtics. As for the Big O, he was king of the "triple-double." Oscar is the first person credited in averaging 10 points, 10 rebounds, and 10 assists per game over an entire season. In just his second season, Robertson put up the following insane stats: 30.8 points a game, 11.4 APG, and 12.5 rebounds a game. Put those stats as well as Zeke from Cabin Creek up with Air Jordan and LeBron and it's a standoff. Oscar narrowly missed a second-triple-double (9.9) rebounds, kept Oscar from that while helping the Milwaukee Bucks to the NBA championship in 1971 and Oscar's height only 6'6".

# CHAPTER 104

## *Family time at Wildwood*

A favorite destination for our family each summer was the seashore resort of Wildwood, New Jersey. This was always a happy and fun time for our entire family. Carol and I would find a nice motel or hotel within two blocks of the boardwalk. The Wildwood boardwalk is two miles long. We would rent bicycles and rode the entire length of the boardwalk. The beach always brought a sense of peace and contentment to my soul, a temporary escape from the acute anxiety which defined my life. Oh how all three children loved to ride the waves of the ocean, and what beautiful sandcastles they made. There were the three piers with the rides and games. Morey's Pier was the most popular with the giant waterslides located adjacent to the ocean. These five days at the shore was such fun times for all of us.

It happened that we usually took our five-day vacation around mid-June. There were two summers that our Wildwood trip coincided with the annual national marble tournament which has been held annually in Wildwood, New Jersey, since 1922. It's a four-day tournament with over 1,200 games played. The Major League Baseball Hall of Famer Harold "Pee Wee Reese," the shortstop of the Brooklyn Dodgers, was a national marbles champion. A small marble is called pee wee, how Harold Reese got his nickname. Our last stop on the boardwalk would always be the Douglas fudge shop. Oh, how I have a sweet tooth! My favorites were maple, peanut butter, vanilla pecan, and chocolate. We always got enough to last a couple of weeks, that is if I didn't get my hands on it.

It's the spring of 1984 and my acute anxiety was getting worse. If I knew that my supervisor was going with me the next day, I couldn't sleep. I would be like a zombie the next day. I just could never handle being one-on-one with another man, especially for an entire day. And after all my research on mental health, I realized it was my having no confidence, fearing he would find something wrong. Yes, my mental illness was sown on that New Year's Day of 1927 and it took root in the spring of 1952 when I wasn't yet eight. In mid-June of 1984 we had planned a family trip to two sports Halls of Fame. I had 99 percent came to the decision that I wouldn't go back to Gibbles. Let me add, I'm not sure why but I feel so much more comfortable being with a woman one-on-one than a man.

# CHAPTER 105

## Cooperstown

In June of 1984, my son David would be turning eight, and like both his grandfather David and his dad Ken, David was already into sports. The Baseball Hall of Fame located at Cooperstown, New York, is a quaint little Hamlet located at the bottom of the Catskill Mountains. By age ten, I'd already read books about the early 1900 Hall of Famers who who played baseball in the "dead ball era," ending in around 1920. It was such a treat viewing the bust and bronze plaques of the Hall of Famers. I'd already memorized many of the baseball greats along with their records by the age of ten. Denton True "Cy" Young won a record 512 Major League games. At age ten, I already knew that Bob Feller the teenage phenom from Van Meter, Iowa would throw three no-hitters along with twelve one-hitters, just a remarkable stat. Yes, just two examples of records frozen in my left temporal lobe.

At age ten, I knew that Rogers Hornsby, arguably the greatest right-handed hitter in history, would hit .424 in 1924. Hornsby not only hit over .400 once, not twice but thrice. I'd come to know of the greatest hitter in baseball history Ted Williams, known as the "Splendid Splinter," who had a lifetime batting average of .344. "Teddy Ballgame" as Williams came to be known would miss playing five years due to his serving in both WWII and the Korean War. If not for missing those five full seasons William's lifetime stats would be "astronomical." Williams career lifetime stats are "mind- boggling" career stats: 521 homeruns; 1,839 RBIs; and 2,654 hits.

Oh, and by the way, Teddy ball game served as the wingman for a young pilot named John Glenn.

Another Hall of Famer whose stats have been frozen in my left temporal lobe for years is Hack Wilson. Wilson was called the "mighty bull," standing only five feet six. Wilson's stats form the year of 1930 are truly remarkable. Wilson drove in 190 runs, along with 56 homeruns. Remarkably, ninety-one years later in 2021, that RBI stat still stands. Wilsons National League homerun record stood for sixty-eight years until Mark Mcguire hit seventy in 1998, and we know how McGuire broke the record; he was aided by taking performance-enhancing drugs. Sadly, Hack Wilson was still in sixth grade at the age of sixteen. Only two things mattered to Wilson in his short life— drinking and playing baseball. Wilson died a "pauper" at the age of forty- eight in 1948.

Another bust at the Baseball Hall of Fame is that of Mel Ott who hit 511 homeruns in his career, all with the New York Giants. Now for the "impossible," Ott stood only five feet nine inches and weighed only 180 pounds—really! The left-handed Ott had the strangest batting stance. He always lifted his right leg high in the air while the pitch was on the way to the plate. Mel Ott was killed in an automobile crash in 1959 at only forty-nine years of age. And yes, I've had Mel Ott's career home run record frozen in my left temporal lobe since 1953, a boy of eight.

As mentioned earlier, the first book that I checked out of the Abilene Public Library was a biography of the man who I most admire in baseball history, the "Iron Horse" Lou Gehrig. For seventy-five years, Gehrig had the Major League record of hitting twenty-three grand slams, and it was broken in 2013 by Alex Rodriguez. But there's a catch. Rodriguez was caught using "PED." Both McGuire and Rodriguez cheated, and I have absolutely no respect for either. Why is it that players who are blessed with the most natural talent given by God are cheaters. Bonds in Ken Mussers baseball almanac had more natural-born skills than any other in baseball history. Barry Bonds had everything plus in his "genes." His dad Bobby Bonds hit for 332 career homeruns, and Bobby Bonds had 461 career stolen bases. Bob Feller's strikeout record of 348 in 1946 stood for nineteen years, until the left-hander known as "The Left Hand of God" Sandy Koufax broke Feller's strikeout record with 382 strike outs. Bob

Fellers strike out record of 348 in 1946 stood for nineteen years until the left-hander, known as "The Left Arm of God," Sandy Koufax broke Fellers' record in 1965 with 382 strikeouts. Yes, the world of sports became my lifeline, along with Grandpa and Grandma Hoover's unconditional enduring love during those years in my albatross.

# CHAPTER 106

## Dr. James Naismith and the St. Andrews of College Basketball

From Cooperstown, New York, we visited the Basketball Hall of Fame in Springfield, Massachusetts. James A. Naismith a Canadian-born physician and chaplain, at the age of thirty in 1891, invented the game of basketball in Springfield. Dr. Naismith first used peach baskets as the basketball goal. Each time the player made a basket shooting a soccer ball, not a basketball, there was a designated person to step up the ladder and throw the ball out of the basket. The first game of basketball was played in December 1891. Naismith was an all-around athlete, playing football, and he won multiple Wickstead Medals for outstanding gymnastics. Wickstead was a slide in which competitors would slide down chutes. At that time in 1891, the international YMCA training school was in Springfield, Massachusetts, where Dr. Naismith was director of physical education. Seven years after inventing the game of basketball, Naismith received his medical degree in Denver, Colorado. In 1898 James Naismith joined the faculty at the University of Kansas in Lawrence. He would remain in Lawrence until his death at the age of seventy-eight in 1939.

And what a coaching tree Dr. Naismith left behind at Kansas University. Naismith coached the legendary Forrest Clare "Phog" Allen from 1905– 1907. Dr. Allen coached basketball for fifty seasons, compiling a 746–264 record. At KU Dr. Allen won a record 590 games while losing only 219 in thirty-nine seasons at Lawrence. Even up to the present day in November 2020, Dr. Allen still has the most wins of any KU coach.

The following is quite the tribute and a quote from Jay Bilas a former Duke star player and at present, a college basketball play-by-play and color commentator, "The game's history comes through Lawrence. Every road in the game leads here—every single road. Adolph Rupp played here, Dean Smith played here. Phog Allen coached here. Naismith was the first coach, he invented the game." Bilas goes on, calling Allen Fieldhouse the St. Andrews of college basketball." Bilas goes on to say, "That building has a soul. You can feel the aura of the building even when empty. That's one of my favorite times to be there." Just let me add, there's no love lost between these two storied programs. KU is the number 2 all-time winningest program in division 1 while Duke is number 4. To have a former Duke player himself a lawyer, feeling this way about Kansas basketball and Allen Fieldhouse just so warms my heart. Jay Bilas, I have so much respect for you. You are a true class act.

The Naismith coaching tree at KU would continue with Roy Williams who played and coached on Dean Smith's North Carolina teams. Williams would become KU coach in the 1988–1989 season, remaining at KU through 2003.

Are you ready for an historic score? On December 9, 1989, the Kansas Jayhawks annihilated Kentucky 150–95 in Coach Williams' second year as KU coach. As head coach at Kansas University Williams had 418 wins and only 101 losses . It's possible that KU's greatest basketball team ever didn't win an NCAA championship. Roy Williams' 1996–1997 squad was number 1 in the land for most of the year. That KU team featured All-Americans and a future NBA All-Pro and future Hall of Famer All-American small forward Paul Pierce, All-American point guard and Academic All-American Jacque Vaughn, All-American first team center Raef LaFrentz, power forward Scott Pollard, starting shooting guard Jerod Hasse who played with a broken wrist. Paul Pierce got his nickname "the Truth" from Shaquille O'Neal in 2001 after an NBA game in which Pierce scored 42 points against the Los Angeles Lakers.

Bill Self left the University of Illinois to become KU head coach in the 2003–2004 season. The KU heart never stopped beating as Bill Self's won lost record in his sixteen years at KU is just mind-boggling with 472 wins and only 104 losses, a winning percentage of .819. KU, under Coach Self's tenure, won fourteen consecutive Big 12 titles, eclipsing Johnny Wooden's record of thirteen consecutive conference titles at UCLA. What's even more remarkable about HCBS's record is that in this era of basketball, many high school stars only attend college for a year or two, while back in the 1960s– 2000, you stayed in college all four years. For example, Coach Wooden had all the following stars for four years as Bill Walton, Kareem Abdul Jabbar, Jamal Wilkes, Lucius Allen, Gail Goodrich, Sidney Wickes, Curtis Rowe to name a few. Coach Self has had his share of five-star players leaving after only a year or two, Devon Dotson, Joel Embid, Josh Jackson, Andrew Wiggins, Thomas Robinson, and Marcus Morris at Lawrence. Coach Bill Self, himself a star basketball player at Oklahoma State, was inducted into the Naismith Memorial Basketball Hall of Fame in 2017.

# CHAPTER 107

## My Argument for Wilt Chamberlain being the Greatest Athlete of the Modern Era

I couldn't give the storied KU basketball program justice without bringing up jersey 13 Wilt Chamberlain. Chamberlain who attended Overbrook High in Philadelphia, was recruited to play basketball at Kansas University in 1955 by the legendary coach Phog Allen. Wilt scored 2,200 points in only three years at Overbrook, recruited by over two hundred colleges. Although Phog Allen won the recruiting war for Chamberlain, Allen would never get the chance to coach Wilt. In that era of the 1940s and 1950s, the NCAA didn't allow you to coach past the age of seventy. Let me share how Allen got his nickname, "Phog." Allen, before coming to Kansas, was a baseball umpire who had a distinctive foghorn voice and that nickname stuck with Forrest C. Allen for the rest of his life.

Wilt, stood 7'1", weighing 285 pounds, a girth of a man. Wilt, in Ken Musser's mind is arguably the greatest athlete in the modern era as was Jim Thorpe, probably the greatest athlete in the first half of the twentieth century. The modern era of sports is generally acknowledged to start at about 1915– 1920. In Wilt's first game at KU, he scored 52 points and 31 rebounds against Northwestern. There is one other athlete who I consider a possible second to Wilt as the greatest athlete of the modern era—that's Jim Brown, the incomparable football legend who wore the number 32. At Syracuse University, Jim Brown was a four-sport star in football, lacrosse, basketball, and track. As a sophomore at Syracuse, Brown averaged fifteen points per game playing varsity basketball. His senior year Brown was named as first team All-American in lacrosse, with (forty-three goals in scoring nationally). Brown was so dominant in lacrosse that rules were changed requiring a lacrosse player to keep their stick in constant motion when carrying the ball (instead of holding it close to his body). Brown is in the lacrosse Hall of Fame. Brown's storied NFL career lasted only nine years as he retired at the age of thirty. Brown's NFL stats are incomparable: 12,312 yards rushing in only nine seasons. Brown played in 118 NFL games averaging 122 yards rushing a game. This dwarfs Ezekiel Elliot's 101.2 rushing yards a game from 2016–2018; and Barry Sanders one of the five greatest running backs in history, averaged 99.8 rushing yards a game from 1989–1998.

Now my argument for Wilt being the greatest athlete in the modern era. The 7'1" Chamberlain ran a sub 10.9 100-yard dash. Wilt triple jumped in excess of 50' and Wilt won the Big 8 conference high-jumping competition three years in a row. Wilt heaved the shot put 56' and many aren't aware that Chamberlain was a world-class volleyball player. In my mind, the only man close to Wilt would be Jim Brown. On March 2, 1962, at Hershey, Pennsylvania, Chamberlain scored an unheard of 100 points against the New York Knickerbockers. In that 1961–1962 season, Chamberlain averaged 50.4 points a game and 25.6 rebounds a game. Are you serious! To add a little icing on the cake, Wilt led the NBA in total assists in 1967–1968 with 702 total assists, coming to almost 9 assists a game. To this day in November of 2020, Wilt is the only center to have led the NBA in total assists for an entire season. In NBA history, Chamberlain is the only player to average 30 points a game and 20 rebounds a game for an entire season and remarkably Wilt did it *seven* times. It's completely unfathomable that a player could average twenty or more rebounds for an entire season, let alone seven times. Michael and Lebron, move over. You two aren't even in Wilt's ZIP code. I'll concede that LeBron James is possibly the most versatile player in NBA history but a case could also be made for the "Big O" Oscar Robertson. Move over Michael and LeBron, try putting up those track-and-field numbers.

And if I haven't persuaded you yet to get into Wilt's corner, I've something more astronomical to share. During that 1967–1968 season,

Wilt had a very rare double-triple-double (25 points, 22 rebounds, and 21 assists) in a game against the Detroit Pistons. Wilt played 14 seasons, 1,045 regular season games, 160 playoff games, 55,418 total minutes, and he never fouled out of a game. When hearing that, Hall of Famer Hakeem Olajuwon stated, "That can't be possible, can it!"

In conclusion, two illustrations of how strong Wilt was: (1) Wilt was getting on an elevator while two delivery men were having trouble lifting a cart. The cart was so heavy that the elevator sunk a few inches under the floor. Wilt took the cart and lifted it on to the lobby floor. When asked about the incident, one of the men said that the cart weighed about six hundred pounds. (2) During a game near the end of Wilt's career against Boston, Paul Silas and Happy Hairston were about to get into a fight. Wilt picked up Celtic Paul Silas and turned him around and said, "Were not going to have that stuff." Silas was 6'7" and weighed 240 pounds.

If I still haven't persuaded the reader of Wilt's being the number one athlete of all time, here's a little icing on the cake for my argument of Wilt's being the greatest athlete ever. At the age of sixty-two, Wilt would pursue a new sport, a gigantic challenge of running in "ultramarathons." A standard marathon race is 26.2 miles. The most common distance for the "ultramarathon" is from fifty miles up to hundreds of miles, normally taking place on roads or trails around the world. At the "ripe old age of sixty-two," Wilt ran in the Honolulu Marathon and a fifty-mile race in Canada. The most common distances are 50 kilometers (31.069 miles), 100 kilometers (62.137 miles), or 160.9344 kilometers (100 miles). Some ultramarathons run in the hundreds of miles.

The "ultramarathon's" beginning is in the early 1800s, beginning in a small village in Norway. Mensen Ernst was born in 1795 in Norway. Mensen made his living running mainly through placing bets on himself to run a certain distance within a certain period of time. The following are two of Mensen Ernst unbelievable accomplishments. First, Ernst run from Paris to Moscow, a distance of 2,500 kilometers, 1,600 miles from Paris to Moscow. The departure date was set for June 11, 1832, the twentieth anniversary of Napoleon Bonaparte's disastrous march on Moscow. It took Ernst fourteen days, averaging over 175 kilometers a day, averaging 120 miles a day. Ernst was given a "hero's welcome" on his arrival in Moscow once his identity had been established described in an excellent 1980 *Sports*

*Illustrated* magazine. Ernst's run was legendary and was full of inevitable stories as (with his disheveled appearance). Ernst had often been mistaken for a beggar. After days of banquets and receptions in Moscow, he traveled to Saint Petersburg, where he was presented by none other than "Tsar Nicholas" himself and added to this was the "4,000 francs" that Ernst won. A favorite true story occurred as Ernst was nearing Moscow. Ernst stopped into a tavern for a drink. The tavern patrons took one look at this crazy running man, thought he was the devil, and locked him in the tavern so he would not be able to harm them. Desperate to continue his run and win the bet, Ernst escaped through the chimney, escaping from the village. Ernst averaging 120 miles a day equals about 4.5 marathons per day. Second, on a later trip from Istanbul to Calcutta and back again, lasting fifty-nine days, he ran 140 kilometers (87 miles) per day. His last trip started in "Bad Muskau," a "spa town" in the historic "Upper Lusetia" region in Germany at the border of Poland. His route took him through Jerusalem and Cairo from where he intended to run along the "Nile" until he found its source. Mensen Ernst died in January 1843 from "dysentery," close to the border between Egypt and Sudan, where he was buried a few days later. The place of his death is now buried by the Aswan Dam. I truly doubt that many Americans knew of Wilt Chamberlain's "ultramarathon" running. I rest my case for Wilt Chamberlain being the greatest athlete, not only in the modern era but in history.

The following are my top 12 NBA players of all time: (1) Wilt Chamberlain. Michael and LeBron, you two aren't even in the same neighborhood with Wilt's staggering stats and forget the argument that Wilt wasn't a team player, how about that season of Wilt leading the NBA in assists and that rare double-triple-double; (2) Michael Jordan; (3) Kareem Abdul Jabbar; (4) Bill Russell; (5) Jerry West; "Mr. Clutch." Jerry West, number 44, my greatest jump shooter ever, and along with Steph Curry my two greatest pure shooters ever. In game three of the 1970 NBA finals, Jerry West would make the greatest Shot ever in basketball history. The New York Knicks with three seconds left scored the go-ahead basket. Inbounding the ball, Wilt Chamberlain throws to number 44 and Mr. Clutch swishes a 63 feet jump shot as buzzer sounds to win game for Lakers. It's Jerry West "silhouette" on NBA jerseys and that is quite the honor; (6) Oscar Robertson, the Big 0; (7) LeBron James. A remainder, Dr. J., Julius Erving, doesn't even have LeBron James on his second all-time team and Dr. J. has Michael Jordan on his second all-time team; (8) Larry "Legend" Bird; (9) Irvin "Magic" Johnson; (10) Karl "The Mailman" Malone; (11) Elgin Baylor "smooth as silk," floating in the air to the basket, the forebear to Dr. J. (12) a tie between the late Kobe Bryant and John "Hondo" Havlicek-perpetual motion. A bit about Bill Russell—he made every teammate around him better, the ultimate team player. Hands down the greatest defensive NBA player ever. Bill Russell is synonymous with "winning." The man has won everything at every level of basketball. In high school, Russell led his team to two state championships in California. At the University of San Francisco, Russell tacked on two NCAA championships too, along with a fifty-five- game winning streak. Next Russell captained the gold-medal-winning US national basketball team at the 1956 Summer Olympics held in November and December in Melbourne, Australia. Russell followed that up by winning eleven NBA championships in thirteen seasons, including eight consecutive titles during a stretch of the 1960s. Russell concluded his sterling NBA career by winning two championships in three seasons as a player coach. No sport has ever seen a winner like Russell, and no sport ever will see a winner like Russell again. Simply put, Bill Russell didn't know how to lose!

# CHAPTER 108

## Our Trip to Beantown

From the Basketball Hall of Fame, we headed toward Beantown. In Boston we toured the famed Boston Commons, the oldest city park in the US dating back to 1634. Being the historian, we toured the old North Church in the north end of Boston where the famous "one by land or two if by sea" was. The signal was to tell Paul Revere whether the British were going to approach Lexington by sea or by land. This phrase is related to Paul Revere's midnight ride of April 18, 1775, which preceded the Battle of Lexington and Concord during the American Revolution.

What would a trip to Beantown be for a sports nut without visiting historic Fenway Park which opened in 1912? David was now eight and playing Little League Baseball. His Little League team was the Cardinals. In that summer of 1984, both the Red Sox and Yankees perennial powers, were having off years and that's the summer the Detroit Tigers started out 30–5 after their first thirty-five games. The Red Sox and Yankees, the fiercest archrivals, would normally be a hard ticket to get. However this mid-June, we struck gold. Unbelievably we were able to get tickets ten rolls up right behind home plate. What an unforgettable experience for our entire family. We were able to get awesome family photos of Fenway. It was such a fun time of being with Carol and the three children and my acute anxiety was ten thousand miles away.

When leaving Boston, we headed forty miles south to Plymouth Rock where the Pilgrims landed in 1620 with their leader, William Bradford. The first known written reference to the rock dates to 1715 when it was described as a great rock. In 1774, the rock broke in half during an attempt to haul it to Town Square in Plymouth. The top portion (the fragment now visible) was moved (to Pilgrim Hall Museum) in 1834 and returned to its original site on the shore of Plymouth Harbor in 1880.

From Plymouth Rock we headed west toward Nantucket, a tiny isolated island off Cape Cod, Massachusetts, with its sand dunes and cobblestone streets. Something a bit humorous happened when eight-year-old David and I were walking the sand dunes. We came upon a couple to our left who were sunbathing in their birthday suits. David and I kept right on walking with a little chuckle to each other. I then heard that sunbathing in your birthday suit isn't all that uncommon a happening in Nantucket. Yes Grandpa Hoover's farm, premium family time on vacation both with my parents as a boy and then as a dad, the world of sports, and the public library were always my refuge and safety net. After returning home in late June of 1984, I turned in my resignation to the snack company due to acute anxiety and job burnout. I remember my boss telling me that he expected the resignation.

# CHAPTER 109

## The Mid-to-Late 1980s

In the fall of 1984, Carol was employed at the Elizabethtown, Pennsylvania, Kmart. David was entering third grade, Carrie in first grade, and Maribeth was four. I just couldn't get sales out of my system. I started selling Fuller Brush door to door. I was a success right from the start. Almost all my selling was cold selling, that's knocking on front doors of homes. A priority of my time was spent in the city of Columbia of ten thousand residents, located four miles west of Lancaster. In September of 1984, I picked up a part-time evening cleaning position at the Rheems Elementary School in the Elizabethtown, Pennsylvania, school district. This four-hour position was often a family affair with Carol and all three children, even four-year-old Maribeth helping.

I was so honored by having a write up of myself in the local weekly newspaper, *The Merchandizer*. Fuller Brush I found out from many housewives, had become almost extinct in the city of Columbia. In the newspaper article, I shared of how so many times, when knocking on the front door of a home, and the lady of the house asked me who I was, I answered with the Fuller Brush man. Her answer, "Where has the Fuller Brush man been all these years?"

I also had my photo taken and put in the *Merchandizer*. If Carol was working the morning shift at K-mart, I would take Maribeth with me. During the 1985–1986 school year, Maribeth would be with me in the mornings. When the lady of the house saw this cutie five-year-old towhead, she just had to let us in. You could say that Maribeth was my security blanket.

285

The day of the week was Tuesday, January 28, 1986, and Maribeth and I were in a home in Columbia. I was about to give my sales pitch when on the TV was a live photo of the space shuttle *Challenger* lifting off from Cape Canaveral, Florida. To everyone's horror, after being in the air for seventy- three seconds, *Challenger* broke apart, exploding, killing teacher Christa McAuliffe and the other six-member crew. I shall forever remember this Tuesday as to where I was. What is it about fatalistic Tuesday? 911 was on a Tuesday.

I so cherish those mornings of having Maribeth with me her kindergarten year. All three of my children had Mrs. Bailey as their kindergarten teacher. What a wonderful person and teacher Mrs. Bailey was. Just a little tidbit about Maribeth, I've always called her Bethie, and if I call her Maribeth, it's not okay with her. Likewise David has always called her Bethie. Carrie has always called her Beth and Carol, Maribeth. That's the names that Bethie has come to be known from each of us since her toddler days.

The decade of the 1980s brought with it, after lying dormant for years, the double whammy which years earlier was sown on my watching Mother's abuse of Daddy and of my own traumatic abuse. It had come full circle. In the mid-to-late 1980s, I was living in my own little world. Many nights if I knew my supervisor was going with me in the morning, I would be up in my bedroom, having my radio on, listening to a sporting event, while the rest of the family was downstairs. Please don't get me wrong. This wasn't a regular happening, if my supervisor was going with me in the morning, I would be up in my little corner of the world, my bedroom. Reflecting some thirty-five years later, I'm tormented with how I hurt my wife and children. Without my knowing it, severe depression and acute anxiety had taken over my life. Unless one hasn't been abused like I was, one can't understand how it effects one's family life. Being abused in childhood can come to define one's life. I tried being a good husband and a loving father.

Several summers after working twelve-hour-days, I would come home to get the rototiller to cultivate a garden and what great tomato and sweet corn crops we had. We had an Irish setter named Sheba, a delight to all of us. There was a small creek right at the back of our home and I often took the children on hikes. My greatest regret, looking back sixty-five years later, is that how being locked up in that outside prison for three years has kept me from reaching my full potential. It hurts even more to realize what a brilliant mind that God has blessed me with has been wasted due to my mother's traumatic abuse.

# CHAPTER 110

## Mother's Mental Illness

It was in the early 1980s to mid-'80s that Mother was twice admitted to Philhaven Hospital, a psychiatric hospital in Mount Gretna, Pennsylvania. It's known as one of the top mental hospitals in the Eastern US, addressing conditions such as acute anxiety, severe depression, bipolar disorder, and PSTD. Please believe me, Mother was afflicted with all the above. Mother underwent shock treatments where the patient is usually awake and alert during these treatments, normally taking from twenty to thirty minutes, administered five days a week. I do remember Mother telling me that her psychiatrist Dr. Walmer, told her that being only five years old and witnessing her mother burning to death was the catalyst for her lifelong depression and mental illness.

My parents for years, had a rocky marriage which led them to go to marriage counseling together. As an eight to sixteen-year-old, I watched Daddy being abused but never once did he strike back. If Daddy had one fault it was that he was too passive, being too passive was his weakness. Year after year I had to watch Daddy being slapped in the face, cursed at; it tore me all up inside. How many hundreds of times would I hear my mother yelling out in anger the initials NH NH NH NH being the initials of my paternal grandfather Noah Harrison. For years I knew that Daddy was being abused but I never gave it a thought that I was being abused. I knew of the first double whammy, but never gave it a thought of my being abused until just a couple of years ago. It took the writing of my memoir the last twenty months to come to the realization that I was abused for years. I'd always felt if one of the two were to die first, it would be so much easier on Daddy if Mother went first.

I drove up to their condo in Mechanicsburg, Pennsylvania, on Sunday evening September 28, 2008. I had prayer with Mother and Daddy before leaving, and I helped Daddy put Mother to bed for her last night's sleep on her Savior Jesus Christ's earth. Jesus was with Daddy his faithful servant. Just as my dear beloved Grandpa Hoover, numerous times being protected by God's guardian angel, so it was with Daddy. The morning that Mother passed on to glory, Daddy was going to have a visiting nurse come around to get something set up for Mother's care, as Daddy could no longer take care of Mother. The good Lord had everything worked out for both Mother and Daddy.

In the last fifteen years of Mother's life, I became closer to her. Going back some twenty years before Mother's passing, I remember my brother Chuck telling me, "Ken, I feel you're closer to Mother than I am." Chuck understood the abuse that I took over the years. Daddy lived on for ten more years, minus thirty-four days, passing away on August 26, 2018. I must make mention that Mother was the best pie baker on God's earth. Her blueberry pie would take the blue ribbon at any County Fair in the entire USA. For eight and a half years after Mother's death, Daddy would drive the eight miles to his church, the West Shore BIC Church, three times a week up to the age of ninety-five. Daddy would drive weekly over to his church to put the Sunday bulletins together for the Sunday morning service. During the last fifteen years of Mother's life, Daddy and Mother became very close. Mother would memorize hundreds of Bible verses. The last fifteen years of their marriage was the happiest of their lives.

By this time in my memoir, I'm sure your aware of the exceptional memory that the good Lord has blessed me with. An illustration of this goes back sixty-eight years ago to the last photo that was taken on August 14, 1951, at the annual Frey reunion. I was sitting on the grass in the front row next to my late beloved Uncle Harry Hoover. Uncle Harry would have been fourteen and I was seven. Just before the photo was taken, my cousin

Muriel Noel said to me in these exact words, "Kenny, I'm so happy to hear that you're coming to Talmage." This was in reference to my beginning the second grade at Talmage to which has been referred to earlier. It's just little quotes like this that I've been able to retain in my left temporal lobe of the brain, under the temple in the hippocampus part of the brain.

# CHAPTER 111

## *Family Fun Times at the Vet*

I have one last sports story to share. Our family would try to get down to Veteran's Stadium in Philadelphia to see the Phillies play about once a year from the mid-1980s to late '80s which were the Phillies' glory years. On those teams were two future Hall of Famers, lefty Steve Carlton, jersey 32, and arguably the greatest third baseman of all time, number 20 Michael Jack Schmidt. There was the "Bull" Greg Luzinski who hit towering home runs and the secretary of defense, the Gold Glove center fielder Gary Maddox. The heart and soul of that team was Darren Daulton, the catcher and three- time All-Star and winner of the Silver Slugger award in 1992. Sadly Darren Daulton passed away from brain cancer on August 6, 2017.

On a Saturday in the summer of 1986 after arriving at Veterans Stadium and parking, we were walking toward the Vet when lo and behold, we ran into the Hall of Famer Richie "Whitey" Ashburn. Ashburn was a two-time National League batting champion in 1955 and 1958. Ashburn led all of Major League Baseball with 1,855 hits in the decade of the 1950s which is just remarkable, averaging 187 hits a season. Ashburn finished his Major League career with a lifetime batting average of .308. Like myself, Richie was a native of the Great Plains, the state of Nebraska. I had a nice ten- minute chat with Richie as we shared our native Midwest roots. I recall telling Richie that as a nine-year-old, I had his 1953 color Bowman baseball card. To this day that 1953 Bowman color and BW set remains the most popular baseball card set ever printed.

The following is a humorous true story about Ashburn during an August 17, 1957 game at Connie Mack Stadium in South Philly. When batting, Ashburn hit a foul ball into the stands that struck spectator Alice Roth breaking her nose. When play resumed, Ashburn hit another foul ball that struck Alice Roth while she was being carried off in a stretcher. What are those odds! Alice Roth was the wife of *Philadelphia Bulletin* editor Earl Roth. Richie and Mrs. Roth maintained a friendship for many years and the Roth's son later served as a batboy. Ashburn along with my favorite player while growing up during the 1950's Gil Hodges, were truly two of baseballs nice guys, well-loved by their teammates and fans. Richie Ashburn was well- known for his dry sense of humor as a broadcaster. On one occasion he was talking to his dear friend and fellow Hall of Famer broadcaster Harry Kalas about his superstitions during his playing career while on air. Ashburn said that he once had a habit of keeping a successful baseball bat in bed with him between games, not trusting the clubhouse crew to give him the same bat the next day. Ashburn while on air, told Kalas that he had slept with a lot of bats in his day. Ashburn got his nickname "Whitey" from his blond hair. Harry Kalas often referred to Ashburn as "His Whiteness," a nickname Kalas would use for the rest of his life for the man he openly adored.

According to his mother, Ashburn planned on retiring from broadcasting at the end of the 1997 season. Richie died unexpectedly of a heart attack at age seventy on September 9, 1997 in New York City after broadcasting a Phillies-Mets game at Shea Stadium. Kalas likewise died of a heart attack on Monday, April 13, 2009 in Washington, DC. He had collapsed in the Nationals Park press box at approximately 12:30 p.m., several hours before the Nationals home opener against the Phillies. Kalas was seventy-seven.

During the summer of 1986 I landed a job that was just so perfect for me. It was driving as a courier for Way messenger service, out of Lancaster, Pennsylvania. I drove a van, a pickup, and a diesel straight truck. My trips took me all over the state of New Jersey, New York State, including downtown Manhattan in the Big Apple, including Long Island, New York, and Brooklyn. I never got lost on a trip to New York City. However, the District of Columbia is another story. DC has it's NW, SW, Southeast, Northeast, plus so many one-way streets. The same can also be said for Arlington, Virginia. Often I've stated how comfortable I am working alone, and more than ever, I've come to realize that its due to those years of being locked in that outside cellar, my prison, my albatross. I can't express the following enough—that it's just been the last two years while writing my life story and doing extensive research on mental illness, I've come to realize how great and damaging the trauma was that I suffered at the hands of my mother from ages eight to sixteen. Her cruel treatment of me has come to define my life. I really enjoyed my time driving for Way Messenger but there were no benefits, so once again, the first week of January 1988, I was back into snack sales.

# CHAPTER 112

## My Nervous Breakdown

Forwarding to January 1988, I was getting back into snack sales and I should have known better. I never seemed to be able to face a new challenge and the thought of failure dominated me. I could never commit myself to anything long-term. It's Sunday evening January 4, 1988, and Monday morning I was to start my new work with Bickel's chips as a salesman. Again I would be with a man one-on-one. It was the fear of failure, the fear of taking criticism, the fear of doing something wrong. For going on sixty years, I had no idea of the two-edged double sword that I was living with—that of chronic acute anxiety and severe depression. These many years later, I would come to accept the fact that my life was defined by those nearly three years of being abandoned, forsaken, darkness without sunshine, God's vitamin D that every child needs to have in their natural physical growing process. Unless one is emotionally and physically abused as a child, you'll never be able to understand how shameful and how worthless one feels on looking at your life.

Somehow with the grace of God, I made it to work that Monday morning, July 4, 1988. I've come to accept the fact sixty some years later, how being alone those hundreds of hours would affect my life years later, in my struggle to meet a new challenge, in my being so afraid of failing in a new job, the reason why I got back into a line of work that I felt most comfortable in, even though it meant the acute anxiety all over again. I found out early that I had a Christian sympathetic supervisor. I was able to share with Mel about my history of anxiety. My daily sales route took me to Delaware five days a week and I couldn't get to my first Turkey

Hill soon enough to get my coffee. During the summers of 1988 and '89, David would often drive with me and what a great helper twelve-year-old David was. Recently David received his master's in religion, and David is currently a special education teacher in the Cumberland Valley school district in Mechanicsburg, Pennsylvania.

My world came crashing down in the fall of 1990. I was still driving daily to Delaware and working eleven-to-twelve-hours a day, and I was hardly sleeping. I do know that I was a very sad man with no purpose in life, no self- esteem, often thinking of taking my life. I don't think that Carol or my three children were aware of my severe depression and neither did I. One late afternoon after running my sales route, I had an appointment with a psychiatrist at Lancaster General Hospital. During that hour-long session with the psychiatrist I recall crying and crying. I had absolutely no idea of how mentally ill I was. I was immediately admitted to the psychiatric ward at Lancaster General. I would be in the hospital for about sixteen days and on so much medication that I was out of it for a long period of time. It was this time while in the psychiatric ward, that I was put on what I call my wonder drug Prozac. While in the hospital I was put on the med clonazepam for anxiety and sleep. Forward thirty-one years later to 2021. I'm on 80 milligrams of Prozac daily which is the highest dosage a person by law can take. If I miss taking my wonder drug Prozac for a couple of days, I'll be so overcome with severe depression. Yes, I thank God for my wonder drug Prozac. As I'm typing here in July 2021, I'm still on 80 milligrams of Prozac daily.

Let me share the symptoms that I've experienced, over the years, of living with acute anxiety and severe depression.

1. Experiencing prolong sadness and feelings of worthlessness
2. Loss of interest or pleasure in hobbies
3. Withdrawing from family, always wanting to be alone
4. Decreased energy or fatigue
5. Difficulty sleeping
6. Constantly worry about the next day; in my case, the supervisor being with me the next day
7. Thoughts often of suicide
8. Constantly living with an inferiority complex

I've now been on Prozac and clonazepam for nearly thirty years. In my case, I should have been on both meds thirty years earlier. It's important to remember that in 1990, when going on my two wonder drugs, David was fourteen, Carrie twelve, and Maribeth ten. By that time, the damage to our family had been done. One of my greatest regrets is that by the early 1990s, I very seldom went to Sunday evening services with my family. I would stay in my tiny little bubble, upstairs in my bedroom, listening to Sunday night football and worrying about the next morning of my supervisor going with me.

# CHAPTER 113

## A Fun Family Vacation and a Life and Death Situation

Our family trips were a fun time as a boy growing up in Kansas, so were our family trips with our children. One of our fun family trips was to the Outer Banks in Cape Hatteras, North Carolina. The Outer Banks are barrier islands off the coast of North Carolina, separating the Atlantic Ocean from the mainland. A must attraction to visit is the Cape Hatteras lighthouse with its black and white candy cane stripes, is one of the most famous and recognizable lighthouses in the world. Its beam of light spans twenty miles into the ocean, and the lighthouse is also the world's tallest brick lighthouse at a staggering 208 feet. We were able to climb the 269 steps from the ground level to the lens of the Cape Hatteras lighthouse, just one breathtaking view.

A highlight of the trip was at Nags Head, North Carolina, with its sand dunes. How fun it was for the children, Carol, and myself, climbing the dunes. A must attraction for us was taking the ferry over to Ocracoke Island, an enchanted island with sixteen miles of pristine undeveloped beaches lined with nineteenth-century ships and restaurants. We also got to Kitty Hawk, North Carolina, where on December 17, 1903, Wilber Wright piloted the record first flight of an airplane, lasting fifty-nine seconds over 852 feet. Cape Hatteras was one of the most beautiful settings I've ever experienced, such a respite from my acute anxiety. The ocean has always brought to me a peace and calmness, a haven of rest for me.

The date was Friday the thirteenth, the year 1993, to take a little pun from FDR, a date that will live in infamy, in this case, the Ken Musser family. David a junior in high school wasn't feeling well that Friday the thirteenth, complaining of an upset stomach and sharp stomach pains. There was also a forecast for snow but it's mid-March so it couldn't amount to much. In what meteorologist called a cyclonic storm had formed over the Gulf of Mexico on March 12, 1993. Snow had begun to fall on Lancaster County on the thirteenth. On Saturday morning David was feeling a bit better. By Saturday evening the snow was coming down heavy with the wind picking up. By about 10:00 p.m., David was experiencing severe stomach pains and both Carol and I knew that the situation was becoming critical. By early Sunday morning, the blizzard of the century was on top of us with seventy-mile-an- hour winds and already eighteen inches of snow. How in the world were we going to get David help?

Carol and I now knew that it had come to a life-death situation. As a last resort we called 911 and a snowmobile was on the way out to our house, a mile and a half away from route 230, the main artery going through Mount Joy. On the way in the ambulance to Lancaster General Hospital, thirteen miles away, David's appendix had burst. Somehow God had let Carol and I know just the right time to call 911. God's guardian angel had protected his child David with his enduring love. To God be the glory! David came through surgery just fine. Just how bad was that blizzard of March 13–15, 1993, in South Central Pennsylvania. The following is a quote from expert senior meteorologist Alex Sosnewski, "The granddaddy of them all."

# C H A P T E R   1 1 4

## The Result of the Two Double Whammies

The year 1994 brought with it an in-house separation between Carol and me. During the last five years of our marriage, both Carol and I were deeply hurt by one another. There was constant in-house fighting and the children couldn't be disciplined. Yes, the seed that had been sown on that fatal New Year's Day of 1927, when an innocent five-year-old being the oldest person to witness the fiery death of her mama, took root in the spring of 1952 when this five-year-old, now a wife and mother, slapped her husband in the face, cursing him while this mother's oldest son—myself—witnessed this abuse on his Daddy which I call the first double whammy. Shortly after, the son would be locked up in an outside cellar where he would be forsaken for hundreds of hours. That seed planted on New Year's Day of 1927, had now sprouted its roots in becoming the second double whammy, the emotional and physical abuse of the son. That seed sown on New Year's Day of 1927 had now traveled to a third generation.

Forwarding to the 1980s and early '90s, that seed sown on New Year's Day of 1927, with the root continued sprouting, had grown to affect a fourth generation in the son's severe depression and acute anxiety and the watching of pornography. It can't be overemphasized how much damage that second double whammy would have on both the third generation—the son—and the fourth generation, the son's children. The separation of her parents was especially hard on thirteen-year-old Maribeth. The emotional and mental development of children with separated parents can never be as healthy as those children with both parents present. I regretfully have firsthand knowledge of this with my mother's physical and emotional abuse on my daddy and I as well of my emotional abuse on my own children by neglecting them, by shutting myself away in my own little world. Thankfully I can say that I never physically abused my wife or my children.

However the power of our Lord and Savior Jesus Christ is a healing power; and as of today in January of 2021, the Lord has healed our family. All three of my children are wonderful Christians, actively involved in their church, are the most loving parents themselves, and prayer is at the center of each of my children's families. Carol has become a great friend. We attend all family fun functions, sit beside each other at our grandchildren's sporting events. You will not find a more tender gentleman on God's earth and that's due to the fervent prayer and power of God's forgiveness.

Our final trip as a family would take place in mid-August of 1994. David right after high school graduation in early June of 1994, would enter the army for his six-week basic training at Fort Jackson, South Carolina. David would make us all proud by receiving a tremendous award. David was honored out of sixty-four young men by being awarded "Soldier of the Cycle" for all- around physical fitness. David has always been a fitness freak. In David's last couple of years of high school, he teamed up with a close friend, Jason Peiffer, to form a successful volleyball team, winning many matches on all surfaces, including on sand.

Both David and my son-in-law Brian Caldwell served together in the Iraq War in the years 2005–2006. Brian's like my late beloved Uncle Harry Hoover, a do-it-all kind of person, mechanic, electrician, carpenter. Brian has often been there for me when my car has broken down saving me lots of silver. After coming back to the States, both were in the army reserves together. David retired several years ago. Just recently Brain retired after being in the reserves for twenty years as a staff sergeant with many men under him, while at the same time, David surprisingly reactivated in the army reserves. I could never have asked for two nicer sons-in-law than Brian Caldwell and Michael Leety. The same goes for David's wife, Meghan Tucker Musser. Meghan is a true jewel of a wife, mother, and daughter-in- law. Meghan like David is teacher certified; and for the last several years, Meghan has been homeschooling their three oldest children, Veronica, Elianna, and Stephen. Wesley the youngest is about to start.

# CHAPTER 115

## *I Begin a New Career*

Carol and I were officially divorced in 1996 with Carrie and Maribeth living with Carol. Shortly after, I started a cleaning business called Ken's Cleaning. In the following twenty years, I would have as my clientele: three restaurants, an auction, over forty residential homes, including a dentist, an orthopedic surgeon. The dentist's home was like a Beverly Hills home with a large Jacuzzi, at least eight sinks in the bathroom, was it a challenge to clean! In September of 1996 I would begin cleaning a new sports bar restaurant. Dawn was the general manager of my two restaurants, Reflections and Portofino's. The new restaurant in Lititz, Pennsylvania, three miles north of Lancaster, was called Scooters as this was Dawn's nickname. With the opening of Scooters in the fall of 1996, Dawn would bring me along with her to clean. I cleaned Scooters for exactly twenty years beginning in the fall of 1996 and ending in October of 2016. In 2016 I had to give up all cleaning due to my persistent neck issues along with three major neck surgeries from 2010–2016 due to a degenerative disc disease in the neck. Yes, I did all this cleaning myself. From 1996–2006 I was cleaning two homes a day and I was living with a herniated disc in the lower back since 1980.

In early February of 1997 I hit a gold mine. I picked up a twenty-thousand square feet brokerage office in the Colonial Park area of Harrisburg, Pennsylvania. It was the lucky break that I'd been waiting for. It was by far the best-paying-job period in my entire life. I would normally clean the office in the evening, rotating areas night to night. From time to time, Maribeth would help me. What a great worker Bethie was. I would have this brokerage office as a client up through May of 2001, when the company filed bankruptcy. I never did get the last month check of two grand.

I must share of an extremely close friendship with a special bonding. Since back in kindergarten thirty-five years ago, Bethie had become friends with a girl named Tanya. Over the years Tanya would become like one of the family and the same went for Bethie and Tanya's family. To the best of my knowledge they've never had as much as an argument. In June of 1999 when David and I took a trip to Kansas and to the Black Hills in South Dakota, both Bethie and Tanya took charge of cleaning the twenty thousand square foot building for two weeks and what an amazing job they did. What's more amazing is that Bethie and Tanya went through license practical nursing school together, both graduating together as LPN's in 2003. Theirs is a very special friendship and have taken numerous cruises together.

# CHAPTER 116

## A Wiser Heart

I must share a fun time and a bonding that Bethie and I had. It centered around a top television hit, *Little House on the Prairie*, about a family living on a farm in Walnut Grove, Minnesota, in the 1870s, 1880s, and 1890s. *Little House on the Prairie* ran for nine seasons, 204 episodes, plus four specials. Many episodes are about the maturation of daughter Laura, growing up from childhood into a young lady who at sixteen, was a schoolteacher. The television show was based on Laura Ingalls Wilder's series of *Little House* books. I can say that I watched every single episode, taping many of my favorites. Bethie and I would watch many of these reruns together. After watching a rerun of an episode or so, I would memorize what the character was about to say and Bethie got such a kick out of this.

One episode of *Little House on the Prairie* will forever live in my heart. It was entitled, "A Wiser Heart." Laura is invited by sister-in-law Eliza Jane to attend a college class on "Great American Writers" in Arizona. On the train, Laura meets a man Mort, who is going to the same class and who takes a liking to Eliza Jane. However, Eliza Jane only has eyes for their class professor, but the professor causes problems between the two women when he propositions Laura. To pay her way, Laura must work long hours as a dishwasher. Later, Eliza Jane is dismayed when she finds out the truth about the professor's feelings toward Laura. When it's time for the professor to give out grades, he fails Laura. Mort stands up in defense of Laura as this is Mort's third or fourth time taking this test. Mort tells the professor that he knows more about the "guest writer" Ralph Waldo Emerson than he does.

Mortimer says, "Professor, I think you made a mistake."

Professor Woestehoff replies, "I made a what?"

Professor states, "I was president of my college debating team."

Mortimer states, "I was president of my college literary society."

Professor replies, "I went to Cambridge."

Mortimer replies, "That explains it. I went to Oxford."

The professor's feelings being hurt tells Mort, "Let's take this outside."

Mortimer's response, "I don't want to, but I will."

Professor Woestehoff, rolling up his sleeves, says, "I hope this is going to be a lesson to you because you are an insufferable odious lout."

Mort, with one quick jab to the professor's face knocking him to the ground, says, "I might be one insufferable odious lout, but I'm one heck of a boxer."

The professor says, "You know you won't get credit for this course." Mortimer replies, "Story of my life."

I have so many priceless memories of watching these reruns with Bethie.

At the conclusion of this episode, Eliza Jane tells Mortimer that she can help him locate a teaching position in Minneapolis. Mort accepts, and the rest is history.

# CHAPTER 117

## *Romance Is in the Air*

In February of 1997 I began to correspond with a lovely Christian lady via US mail who lived near Charlotte, North Carolina. Her name was Sandy whom I had met through Christian Singles, a Christian dating network out of Allardt, Tennessee. Sandy and I began to chat nightly on the phone, it's like we bonded without ever having met. After about six weeks of letters and nightly chatting, we agreed to make our initial meeting at the Natural Bridge in the beautiful Shenandoah Valley of Virginia near Lexington, Virginia, where the great commanding general of the South during the Civil War, Thomas Stonewall Jackson, is buried.

On the evening of May 2, 1863, Jackson was shot by friendly fire and lost his left arm to amputation. Weakened by his wounds, he died of pneumonia eight days later. Military historians regard Jackson as one of the most gifted tactical commanders in US history. On hearing of Jackson's death, the Confederate general Commander Robert E. Lee told his cook, "I have lost my right arm and I'm bleeding at the heart." Stonewall Jackson was a devout Christian, a deacon in the Presbyterian Church. Jackson's biographer, Robert Lewis Dabnex, suggested that, "It was the fear of God which made him so fearless above all else." Jackson himself is quoted as saying, "My religious belief teaches me to feel safe in battle as in bed." Jackson viewed himself as an Old Testament warrior—like David or Joshua who went into battle to slay the Philistines. Robert E. Lee, the great commander of the Confederate States Army himself was a devout Christian.

What a breathtaking setting is the Natural Bridge, located in the beautiful Shenandoah Valley of Virginia. The Natural Bridge is a 215 feet high, natural arch with a span of 96 feet, consisting of horizontal limestone. When Sandy and I met for the first time at a motel, it's as if we bonded immediately. I caressed and just held her in my arms for the longest time. Truly Sandy became the soul mate that I never had. What an unforgettable weekend! Sandy three years my junior, had often told me via our phone conversations that she had been in an abusive relationship throughout her entire marriage. Sandy often had told me that she thought that her ex had connections to the Mafia. Sandy had two lovely daughters, Ashley and Irene.

Shortly after our initial meeting at the Natural Bridge, Sandy moved up to Pennsylvania with me. I will never forget Sandy's first night arriving at my apartment in Elizabethtown, Pennsylvania. I was to learn that Sandy arrived shortly after midnight. Instead of coming up the porch steps and knocking on the door, Sandy slept in her car all night. That tells you a lot about Sandy. She was so selfless and sensitive like me. I loved Sandy with all my heart and soul. Sandy's youngest daughter Irene, was getting married on Saturday May 10, 1997. Several days before the wedding, Sandy drove her car to North Carolina in preparation for the wedding. Sandy requested that I come to the wedding for her support.

On Thursday May 8, I would take a flight out of HIA, Harrisburg International Airport, heading for the Queen City of the South, Charlotte, North Carolina. You know the saying "it's a small world?" Well, on this Thursday morning, May 8, 1997, it truly was a small world. Can you believe who was standing right behind me in line at HIA? None other than my brother Chuck and his wife Cara. What are those odds? Chuck and Cara just happened to be flying to Florida to spend a week at a church friends' cottage near the Atlantic. Are you ready for more? Sitting right beside me on that flight was a classmate of Bethie's, her name was Tanya Adcock. Upon landing at Charlotte, Chuck, Cara, and I all got off as they had to change planes. So instead of one person to greet Sandy, there were three.

It was such a beautiful wedding on a perfect spring day. I got to meet both daughters, Ashley the oldest, and the bride that day, Irene. I also got to meet Sandy's ex, Robert, and we hit it off. On that Sunday, May 11,

GRANDFATHER'S ENDURING LOVE

1997, Sandy and I were sitting on her sofa in her trailer. Sandy wanted me
to know about her financial situation. She shared with me about her credit
card debt. Can you believe that she was $23,000 in debt? I was a bit taken
aback but I thanked her for her being honest with me and that we would
work it out. Sandy had never kept anything from me, but in about two
years, it's another story.

Sandy rented a U-Haul and I drove it back to Pennsylvania while Sandy
drove her car. Sandy truly became my very best friend on God's earth. A
true void had filled my empty heart. My tender heart was aching and
starving for love. Yes, I've always up to the present day, had an extremely
tender heart. I think it's because my heart had missed out on love and
tenderness as a boy growing up and being cruelly and emotionally abused.
Sandy and I had already gotten a lovely second floor efficiency apartment
at 80 East Main Street in Mount Joy, Pennsylvania.

# CHAPTER 118

## *Carrie Has Quite the Honor*

I must share a terrific honor that my oldest daughter Carrie received in her senior year at Donegal High. Carrie was honored by being nominated to the Homecoming Queen Court. During Carrie's senior year, she attended Mount Joy Vo-Technical School to study cosmetology. It was especially an honor for Carrie as that entire senior year, she wasn't in much contact with her closest friends at Donegal High. I was so honored to be able to walk Carrie out onto the football field at halftime of the homecoming game. What a proud Dad I was. Carrie for the past eighteen years, has had her own cosmetology business with many professionals being her clients. Carrie was also an outstanding field hockey player winning the Team MVP on defense.

# CHAPTER 119

## Sandy and Ken's Wedding

On October 25, 1997, Daddy performed our small wedding in our apartment with my son David being best man. My close friend and first cousin Mahlon Thrush was to have been the best man, however he failed to show up but I understood and later will share about Mahlon's demons. Sandy's oldest daughter Ashley was the maid of honor. Also attending were my two daughters, Carrie and Maribeth, as well as my late mother. Like myself, Sandy loved to cuddle, and it seems like we were always holding hands. I must make mention a bit about Ashley. During Sandy's and my courting via telephone, and even after our marriage, Ashley wrote me the most beautiful poems. I'm sure that Ashley was aware of her mother's turbulent marriage to her daddy.

On March 22, 1998, Carrie gave birth to a son Cole Michael Leety my first grandchild, and the daddy being Michael Leety. Sandy simply adored Cole. I shall forever remember that Saturday evening when Sandy and I were babysitting nine-month-old Cole. We were in the food court at the Park City Mall in Lancaster, Pennsylvania. To this day I can't get the following event out of my mind. I remember that Saturday evening in December 1998, Sandy holding Cole and just simply beaming with a wide smile and pride. Sandy was truly loved by all three of my children and the feeling was completely mutual. Sandy was such a loving and giving helpmate. Sandy got a job at the local QVC, located only seven miles from our apartment in Mount Joy. Often when Sandy had a night off from QVC, she would help me clean the twenty- thousand foot brokerage office. Not a day went by that we didn't tell the other I love you.

Sandy always went out of the way to do little extras; the Kirby vacuum cleaner that I used when cleaning my three restaurants would get all the grease and dirt which was so sticky and hard to get off the sweeper. The residue felt like clay, resulting my taking the kirby to AAA vacuum cleaner shop. Sandy had a tender heart, but when it came to something that she wanted to do, she did it with a touch of stubbornness. Sandy would get on her knees, open the engine, and for several hours, she would clean and scrape all that black dirt and clay out. Sandy wanted to help in saving a little money and she was so selfless.

# CHAPTER 120

## *Deception*

As was the case in ancient Jericho, the walls were about to come tumbling down on Ken. Sandy and I for almost a year, had been planning a June 1999 trip to my native Abilene, Kansas; and from there, we would drive to the Black Hills in South Dakota. We had done extensive planning and had purchased tickets to attend the annual Passion Play, held every summer in Spearfish, South Dakota, with professional actors acting out the crucifixion, death, and resurrection of Jesus Christ with the rugged Black Hills as a background setting. It's the first week of May 1999 and Sandy and I were doing the evening dishes after supper. She always washed and I would dry. Spontaneously Sandy gave me one huge tender loving hug and said to me in these exact words, "Ken, I'm so excited about our trip." Sandy was so blessed by God with one exceptional talent, that of being a wonderful seamstress. Sandy was working on Carrie's wedding gown for her upcoming August 14, 1999, wedding.

Let me backtrack for a moment. Remember how Sandy had shared with me of her astounding credit debt of $23,000? After over a year into our marriage, Sandy willingly went with me to my attorney to file bankruptcy and she was successful. Now back to the present day Thursday May 27, 1999, Memorial Holiday weekend. There came a knock on the backdoor which was a bit unusual as almost-always, visitors would ring the front door. It was none other than Ashley Sandy's oldest daughter, who had written me the beautiful poems. What followed at the time seemed a bit strange. Ashley told Sandy and me that she had an interview nearby in

Chester County for an interview to be a nanny. I recall looking at Sandy as this seemed a bit odd. However I didn't give it much more thought.

And now the walls of Jericho came tumbling down on me. Little did I know of how coy both Sandy and Ashley were being, and little did I know of their sinister plot. At around noon on Friday, May 28, 1999, Sandy and I were sitting side by side on the living room sofa when completely out of the blue, I would get the shock of a lifetime. Sandy coyly remarked, "Ken, I'm leaving you. I'm moving back to North Carolina and I'm never seeing you again."

I was completely dumbfounded in total shock. On reflecting twenty years later, I've come to realize how perfect their sinister plot had been planned and what of Sandy's deception. Let me be totally honest, I'm truly a nice guy. I've been told by friends that I'm too nice a guy, an extremely sensitive man. Why is it that my entire life seems to have always gone from a high to a low? I recall one night lying in bed, Sandy was lying in my arms, hugging me and saying these exact words to me, which I'll forever remember until the day I die, "Ken I'm so thankful for your giving me back my self-esteem." Really, you've got to be kidding! Here I was, a man with no self-esteem and inferiority complex second to none, taking this all in. Sandy many times during our nineteenth-month marriage, had told me of her years of being abused by her ex.

While sitting in stunned silence, Sandy had the gall to say to me, "Ken I'll go with you on vacation, but as soon as we return I'm leaving you." For a moment I thought to myself, *Are you kidding*!

I then told her plain and simple, "No way." Honestly I don't ever remember Sandy ever saying a word to me again. Within an hour of Sandy's shocking announcement, Ashley had returned. Wasn't that preplanned perfectly? No sooner had Ashley arrived back from her supposedly Chester County trip, ha! Ashley started out in a profanity-laced tirade at me all while Sandy was completely stoic, not ever saying a word to me again. I remember Sandy, like she was being hypnotized, in a trance, being subservient to Ashley. Ashley went on cursing me, having blamed me for her mother's filing for bankruptcy when it was Sandy's decision alone. I would cry and cry, I couldn't stop crying. Never again would Sandy ever utter a word to me again.

That Friday evening May 28, 1999 Sandy would sleep in the spare bedroom with Ashley. I was stunned, in total shock, in utter disbelief. I called up David who at the time was living with Carol in Marietta, four miles away, telling him of the current situation. David drove over to console me and then I drove back to his apartment, not getting a bit of sleep that night. On reflecting twenty years later, I believe that Ashley was schizophrenic, a personality disorder. Sandy had previously told me that Ashley had some mental issues.

Here we have two spouses whose families were truly dysfunctional. Sandy had gone to rent a U-Haul and I spent the entire Saturday May 29, with Carrie at her apartment in Elizabethtown. Several days after Sandy's leaving, I called up Irene Sandy's youngest daughter, hoping that she could shed some light on what had just taken place. Irene instantly hung up on me as apparently the entire family was in on this sinister plot. Several days later I received a most disturbing phone call from Sandy's ex Robert, telling me in these exact words, "If you make another call to any of my family, I'll come up there and I'll wipe you out."

For the next several months, I felt like I had to have eyes in the back of my head. I was extremely fearful for my life. The brokerage business in Harrisburg that I cleaned nightly had very poor lighting in the back where all employees had to park. For a while, I felt like someone was waiting there for me as Sandy, who often helped me clean, knew where I could be found. I've often thought that with all that had happened to the Irvin Hoover family, beginning on that fatal New Year, a Lifetime movie could me filmed about this Irvin Hoover family and it's tragic four generations.

# CHAPTER 121

## Our God Is an Awesome God

Our God is an awesome God in that even during the lowest and hurting of times, God's with his children. In this instance God's timing was just right for my being able to make the Black Hills trip. Our awesome God does work in mysterious ways. The exact right timing being that David's youth group at the Lancaster, Pennsylvania BIC Church was going back to the Wichita, Kansas area to help victims in the deadly tornado that had killed fifty-four people. It's certainly not how I had planned my trip but our amazing God is perfect in his timing of life events.

David and I took the trip and what a great trip it was. We must remember that God's timing of these two trips, even though my loss of Sandy and of the fatalities in the Kansas tornado, was perfect. "There is a time for everything, and a season for every activity under the heavens. Time is never meaningless for Him" (Ecclesiastics 3:1). Yes, I was in a most difficult time and remorse with losing my best friend and soul mate. God is not ignoring us when time seems to stand still but rather keeping with the present so we may prepare for the upcoming season. God's perfect timing for these two trips can't be overemphasized. David and I lodged at Uncle Virgil and Aunt Carol Wenger for a night. David and I then left for the Black Hills for four days. We had a scare when driving through Nebraska. There was a tornado warning out for the area in Nebraska that we were driving. The other scare was our gasoline gauge was running close to empty for the longest time. The good Lord had us come upon one when we were so distressed. I must add that David drove most of our trip due to my being emotionally exhausted from those last couple of weeks.

As I shared earlier in my memoir, family trips were the fun and happy times, a respite from my prison basement. I had so many fun memories from our 1956 trip to the Black Hills. Our first stop would be the Badland National Park with bison, bighorn sheep, and prairie dogs. I couldn't wait to visit Mount Rushmore with its spectacular breathtaking sculpture of four of our greatest Presidents: Washington, Jefferson, Lincoln, and the cowboy roughrider, Teddy Roosevelt. All four faces are roughly sixty-foot-high granite. David and I would take the walk where you can get so close to being underneath the presidents. Near Mount Rushmore is the site of the historic mining town of Deadwood where both "Wild Bill" James Butler Hickok and Calamity Jane rest in a cemetery above Deadwood's main street. Calamity Jane was an American frontierswoman and professional scout and a close friend of Wild Bill. One evening David and I had our evening dinner in an 1870s-style restaurant and waitresses who were dressed in that era's style of dressing. David and I concluded our Black Hills trip by attending the annual Passion Play of the crucifixion and resurrection of Christ, acted out by professional actors with a spectacular background setting of the Black Hills.

When leaving the Black Hills, we headed south fifty miles to Hot Springs, South Dakota. In Hot Springs, is a large inside water park called Evans Plunge. It's a gigantic indoor pool, featuring naturally warm mineral from a thermal spring and waterslides. Evans Plunge is the world's largest natural warm water indoor swimming pool. The water temperature is consistently 87°F year-round. The highlight for both David and me was the giant rope that you could hang onto, while jumping below some twenty-five to thirty feet into the pool. David met a very nice sixteen-year-old-girl and they were together a great deal of the time. I kidded David about staying in touch with her but nothing came of it. David would have just turned twenty-three.

On returning to Abilene, we arrived just in time to make the BIC Sunday morning worship service, the same congregation that Daddy pastored from 1955–1960 but not the same building. On Sunday afternoon, Uncle Virgils drove David to the exact site near Wichita where David joined his youth group for the second week of helping the tornado victims. How many times had Aunt Carol and Uncle Virgil been there for me over the years? It's such a joy of their selflessness.

# CHAPTER 122

## My Years of Babysitting—My Beautiful Grandchildren

On August 14, 1999 Carrie Joy Musser and Michael Leety were united in marriage, officiated by Carrie's grandfather, Reverend David Musser, at a beautiful outdoor setting at the Harrisburg, Pennsylvania, Holiday Inn. The ring bearer was Carrie and Mike's fourteen-month-old son Cole Michael Leety. Carrie and Mike would be blessed with a daughter Madison Kylie Leety, born April 22, 2003. In future years I was to have an extra-special relationship with both Cole and Madison. I would be their chief babysitter. Madison being five years younger than Cole, would allow me to spend more time with her. I would babysit Madison from about the ages of three to ten.

One TV show that Madison would always like to watch was *The Suite Life of Zack and Cody* which debuted on March 18, 2005. Her other favorite shows were *It's so Raven* and *Hannah Montana*. Madison has come to be known as Maddy by family and friends. I was Maddy's main chauffeur to her gymnastic practices, beginning at ages four to twelve. Madison had quite the honor when she was eight years old. Madison won the Pennsylvania State Championship for all eight-year-olds on the balance beam, receiving the Gold Medal. Madison quit gymnastics at the age of fourteen due to stress issues in her legs and some burnout. Can you believe that during the school year, Madison would have gymnastics practice from 3:30 p.m.–7:30 p.m.? Monday through Friday. Maddy had two great coaches in a husband-and-wife team Tony and Jen. As I'm typing this memoir in January of 2021, here's an update on Madison. As a sophomore in 2018, Madison was on the Donegal High School varsity team that won the Pennsylvania State Championship in field hockey in class 2A for its second Pennsylvania championship in three years and finishing as the number 1 team in the USA. In 2014 the US Ladies National Field Hockey moved from California to Lancaster County, Pennsylvania at Spooky Nook Sports Complex. In the entire US South Central Pennsylvania is the hotbed of field hockey. Spooky Nook is located only eight miles from my apartment in Elizabethtown, Pennsylvania. It happens that Madison had a teammate Mackenzie Allessie, who broke all high school field hockey records by scoring 351 goals and was recently named to the US Women's National Olympic team at only eighteen, the youngest player ever chosen. Just recently, in the fall of 2020, Madison was awarded a tremendous honor by being named to the Pennsylvania high school girls' all-state first team field hockey team. Madison has recently accepted a field hockey scholarship to Kent State University in Kent, Ohio, in the fall of 2021.

Cole twenty-two, is currently a senior at Penn State University at State College, Pennsylvania. He's majoring in economics. Cole played Little League Baseball growing up and was a star football lineman on his varsity football team at Donegal. I'm proud to say that after myself, my grandson is the second biggest KU Jayhawk basketball fan in the state of Pa. Mike is a supervisor at a Cheese Factory. For several years I cleaned Carrie's nail salon until I physically couldn't do it anymore.

On June 19, 2004, Maribeth was united in marriage to Brian Caldwell. Brian for twenty years, was in the US Army Reserves and was elevated to staff sergeant his last several years. Recently Brian retired from the army reserves. Brian is a corrections officer at the Camp Hill, Pennsylvania, state prison. You know the saying "it's a small world?" Brian is a corrections officer in the very same room that my brother Chuck taught Spanish inmates at the state prison.

As previously mentioned, Maribeth is an LPN. Maribeth has a son Keiton who recently turned twenty, a graduate of Elizabethtown High School. Keiton's Daddy is Donald Hack. Brian has a beautiful daughter Cara, age twelve. Brian and Bethie have three children of their own: Gage, age sixteen, a sophomore at Elizabethtown Area High School, Elizabethtown, Pennsylvania, and a star football player, a defensive end and linebacker. In a game in the fall in 2019 on the first play from scrimmage, Gage sacked the quarterback for a fifteen-yard loss. Grace thirteen is a talented field hockey player and really enjoys running. Faithe ten is a future soccer star and possibly a future actress as she is so expressive. Recently Gage has taken up rugby. What a rough and tough sport that is.

I now come to my oldest child, David Kenneth Musser. David was the last of my three to get married. David, like myself, was age thirty-one when he married. On December 21, 2007, David and Meghan Tucker were united in holy matrimony with the groom's grandfather, the Reverend David Musser, officiating. David got a jewel in Meghan. Both are devout Christians with four beautiful children: Veronica, age eleven; Elianna, age nine; Stephen is eight; and Wesley recently turned six. Just a note about David's steadfast Christian faith: when Veronica was three and four years old, David read through the entire Bible with Veronica.

I must share a special honor that was bestowed on David on June 25, 2013. David at the time was in Israel with his Lancaster Bible College classmates while working on his master's in religion. On June 25, David's birthday, he was baptized in the River Jordan. What a supreme lifetime experience. David presently is a special education teacher in the Cumberland Valley school district in Mechanicsburg, Pennsylvania. What are the odds of a daddy being a custodian at an elementary school while going for his college degree, and forty-six years later, his son is a special education teacher at the same school? That occurred in the 2019 school year when David was a teacher at the Middlesex Elementary School in the Cumberland Valley school district, the same building that I cleaned forty-six years ago! Yes, David and I share those unsurmountable odds. I must share a special gift that Veronica has and that's rock climbing. She is eleven and has been climbing for several years, winning multiple awards. Veronica climbs in indoor gyms which replicate outdoor climbing experiences with the use of artificial walls, handholds, and footholds. Look out! In about eight years, we could have an Olympian in the family. Stephen and Elianna are really outstanding on their Ninja Warrior team, an American sports entertainment competition based on the Japanese television series *Sasuke*.

# CHAPTER 123

## Irvin Hoover, Second-Generation Circle Is Broken

The family circle of Grandpa Hoover's children was broken in early February of 1997 with the sudden death of the oldest child Rozella, at age seventy-eight from a massive heart attack. I have so many cherished memories of Aunt Rozella and family. It was that awesome summer of 1963 between my freshman and sophomore years of college, that I lived with Uncle John's when working on the new Highway 81. The year 1997 was such a cruel year for my Grandpa Irvin Hoover's children. Aunt Rozella's two half-brothers, Uncle Glenn age sixty-four, and Uncle Harry age sixty, both died from massive heart attacks. Ironically Uncle Harry, who I was so close to, was laid to rest on his father's birthday, December 4, 1997. At the time of Uncle Harry's death, he was building a project in his church, the Evangelical United Brethren in Abilene. What's so amazing is that from his church on old Highway 40, you can see the cemetery where Uncle Harry is resting with God's angels. What cherished memories I have of my two best friends ever on God's earth, my Grandfather Irvin Brechbill Hoover and my Uncle Harry Dwayne Hoover.

Since the three sibling deaths in 1997, the following sisters and brothers have passed on to the glorious home of their Lord and Savior Jesus Christ: my mother in 2008, Aunt Virgie shortly after, Uncle Herbert, and Aunt Eunice the latest to pass on to glory. Only two of the ten children remain on God's Earth. Ten days ago on January 25, 2021 Aunt Mary Lou, the three- month-old baby girl asleep in her crib at the time of her "Mama

Anna's tragic January 1, 1927 death," passed away with God's angels flying her home to heaven at the age of ninety-four. Aunt Mary Lou was welcomed by her Lord and Savior Jesus into heaven's pearly gates where she will spend ten thousand years. The two remaining children are Aunt Carol, age eighty-six, and Aunt Delores, age eighty-five.

# CHAPTER 124

## Tragedy Continues to the Irvin Brechbill Hoover Third Generation

As previously mentioned on August 2, 1982 tragedy would come upon a third generation of the Irvine Brechbill Hoover Family when Johnny Thrush, Uncle John and Aunt Rozella's oldest child, was crushed to death on his parents' wedding anniversary. The sad tragic deaths of the Irvin Hoover family third generation continued with the death of Mahlon Thrush who passed away in early 2015 at the age of sixty-six. Mahlon was a dear friend. After my ex Diane mysteriously left me on Memorial Holiday of 1999, Mahlon helped me to move with his pickup truck. Mahlon was a man with such a tender heart who was haunted by a lifelong-anxiety and mental health issues. Shortly after his high school graduation in 1966, Mahlon took some alternative 1W service, at the Norristown State Hospital located near Philadelphia. It was about this time that Mahlon suffered his mental illness.

When I was living in Mechanicsburg in the early 1970s, Mahlon would make the fifty-minute drive to Mechanicsburg to shoot basketball with me. We had some great one-on-one pickup basketball games. I always felt a special closeness to Mahlon as we both suffered from mental illness. I truly feel that Mahlon's mental illness had to do with our grandmother Anna's tragic horrific death that fatal New Year's Day of 1927 as well as my own mental illness. As previously stated, the two oldest siblings, Rozella and Virgie were spending New Year's Eve of 1927 at an uncle and aunts. However, how could that not have affected Aunt Rozella, the oldest of the siblings? Possibly a guilt that she wasn't there at her mother's burning to death. There's just so many scenarios that could play havoc on these young siblings losing their mother.

Mahlon and I both shared the following—acute anxiety. Mahlon was to have been my best man on my October 25, 1997, wedding but he failed to show up and I completely understood. Unless you've never suffered acute anxiety, it's a hell I wouldn't wish on anyone. I forgave Mahlon for not showing up as I personally knew his life of demons of acute anxiety and depression. Mahlon took his life by way of a shotgun. The third and most recent tragic death of a third generation, was the death of the youngest child of Aunt Delores. Derise living in Texas at the young age of forty-nine, passed away in 2017 from a ruptured appendix. I recall years ago when visiting my beloved hometown of Abilene, I drove out to Abilene's west wide to the Dairy Queen where Derise was employed. What a delicious strawberry sundae Derise made for me. I'll forever remember her A-plus personality and cheerful smile. May all three of my first cousins be at rest for all eternity in God's presence.

I must share a bit about my late dear Uncle Virgil Wenger. Uncle Virgil and Aunt Carol were like second parents to me in the mid-1960s to mid- 1970s. Uncle Virgil was a basketball star at Abilene High and served in the Korean War. Uncle Virgil's death on July 1, 2017, came just six days of celebrating what would have been Aunt Carol and Uncle Virgil's sixty-fourth wedding anniversary on July 7, 1953. Just a humorous note on Uncle Virgil: in the late 1950s, when Daddy was pastor of the Abilene BIC congregation, I would always sit with Uncle Virgil and Aunt Carol on the Wednesday evening prayer meeting. Every now and then, Uncle Virgil and I would share a bit of humor and we both would get a little chuckle. It's just small memories like this that will live long in my heart. Mother and Chuck seldom went to Wednesday night service. Uncle Virgil was such a great friend and uncle and I'll miss him dearly until we reunite in heaven's pearly gates.

# CHAPTER 125

## A Most Loving Aunt

Aunt Carol Wenger truly is the most loving, most giving, and most hospitable person that I've ever known. God has so blessed Aunt Carol with the supreme gift of hospitality and of being a prayer warrior. Aunt Carol has always given of herself so tirelessly and so unselfishly. Numerous times during the mid-1960s to mid-1970s, when going through the darkest valley of my life, Aunt Carol and Uncle Virgil were always there for me to give me a place of lodging. Aunt Carol has been faithful in keeping all the Hoover family birth dates, weddings, and deaths. In 2009 Aunt Carol's body was ravished with cancer; she was near death's door and then entered my Daddy, David Musser. Daddy would often call Aunt Carol up via his smartphone twice a week or more to pray with Aunt Carol for her healing.

Today going on twelve years later, Aunt Carol is God's living walking miracle. With her steadfast faith in her Lord and Savior, Jesus Christ, and with fervent prayer having gone up to heaven on her behalf, Aunt Carol is again back playing pool with Aunt Delores and the men at the Abilene, Kansas, senior center. Aunt Carol almost always makes it to church three times a week. Several years ago, Aunt Carol sent me an e-mail in which she stated, "If any man is getting into heaven's pearly gates it's your Daddy." Yes, Daddy's fervent prayers for Aunt Carol in the years 2009–2010 went up to heaven and God answered his faithful servant whose fervent prayer on Aunt Carol's behalf availeth much. Daddy would continue his fervent prayer for Aunt Carol up to his recent death and illness at age ninety-seven. Yes, the fervent prayer of a righteous man availeth much (James 5:11). Aunt Carol, during my most depressive summer of 1974, you continued the Hoover generations of enduring love, beginning with my Grandpa Irvin Brechbill Hoover's enduring love for his five little angels. Aunt Carol, you are truly so very special to me and our entire Hoover family loves you.

# CHAPTER 126

## Neck Surgeries and Missing Senior Games

Since 2010 I've been beset with major health issues. I had major neck surgery in June of 2010 for spinal stenosis along with degenerative disc disease of the neck. That neck surgery was a success for exactly six years, when in June of 2016 neck issues hit me again. On October 25, 2016, I literally had to crawl throughout my apartment until Maribeth and my grandson Keiton drove me to the ER at Norlanco Medical Clinic. I had to have another neck fusion, followed by another major neck surgery. On May 17, 2018, I had to have a total left shoulder replacement surgery which is now all plastic. I do believe that the twenty years of cleaning took its toll on me. However years ago, I was first diagnosed with a degenerative disc disease in the neck. After doing research on my memoir in the past nineteen months, I wonder now if those years locked up in the outdoor cellar might have had something to do with this degenerative disc disease of the neck.

What I miss more than anything since my four major surgeries are not being able to shoot basketball with my grandchildren. Every May in Lancaster County there is the senior games. Senior citizens from the age of fifty-five to ninety-nine can compete in dozens of different sporting events. As early as my midthirties, I thought about that time when I turned fifty-five that I could compete in these senior games. I so looked forward to the basketball shooting events; hotshot shooting—shooting from anywhere, free throw shooting, and three-point shooting. I truly know in my heart that if I was physically up to it, I could have won the basketball shooting events, at least I would place in the top-three shooting events. I consider myself a pure shooter. Back in my twenties to midthirties, numerous times, I would swish the net on twenty or more straight shots from the left corner without a miss.

In writing my memoir, I realize how much emphasis I've put on the world of sports and history. Please remember for those nearly three years of being locked up in that cold damp outside cellar, forsaken, abandoned, in complete solitary, with no sunlight, and remember this abuse lasted from the age of eight to seventeen. It was in that cellar that I was reading sports books, history books, and I would shoot basketball for hours on end, my escape, my refuge, my time of peace and contentment.

# CHAPTER 127

## Mother and Daddy's Last Years

It was eleven years this past September 29, 2019 since Mother entered heaven's pearly gates. I want to make clear that in the last few years of Mother's life we did become closer. I remember some twenty years ago, my brother Chuck telling me that he felt that I was closer to Mother than he was. That was a bit of a shocker to me. Just a few months ago I met Chuck for brunch, and he told me that growing up, he felt controlled by Mother. Please know that the past nineteen months, working on my memoir has been a time of healing for me and has enabled me to understand better of why I was emotionally traumatized for years. Yes that innocent five-year-old witnessing her mother burning to death had to have left that child with a big gaping hole in her heart. I do rejoice in knowing that for the past eleven years, Mother has been reunited with her Mama Anna, her loving stepmother Carrie, and her beloved Papa Irvin for all eternity. What a glorious reunion that must have been.

I must give kudos to both Daddy and Mother. Over a ten-year period in the mid-1990s to early 2000, both helped out at the Messiah Village in charge of chapel services. Mother who for a lifetime could play the piano by ear led in the opening playing and singing of hymns. Daddy would have a short message for the residents of Messiah Village. Messiah Village is a lovely retirement home affiliated with the Brethren in Christ Church. My parents' home was only a mile from the village. After for so many years of being a dysfunctional family, Mother and Daddy in their golden years, became much closer. Every fall for the last ten years of their marriage, they traveled up to Vermont by car. They had a special motel where they stayed for about a week. It would always be the peak season of fall foliage. Over time their relationship did heal, but sadly it came a bit too late for our dysfunctional family.

It was Wednesday June 22, 2011 that our family got to celebrate Daddy's ninetieth birthday at a local park. Aunt Francis, Daddy's older sister by a year, flew out to Pennsylvania with a granddaughter from California. Daddy's younger sister, Aunt Faithe from Palmyra, Pennsylvania, made the birthday party as well as Chuck and all his family and all three of my children and Daddy's great-grandchildren. What a rejoicing time of reminiscing and thanking the good Lord for the longevity of both Aunt Francis and Daddy's lives. My aunt Francis lived to ninety-nine, and Daddy lived two months after his ninety-seventh birthday.

# CHAPTER 128

## Daddy's Last Eighteen Months on God's Earth

I must share about Daddy's last eighteen months on God's Earth. On Sunday evening, August 26, 2018, at the age of ninety-seven, Daddy departed this life and entered into heaven's pearly gates to be with his precious Lord and Savior, Jesus Christ. I was so thankful that I got to be with Daddy, along with my son David and family, as Daddy took his last breath. What's so amazing is that on Sunday June 18, 2018, Father's Day, Daddy was picked up at his nursing home by church deacon Roger and driven to Daddy's home church, the West Shore BIC congregation, Mechanicsburg, Pennsylvania. That Sunday morning Daddy, his body ravished with prostate and bone cancer, preached standing behind the pulpit. Up through the age of ninety-five and a half, Daddy was still driving. Daddy drove the eight miles three times a week to his church, including putting together the church bulletin for the upcoming Sunday service. Daddy's Godly life and his mentorship has left a legacy and spiritual impact on many of the worshippers at the West Shore BIC. Each time I visited there, many people would come up to me to let me know how much they thought of Daddy and of his impact on their personal relationship with Jesus Christ. Each fall the West Shore BIC would have an apple festival, and even at the age of ninety-five, Daddy would spend an entire day helping with the canning.

In early summer of 2017 shortly after Daddy had turned ninety-six, he fell on the sidewalk outside of his condominium. Daddy was taken by ambulance to the Geisinger Holy Spirit Hospital where Daddy was found to have an extremely low red blood cell count. For the previous nine years since Mother's death, Daddy had lived by himself and cooked his own meals. Daddy was extremely independent. In 2013 Daddy was diagnosed with prostate cancer. However Daddy along with Chuck and I, agreed that he should live with it as many seniors that age can live indefinitely with prostate cancer. The good Lord so blessed Daddy with his longevity on this earth by being God's loyal servant his entire life.

Up to the summer of 2017, Daddy had only been hospitalized once in his entire life and that was a hernia in his early thirties. About a month before Daddy's death, he had been diagnosed with bone cancer. On the morning of August 26, 2018, Daddy had gotten out of his hospital bed and was walking with his stroller to the bathroom. Daddy fell and hit his head on the floor and began bleeding in the brain. Daddy never regained consciousness. That Sunday evening, David and I were at Daddy's bedside shortly before his passing. I'll forever remember nine-year-old Veronica gently rubbing Daddy's arm and forehead before he took his last breath on earth. Chuck and Cara had been there all day with Daddy and had left when David and I arrived.

Daddy I so wanted you to reach the age one hundred but Jesus wanted you a bit sooner at his residence in Heaven. Veronica, the good Lord in heaven will forever remember your extreme loving tenderness with Great-Grandpa in his last moments on earth.

Daddy, it's been three years since you passed into eternal glory. I've already missed your wisdom about many areas of my life, including my spiritual and emotionally wellness. I'm so missing our three-four-times-a-week chatting on the phone about KU basketball and Penn State football and how you enjoyed watching Tiger Woods in his comeback. Daddy, you were of such spiritual strength during my two divorces. I'll forever cherish our twice-a-week meetings at the Camp Hill Dunkin Donut. Daddy, you never had cable TV so I would always call you on my cell that Penn State football was on TV and you would listen to the Penn State radio team with play-by-play announcer Steve Jones and color voice of Jack Ham. Daddy, rejoice in heaven with Mother for all eternity. I'll see you both again on the golden streets of heaven. Daddy, your love for Mother through all those years of thick and thin was an enduring love and you'll have your reward in heaven.

# CHAPTER 129

## I'm a Survivor of the Addicted World

Four years ago in 2017 I began working in special education with the autistic and the behavioral problem child. My work takes me to the school districts in Lancaster County, Pennsylvania. The ages are early intervention, ages three to six and up through twenty years of age. For years I've regretted not being a teacher. I can now say as a para-educator, I'm in the classroom if only for half-days. I'm finally using my college degree to good use. It's a challenging field, and from day to day, you might be working with early intervention children, ages three to five, or with the behavior problem student up to age twenty. Recently I worked a half-day with children ages three to five and none of them can speak. That was the first time I had worked with those children.

Now so many years later, I've come to accept the fact that the traumatic abuse which I suffered at the hands of my mother was the catalyst leading me into a life of severe depression, acute anxiety, and sexual addiction. A person in sexual bondage feels safe in his own little corner of the world. The man or woman into sexual bondage lives in a lonely world since his primary energy is directed inward. The addict whether he or she is a drug, alcoholic, or sexual addict, can resist the bondage, keeping it secret while planning his or her next fix.

The Apostle Paul fully understood what it meant, fighting the demons that he so despised. In Romans 7:17–19 Paul writes, "As it is no longer I myself who do it but it's sin living in me. For I know that good itself does not dwell in me, that is in my sinful nature. For I have the desire to do the good I want to do, but the evil I do not want to do I keep doing."

The Apostle Paul gives hope to the addicted in Romans 8:5–6, "For they that are after the flesh do mind the things of the flesh but they that are after the spirit the things of the spirit. For to be carnally minded is death, the spiritually minded is life and peace." In this scripture, Paul is telling us that those who struggle with an addiction and who try to overcome it by his own flesh is fighting in vain. Paul reminds us to offer up to the Lord the weakness of your sinful nature. It's God who sent his only begotten Son to be in the likeness of sinful flesh for it's in the death and resurrection of Jesus Christ that we can be free from the law of sin and death.

I'm a survivor of both witnessing abuse and of experiencing it. Patrick Carnes in his book *Out of the Shadows* tells us that in the addicts' life, there are two worlds we live in—guilt and shame. Carnes continues, "There is a difference, guilt is about what we have done, shame is who we are. With the guilt feeling we can always be forgiven Jesus will always allow us a fresh start. With shame it's like we are caught in a 'noose' since the addictive cycles and problems stay with us, we ourselves are the problem."

In these latter days, with all the mass media, the Internet, it's so easy for the Christian believer to get trapped by Satan into his or her addiction, whether it be sexual, alcoholic, or drugs. Let that person fall back into one of these addictions, the shame factor rises to the sky. He or she has nowhere to go, no one to talk to. Hebrews 10:2 tells us that Christ, for the joy set before him, endured the cross, the scorning, and shame. The cross is the only answer to the shame that can be so much a part of our lives in this fallen and addicted world.

There's a true story about a guest speaker who shared about how those with addictions need to be open about his or her weakness and struggles. A man came up to this guest speaker after the service and said, "You understand, don't you?" The speaker asked him what he meant. It turned out that the man hadn't been in church since he was a young boy. He was struggling with alcoholism. The speaker hadn't mentioned a word about the fact that he had battled alcoholism for years, and somehow, this alcoholic had picked upon the fact that the speaker knew what it meant to struggle. This young man committed his life to Christ that very day to walk out of the hell that he had lived for years.

Yes, the addicted world can be lonely and cruel as he is in bondage to Satan and his energy is directed inward. I spent enormous amount of energy to bondage of sexual addiction and kept it secret. The addicts' weakness to bondage can only be overcome by seeking after the cross that Jesus Christ himself shed his blood on that cross for our sin. If the addict can do that, he'll be filled with the Holy Spirit who will challenge him or her daily to give praise to God, our Father, in heaven. The Apostle Paul, who called himself the chief of sinners in Romans 8:2, writes, "The Spirit helps us in our weakness. We don't know what we ought to pray for, but the Spirit himself intercedes for us with groans that words cannot express."

I want to give praise to my Lord and Savior, Jesus Christ, for his enduring love by giving his life for us sinners on the cross. Christ's forgiving love has enabled my family relationships to be restored. Depression is and will always be a lifelong battle for me. My depression can partly be due to the result from a chemical imbalance in the brain but one thing I'm certain of—I do know that my depression was sown on that fateful New Year's Day of 1927 when an innocent five-year-old witnessed her mama burning to death.

Acute anxiety and depression are so evenly woven together. Having a blood relative with depression or anxiety can run in family genes for generations. It's going on fifty-six years since I lived through that bout of pure agony without being able to void while driving through three states. In my research on mental illness, I've come to accept the fact that young children who have been exposed to multiple traumas, as did my mother, that child will almost surely have a history of severe depression as well as her son will have a much higher risk of acute anxiety and depression. Let me be clear that PTSD is a mental health condition that's triggered by a terrifying event, either experiencing it or witnessing it. Watching her mama burning to death was the catalyst for this five-year-old growing up to be both an abusive wife and mother.

# CHAPTER 130

## Enduring Love

Jodi Eareckson Tada and Ken Tada's marriage is an illustration of a long lasting and enduring love. Joni grew up in Baltimore, Maryland, the daughter of athletic parents. Her father had been an alternate for the US wrestling team at the 1932 Olympics in Los Angeles. Joni enjoyed horse riding, hiking, and swimming. On July 30, 1967 the world came crashing down on her. Joni dived into the Chesapeake Bay after misjudging the shallowness of the water. The result left her with a fracture between the fourth and fifth cervical level and Joni, in the blink of an eye, became a quadriplegic, paralyzed from the shoulders down, including the use of her hands. During Joni's two years of rehabilitation, she experienced anger, depression, suicidal thoughts, and religious doubts. However, during occupational therapy, she learned to paint with a brush between her teeth and began selling her art. Joni founded Joni and Friends in 1979, an organization to accelerate Christian ministry in the disability community throughout the world.

Joni pronounced Johnny due to her closeness to her daddy, met Ken Tada in 1980 at the Grace Community Church near Burbank, California. Ken the son of Japanese parents, was a high-school football star, having a scholarship to play football at the University of Hawaii. However Ken wanted to stay closer to home and attended San Fernando Valley State College. In 1982 Joni and Ken were married. In 2010 Tada announced that she had been diagnosed with stage 3 breast cancer. She underwent a mastectomy and chemotherapy and as of 2019 is cancer free. Now married for thirty-seven years, both laugh about the time on their first date at the drive-in movie theater that Ken had to change her leg bag, emptying the urine outside behind a tree. In 2001, Family Life awarded Ken the Robertson Mcquilkin award, honoring the "courageous love of a marriage covenant keep." Ken Tada remarks, "People wondered, here is an able-bodied man and disabled woman, what is the attraction, why did they fall in love?" He said, "Those who know her know she has a beautiful heart and is beautiful on the outside. I fell in love with her."

Joni responds, "We pray and read the Bible together and I let my husband keep his dreams. One of those dreams is fly-fishing." And Joni states, "I do all to encourage him. I'm his cheerleader." Joni continues, "Disability hasn't stood in the way of our physical intimacy. We understand that there is more to romance than what happens below the waist."

However there came a crisis in their marriage. One night after Ken had to turn Joni over in bed three extra times, he collapsed in exhaustion on the bed. Ken sighed deeply and confessed, "Joni, I'm so tired. I just don't feel like I can do this. I feel so trapped."

Joni replied softly, "Ken, I don't blame you one bit for feeling trapped, and if I were you, I'd feel the same way. I just want you to know I understand and I'm going to do everything in my power to support and to help you. I think you are amazing, and with God's help, we can do this."

"That moment was a turning point in our marriage. Somehow we knew we'd make it and we'd make it as best friends."

Enduring love, it all starts with God who gave his only begotten Son to shed his blood on the cross for all sinners. Yes, what God did was enduring, everlasting love. Just as God's enduring love was the center of my grandfather Irvin Hoover's family, it has been an enduring love in Joni and Ken Tada's marriage. Enduring means long-lasting. Enduring has roots that go back 1,500 years to the late Latin period. The original root of enduring meant *hard* so your enduring friendship or your enduring love is solid enough to stand the test of time. After thirty-seven years of marriage, Joni and Ken's marriage still thrives.

The noted psychiatrist Dr. Karl Menninger, gives us the following illustration of an enduring love: "Love is the medicine for the sickness of the world." Dr. Menninger summarized his therapeutic approach this way: "Love cures. It cures those who give it, and it cures those who receive."

# CHAPTER 131

## A Father's Enduring Love

As I've come to do much research on anxiety and depression, I've looked daily to the scripture in Philippians 4:6–7 as my daily motto, "Do not be anxious about anything, but in everything by prayer and supplication with thanksgiving let your request be made known to God, and the peace of God which surpasses all understanding, will guard your hearts and your mind in Christ Jesus."

One of my favorite passages in all the Bible demonstrates a father's enduring love—that of the prodigal son. The word *prodigal* means being wastefully extravagant. Although the prodigal's addiction may have corroded his soul by his becoming destitute in his heart, in that very moment, when the young rebel comes to himself in that pigsty, that's the moment that he still knew he could go back to his father. No matter how great our bondage or addiction, Jesus is always there to welcome us home. The one thing that the prodigal son had left was his freedom of choice. Jesus Christ will not ever take that away from us. Why? Because Christ gave his life for us on that cross and neither would the prodigal son's father take that freedom of choice away from his son.

In Luke chapter 15, in the cultural text of Palestine, the father's house was part of a village and the son came through the fields of all his father's neighbors, the entire village would know of his return. The father could have allowed the son to make the long shame-filled walk to him or the father could sacrificially run to his son in unconditional love; the father chose the latter.

Jesus Christ's love is enduring, his love is everlasting, constant, without end as was my Grandfather's enduring love for his five young daughters, ages seven to three months, to whom Papa Irvin often called his five little angels. The five daughters had severed forever here on earth the unconditional love of their Mama Anna. Unconditional love can also be known as true love or complete love, an affectionate love without any limitations. Papa Irvin, no matter how great the calamity, no matter what the circumstances, no matter that he had lost his true loving soul mate, Anna, on that fateful 1927 New Year's Day, his enduring love for his five young daughters would be unchanging, no matter what life's happening befell him.

Jesus Christ was publicly humiliated and so shamed that we can be free from sin's shame. The blood of Christ shed on that cross is the answer to every addiction that buffets men souls. The prodigal longed to be perfectly whole and Jesus Christ is there for us to break down every idol, every addiction, casting out every foe, and washing away our sins as white as snow.

My Grandpa Irvin Brechbill Hoover

The Red Barn at Grandpa Hoovers, so many precious memories

One of my favorite photos. Myself on the left, my cousin Janet
and brother Chuck and my pet dog Trixie 1952

Late fall 1956 at age 12 of my shooting basketball in the Minners backyard

Daddy's highschool graduation photo at age 18

Grandpa Hoover's two families the first five daughters standing with my Grandpa and my Step- Grandmother left to right; Rozella, Mary Lou, Eunice, Virgie, Faithe and standing in front the second family left to right, Delores, Herbert, Harry, Glenn, Carol.

My family 1958 in front of the Abilere Brethren in Christ
Church, where Daddy Pastor from 1955– 1960
I'm standing beside my mother

Yes, two objects I always held in my hand a book or a basketball.
My friend Larry Minner and I reading. I'm on left

Grandpa Hoover and my mother. May of 1957 Grandpa age 64,
mother age 35. Grandpa looked so old for his age

Daddy and mother in 2006, 2 years before Mother's death

Photo of the Wedding of The Frey Patriarch Adam Frey and Mary Ann
Hershey on January 19, 1869 my Maternal Great Great Grandparents

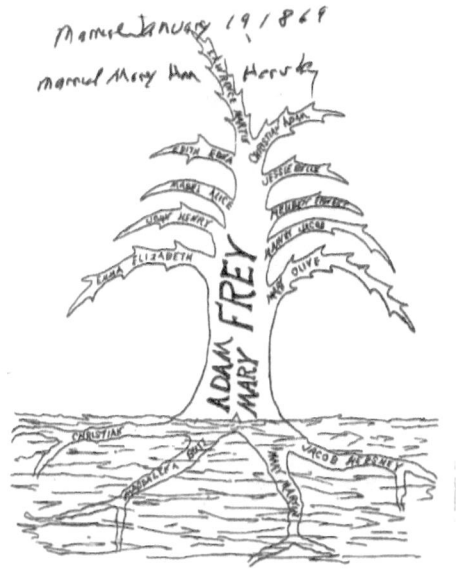

Family Tree

10 Hoover children of my grandfather Irvin Brechbill Hoover taken on August
12, 1995 the last living photo of Grandpa Hoover's ten Children together
Front row—Mary Lou, Delores, and Eunice
Middle row left to right—Carol, Faithe, Rozella, and Virgie
Back row left to right—Harry, Glenn, and Herbert

My dearest aunt Faithe Hoffman, Daddy's younger sister, dining with
Daddy and Mother at my parents' favorite diner photo 2004

I am standing on the center court inside Allen Fieldhouse, at
Kansas University, Lawrence, Kansas, in June of 1999

My son David, sitting on a fifty-yard line at Memorial Field
University of Kansas, Lawrence, Kansas, June 1999

# ABOUT THE AUTHOR

Kenneth David Musser is a native of Abilene, Kansas, the hometown of the thirty-fourth president of the United States Dwight David Eisenhower. Kenneth's daddy, David Musser, was the pastor of the Abilene, Kansas, Brethren in Christ Church in the 1950s, the same church that Eisenhower attended, growing up in Abilene. Musser is a 1962 graduate of Abilene High School, the same high school that President Eisenhower graduated from in 1909. As a young boy, growing up, Musser was a victim of emotional and physical abuse. Musser has three children: David, Carrie and Maribeth, and at the present time eleven grandchildren.

Musser is a 1973 graduate of Messiah College, now known as Messiah University, located in Grantham, Pennsylvania, with a BA degree in religious education. Musser is a scholar of US history as well as a historian of Major League Baseball; in addition, Musser has immense knowledge of NCAA basketball and football as well as professional basketball and football.